THE MAKING OF THE READER

THE MAKING OF THE READER

Language and Subjectivity in Modern American,
English and Irish Poetry

David Trotter

St. Martin's Press   New York

ISBN 0-312-50124-2

Library of Congress Cataloging in Publication Data

Trotter, David, 1951–
  The making of the reader.

  Includes bibliographical references and index.
  1. American poetry—20th century—History and
criticism. 2. English poetry—20th century—History
and criticism. 3. Authors and readers. 4. Reader
–response criticism. 5. Subjectivity in literature.
I. Title.
PS323.5.T76   1983   821′.91′09   83–3385
ISBN 0-312-50124-2

Contents

Acknowledgements

I am very grateful to those who read and commented on parts of this book in typescript, and will remember their courtesy. My greatest debt is to Colin MacCabe, without whose advice the book would have been worse than it is, and without whose encouragement it would probably not have been written at all.

The amount of quotation has had to be reduced to a bare minimum, because of the very high fees sometimes charged for permission to quote. Since I am not sure what some estates and publishers have to gain by hindering in this way serious discussion of the writers they represent, I can only apologise to the reader for any resulting scantiness.

Lines from an unpublished draft version of Seamus Heaney's 'Casualty' are quoted with the author's permission.

References are given at the end of the text. To avoid breaking up the reading of the text, note markers are not used, but the page number and first words of the quotation are given in the references section.

The author and publishers wish to thank the following who have kindly given permission for the use of copyright material: Georges Borchardt Inc. on behalf of the author for an extract from 'Parergon' in *The Double Dream of Spring* by John Ashbery, copyright © 1970 by John Ashbery; Jonathan Cape Ltd on behalf of the Estate of Robert Frost, and Holt, Rinehart & Winston for extracts from *The Poetry of Robert Frost* edited by Edward Connery Lathem; Andre Deutsch Ltd for extracts from *King Log, Mercian Hymns* and *Tenebrae* by Geoffrey Hill, and an extract from 'Soliloquy in an Air-Raid' by Roy Fuller; Faber & Faber Ltd for an extract from *The Whitsun Weddings* by Philip Larkin and extracts from *The Collected Poems of Louis MacNeice*; Faber & Faber Ltd and Farrar, Straus & Giroux Inc. for an extract from 'The Death of Saint Narcissus' in *Poems Written in Early Youth* by T. S. Eliot (copyright © 1967 by Valerie Eliot), extracts from *High Windows* by Philip Larkin, and extracts from *North, Death of a Naturalist* (in the US entitled *Poems 1965–1975*) and *Field Work* by Seamus Heaney; Faber & Faber Ltd and Harcourt Brace Jovanovich Inc. for extracts from 'The Waste Land' and 'Little Gidding' in *Collected Poems 1909–1962* by T. S. Eliot; Faber & Faber Ltd and Harper & Row, Publishers, Inc. for extracts from *Crow* (US copyright © 1971), *Wodwo* (US copyright © 1967) and *Lupercal* (US copyright © 1960) by Ted Hughes; Faber & Faber Ltd and New Directions Publishing Corporation for extracts from *The Cantos of Ezra Pound*, copyright 1934, 1940 by Ezra Pound; Faber & Faber Ltd and Random House Inc. for extracts from *The Collected Poems of Wallace Stevens*, and extracts from *The English Auden: Poems, Essays and Dramatic Writings 1927–1939* and *Collected Poems* by W. H. Auden; Four Seasons Foundation for extracts from *The Collected Poems* by Edward Dorn, copyright © 1975 by Edward Dorn; Hogarth Press Ltd and the Author's Literary Estate for an extract from the 'Fifth Elegy' of R. M. Rilke's *Duino Elegies*, translated by J. B. Leishman and Stephen Spender; Alfred A. Knopf Inc. for extracts from *The Collected Poems of Frank O'Hara* edited by Donald Allen; Marvell Press for an extract from 'Church Going' in *The Less Deceived* by Philip Larkin; New Directions Publishing Corporation for an extract from *Imaginations* by William Carlos Williams, copyright © 1970 by Florence H. Williams; Oxford University Press for an extract from David Gascoyne's *Collected Poems* edited by Robin Skelton, copyright Oxford University Press 1965; J. H. Prynne for extracts from *The White Stones* and *Brass*, republished in *Poems* by Agneau 2, London and Edinburgh; Routledge & Kegan Paul Ltd for an extract from *Force of Circumstances and Other Poems* by J. H. Prynne; A. P. Watt Ltd on behalf of M. B. Yeats and Anne Yeats, with Macmillan London Ltd and Macmillan Publishing Company Inc., for extracts from *Collected Poems* by W. B. Yeats (US copyright renewed 1940, 1944, 1947, 1952 by Bertha Georgie Yeats); and Wingbow Press for an extract from *Gunslinger* by Edward Dorn.

Every effort has been made to trace all the copyright holders but if any have been inadvertently overlooked the publishers will be pleased to make the necessary arrangements at the first opportunity.

1 The secret complement

Tristram Shandy was convinced that no author who understood the 'just boundaries' of decorum and good breeding would 'presume to think all':

> The truest respect which you can pay to the reader's understanding is to halve this matter amicably, and leave him something to imagine, in his turn, as well as yourself.
> For my own part, I am eternally paying him compliments of this kind, and do all that lies in my power to keep his imagination as busy as my own.

It could fairly be said that modern poets have been paying the reader compliments of this kind for some time now, and that they have long been content to halve the matter as amicably as Tristram once did. 'Every work,' Paul Valéry explained, 'is the work of many things besides an author.'

Valéry's testimony demands our attention, not least because three of the poets who will figure prominently in this book (T. S. Eliot, W. H. Auden and Wallace Stevens) contributed prefaces to the English translation of his *Collected Works*. We could follow up that testimony by referring to his use of a famous metaphor, the metaphor of a filament which incites chemical agents to combine while itself remaining unchanged. For Eliot, the filament represented the poet's mind, working on his material; for Valéry, it represented the poem, working on the reader:

> The action of its presence modifies minds, each according to its nature and state, provoking combinations latent within a certain head, but whatever reaction is thus produced, the text is found to be unaltered and capable of indefinitely generating other phenomena in other circumstances or in another person.

1

With Valéry the emphasis moves from the relation between poet and poem to the relation between poem and reader; there, among the combinations provoked by a certain text within a certain head, something at last makes sense. There the reader repays the compliment paid him by the gallant Tristram, the compliment of not presuming to think all.

During the past twenty years much effort has been devoted to analysis of the way in which the reader does his or her share of the imagining. Critics have defined and redefined the 'grammar' which enables us, in Jonathan Culler's words, 'to convert linguistic sequences into literary structures and meanings'. Our 'grammar' allows us to recognise those sequences as belonging to a poem of a certain kind, to interpret them in the light of what we expect a poem of that kind to say, and to evaluate them. Such are the combinations provoked within a certain head, the combinations on whose benevolence an author like Tristram must rely. Their power over all literature at all times now constitutes the object of 'reader-response criticism'.

But might not Valéry's interest in 'reader response', unlike that of more recent critics, have been due to a suspicion that the reader sometimes does not respond at all? That his or her grammar will not be capable of converting linguistic sequences into the right literary structures and meanings? It is a suspicion which has been written into the recent history of American, English and Irish literature by a perpetual concern with the disappearance of the Common Reader. This concern has touched poets more closely than anyone else, because their art is felt to be peculiarly at odds with modern civilisation.

So secure and so widely-shared was the 'grammar' of the Common Reader, that he or she could convert a wide range of linguistic sequences into literary structures and meanings without hesitation. As F. R. Leavis put it, 'to be born into a homogeneous culture is to move among signals of limited variety, illustrating one predominant pervasive ethos, grammar and idiom (consider what the eighteenth century did with Homer) and to acquire discrimination as one moves.' The reader born into a homogeneous culture develops a linguistic and a literary 'grammar' at one and the same time; to make sense of the culture is to make sense of the literature which it has produced and which confirms it. But Leavis's reference to the eighteenth century was not accidental. For he held that the Industrial Revolution had destroyed the homogeneous culture of eighteenth-century England, replacing the community of citizens and the community of readers by an aggregate of isolated and internally divided units; and that the 'signals' emitted by mass society, far from illustrating one pervasive ethos, brought only confusion. 'By what standards,' he asked, 'what criteria, what principles can we bring order into our reading . . .?'

It seemed to Leavis, as it has to many others before and since, that the stable and easily identifiable Common Reader had given way to an anonymous crowd of uncommon readers, each loyal to a tiny sect or to himself alone. It seems to Malcolm Bradbury, for example, that during the nineteenth century writers came to rely more and more upon 'the cohesion of a changing intelligentsia now fairly well divorced from its bourgeois origins,' and to find their readers among 'fellow-citizens of the independent gypsy land of Bohemia'. From about 1880, Bradbury suggests, English culture failed to provide the homogeneity which would have nurtured Common Readers; after that, there were a few colourful camp-followers in the foreground of literary life, but elsewhere only retreating backs.

Whether this sociology of readership is accurate or not, it has certainly been believed by a large number of modern poets and critics, some of whom I shall call in evidence; and it has usually taken the form of a concern about quality rather than about quantity. Common Readers were useful people not because there were so many of them, but because they were easy to identify. Since both poet and reader had been trained to respond to the same 'signals of limited variety', one could have some confidence that a poem would be read for the right reasons, for the reasons which had provoked its creation. The advantage of the Common Reader was that he wore his competence on his sleeve. It was this identifiable competence which became lost in the subsequent massing and diffusion of the audience for literature; a development, Bradbury remarks, which freed the writer from dependence on a patron or a particular class, but also 'made it harder to see for whom he was writing'. While the overall number of readers increased, particularly for the novelists, the identity of the individual reader could no longer be known or deduced.

In which case an author might want to identify the few individual readers who, among a mass of the idly curious, read him for the right reasons. Where competence could not be taken

for granted, it would have to be built up or singled out – somehow
– by the poem itself. The English Romantics knew this.
Wordsworth insisted that his work would not have any effect on
those who 'do not *read* books' but 'merely snatch a glance at them
that they may talk about them'; such people were clearly
incompetent, and the poems would make no effort to capture their
idle glances. 'My glory,' Keats wrote, 'would be to daunt and
dazzle the thousand jabberers about Pictures and Books.' He told
Reynolds that the original preface to *Endymion* was characterised
not by 'affectation' but by 'an undersong of disrespect to the
Public'. The problem was neatly if high-handedly summarised by
Rudolph von Langen, quoted in Coleridge's essay 'On the
Communication of Truth': 'But how are we to guard against the
herd of promiscuous Readers? Can we bid our *books* be silent in
the presence of the unworthy?' Modern society had created a
mass of promiscuous and incompetent readers, among whom the
writer would have to select rigorously if he was to find a proper
audience. Marilyn Butler has pointed out that Coleridge's prose
style did just that, 'since the strangely specialized tone made a
kind of compact with the reader, flatteringly promoting him to
membership among the elect'. These poets expected – during
certain phases of their careers, at any rate – to confront not so
much literary competence as a literary incompetence out of which
competence would have to be *made*. Some of their books sought to
identify the worthy by remaining incomprehensible to the
unworthy. Readers who understood had thereby proved their
competence; they, at least, could be known.

With this is mind, we should return to Valéry's remarks about
the action of the text, and to the circumstances which prompted
them. A friend of his had lent a copy of *Charmes* to a philosopher
who, observing that the book had wide margins, filled them with
his own reflections. The friend seems to have taken this very
calmly. He passed the annotated copy on to Valéry, who was so
impressed that he decided to incorporate the philosopher's
commentary into a special edition:

> To consider these annotated pages is to see, along the borders
> of the poem, a man living what he reads. As one deciphers, one
> hears, alongside the verses, the murmur of the discursive
> monologue responding to the reading, cutting across it,
> supporting it by a more or less restricted counterpoint,

continually accompanying it by the speech of a second voice, which sometimes breaks out.

On these pages, fluid handwriting 'besieges' the rigid structure of the typography, a conjunction which 'presents to the eye the secret complement of the text, shows the reader's function, brings out the spiritual environs of a reading'. Here, indeed, is matter for reader-response criticism.

But we should not neglect Valéry's reminder that the action of this secret complement, this counterpoint to the text, is 'more or less restricted'. After all, the handwriting appears only in the space left for it by the typography; it takes its form from the blocks of print around which it flows. Following Valéry's metaphor, we might add that the philosopher's commentary occupies only the semantic 'space' left for it by the poems. Readers may make sense, but they do so in a rhythm and a circumstance prescribed by the text. For the rhetorical devices of the text will be aligned in such a way as to allow their secret complement only a certain 'space' in which to appear; they will provoke their secret complement into making sense, but on their own terms; they will encourage it to make a certain kind of sense. Whether or not this is true of all literature, it is quite likely to hold good for writers anxious to identify those among a herd of promiscuous readers who might read their work for the right reasons. Such writers might well aim to provoke only a particular variety of secret complement, an elect and thus identifiable readership; and they might well set their rhetorical terms accordingly.

I shall be concerned in this book not so much with literary competence as with the way competence has been made out of assumed incompetence by poets who did not know for whom they were writing. Imagining the Common Reader (the reader identified by origin and upbringing) to have disappeared, they have set about recreating him or her by all the means at their disposal. Up until fairly recently, the means at their disposal have amounted to a selection of thematic and rhetorical choices. Versions of subjectivity and effects of language have brought into play and identified a reader. To describe this process is not to provide a complete account of any one poem, or a complete survey of nineteenth and twentieth-century poetry; but it is to understand more about the way many modern poems, some of them recognised masterpieces, have made sense.

* * *

According to Marilyn Butler, the 'strangely specialized tone' of Coleridge's prose served 'to find out an élite, and to help remould it in better accordance with his ideal'. The secret complement brought into play by that strangely specialised tone was also a secret complement to the state, a reader identified by a certain moral and political apartness. An author might see more clearly for whom he was writing if the reader he imagined could somehow be made to stand away from society. In consequence, the making of readers has often involved the making of moral and political dissidents. Thus we might regard the obsessive patrolling of margins and thresholds in poetry since Wordsworth, the journeys outward from centre to periphery, as part of an attempt to marginalise the reader. Out there, at the edge, the issues must be starker; those citizens and readers who acknowledge the value of such extremity are brought into focus by their decision, and so the poet is able once more to see for whom he has written.

Of course, the vagabondage would have to be of a particular kind and a particular quality if it was to serve as a convention for the making of readers. We must explain the power of these Romantic margins and of the men who patrol them, the power of these journeys to distinguish (if that is what they do) among the herd of promiscuous readers. I shall suggest that they do have such power, and that they have it because they re-enact for us an immemorial ceremony of separation and discovery.

Anthropologists studying the 'rites of passage' which in most cultures accompany any change of place or condition (birth, puberty, marriage, coronation, death and so on) have evolved a precise and useful set of terms. Arnold van Gennep, the first person to theorise these rites, distinguished in them three phases: a rite of separation, from a fixed point in the social structure; a marginal or liminal (threshold) phase, when the ritual subject passes through a cultural realm unlike either his past or his future state; and a rite of reincorporation into society. It is as though the justice and scope of Leavis's 'signals of limited variety' have been tested periodically by a step outside into a different realm, into a common subjectivity independent of (yet essential to) organised society.

This realm, van Gennep's marginal or liminal phase, has been analysed by Victor Turner in a number of acute essays. Turner points out that those who have entered the liminal phase in a rite of passage 'are neither here nor there; they are betwixt and between the positions assigned and arrayed by law, custom, convention, and ceremonial'. Such 'liminal entities' have been stripped of social status and possessions. 'It is as though they are being reduced or ground down to a uniform condition to be fashioned anew and endowed with additional powers to enable them to cope with their new station in life.' This is no visit to the finishing school or health farm, but a beginning again, a levelling down to some fundamental subjectivity. According to Turner, the margin or threshold is 'open and unspecialized, a spring of pure possibility as well as the immediate realization of release from day-to-day structural necessities and obligatoriness'. It offers the ritual subjects a chance to recreate themselves from the ground up.

The ground they level down to is a recognition of an 'essential and generic human bond'. Momentarily apart from the 'structured, differentiated, and often hierarchical system of politico-legal-economic positions' which constitutes their society, they rediscover a sense of common humanity, a crucial but often obscured cohesion. So the rite offers the chance to begin again, but from a more absolute and secure foundation; hence its enduring power.

Such rites are endemic in the cultures studied by Turner, occurring at predetermined points in the life of every citizen, with each phase accompanied by public ceremony and each margin located in a holy place. They have to some extent persisted in the Christian world. 'A pilgrim,' Turner writes, 'is one who divests himself of the mundane concomitants of religion . . . to confront, in a special "far" milieu, the basic elements and structures of his faith in their unshielded, virgin radiance.' Pilgrims have always abandoned their social status in order to begin again, to rediscover a generic human bond. But although the shrine they worship at is a holy place, legitimised by public ceremony, their pilgrimage is voluntary. Not everyone will go, and there does not seem to be a particular moment or season in your life when you must set off. Already the rite of passage has become selective, distinguishing the passionately faithful from those who merely 'snatch a glance' at Christ.

The function of these rites changed yet again in the Romantic era when they became internalised and secular as well as voluntary and selective. Pilgrimages still occurred, but no public ceremony blessed their real or imaginary shrines. The pilgrim now had to create for himself the convention which would attribute meaning to his journey. Unlike his Christian precursors, he identified himself not only by his decision to depart from society, but also by his obedience to a convention which had no generally accepted validity. He hoped to enter at the margin into a generic human bond. But who now could tell him when he had arrived at the margin? Who could tell him where to look? Such was the predicament of those Romantic poets who, as Heidegger said of Hölderlin, lived during the time between the departure and the return of the gods.

A poet who decided to make the best of it – to define aesthetics as a voluntary, internalised and secular rite of passage – was Friedrich Schiller. The first version of Schiller's *On the Aesthetic Education of Man* was written in 1793, during the Reign of Terror in France, and he told Goethe that it represented a profession of political faith. It certainly made large claims for the distinguishing and regenerative power of aesthetic experience.

According to Schiller, two drives or determinations govern human behaviour: the sensuous, which we acquire first, and the rational. Sensuousness is a passive state, while thought is active and free. But we cannot move directly from one to the other, substituting freedom for passivity. We must rather allow one drive to be cancelled by the other, becoming 'momentarily free of all determination whatsoever', entering a 'state of pure determinability'. If we submit ourselves to this liminal phase, and afterwards keep the memory of it alive, we can be confident that reason will govern our actions without obliterating the sensuous drive altogether. As children we knew such a liminal phase or state of pure determinability; but how can we rediscover it in the unforgiving adult world?

> This middle disposition, in which the psyche is subject neither to physical nor to moral constraint, and yet is active in both these ways, pre-eminently deserves to be called a free disposition; and if we are to call the condition of sensuous determination the physical, and the condition of rational determination the logical or moral, then we must call this condition of real and active determinability the aesthetic.

Aesthetic experience is an internalised rite of passage which perpetually offers us the chance to begin again, the 'gift of humanity itself': 'Here alone do we feel reft out of time, and our human nature expresses itself with a purity and integrity, as though it had as yet suffered no impairment through the intervention of external forces.'

English Romanticism tended to be less systematic and more overtly social in its revisions of sacred impulse. Childhood became, as David Simpson has shown, an important metaphor for pure determinability. So did the prospect of emigration and the founding of ideal communities. 'I am convinced,' Coleridge wrote to his brother on 23 March 1794,

> that a man once corrupted will ever remain so, unless some sudden revolution, some unexpected change of Place or Station shall have utterly altered his connection. When these Shocks of adversity have electrified his moral frame, he feels a convalescence of soul, and becomes like a being recently formed from the hands of Nature.

Coleridge's moral frame was more easily electrified than most, but even he had some difficulty in finding a threshold or margin where he might once again become like a being recently formed. On 21 October 1794, he recommended to Robert Southey a book by Thomas Cooper, *Some Information respecting America,* which had been published that year. Cooper represents America as a space wonderfully uncontaminated by structure and hierarchy, where a 'pure and equal republican form of government' has been introducing virtues 'consonant to the true nature of our species': a margin, in short, the biggest margin in the world. Even Southey's rather sturdier moral frame registered the occasional spasm. He told his midshipman brother that he and Coleridge, with a view to settling in America, had preached Pantisocracy and Aspheterism everywhere. 'These, Tom,' he added helpfully, 'are two new words, the first signifying the equal government of all, and the other the generalization of individual property.' In the event, Southey proved somewhat reluctant to generalise his own property, and the scheme collapsed. But it has remained a potent dream, for D. H. Lawrence and many others.

Wordsworth seems to have been less interested in the discovery of new margins than in the resurrection of the bizarre figures who populated the old ones. He had more faith than any of his contemporaries in the reality of an essential and generic human bond, yet he haunted some unlikely margins and nominated some unlikely people as 'liminal entities': the Old Cumberland Beggar, for example, whose main characteristic is his purposeful lack of purpose. A solemn lassitude sets the beggar apart. People make exception for him: they open gates, hand him money they might otherwise have thrown in the dirt. He in turn is utterly self-absorbed:

> Thus, from day to day,
> Bow-bent, his eyes for ever on the ground,
> He plies his weary journey . . .

'Plies' is exact, with its suggestion of a body and a will bent almost to nullity. The beggar has been weathered to an irreducible minimum; he seems to *subsist* rather than *exist*. (The plethora of 'under'-compounds in *The Prelude* – under-powers, under-presence and so on – makes one think that Wordsworth might have conceived of a literal subsistence.) The beggar's 'motion' is so 'still' that the dogs give up barking while loafers and babes overtake him at will.

A note informs us that the class of vagrants he belongs to 'will probably soon be extinct'. It is here, with the recognition of his social status, that the remote and utterly incompatible old man accedes to the virtue of a 'liminal entity'. He reasserts the strength of an essential and generic human hond partly by his weathered near-nullity and partly by his 'stated round' of begging:

> While from door to door,
> This old Man creeps, the villagers in him
> Behold a record which together binds
> Past deeds and offices of charity,
> Else unremembered, and so keeps alive
> The kindly mood in hearts which lapse of years,
> And that half-wisdom half-experience gives,
> Make slow to feel . . .

This stated round of begging serves to reawaken the kindly mood (both a generous impulse and a sense of community) which other cultures had located in the liminal phase of a rite of passage, or in some shrine. The beggar, Wordsworth says, becomes a 'silent monitor' of social actions, reminding us by his very apartness that 'man is dear to man'.

However, Wordsworth does not seem altogether convinced that his readers will see in the old man what he himself has seen, and stoops to rather pompous exhortation: 'But deem not this Man useless. – Statesmen!' So idiosyncratic is his choice of liminal entity that it barely functions at all as a device for selecting among the herd of promiscuous readers. Exhortation might jog the occasional statesman-like elbow, but what are the rest of us supposed to think? I shall return to this problem shortly, but first I want to show how the fascination with marginal places and figures persisted into the nineteenth century, sometimes becoming (rather hesitantly) a way to make readers.

Since so many discussions of culture and society focus on Wordsworth's disciple Matthew Arnold, it is worth considering what his poems have to say about rites of passage. In 'Lines Written in Kensington Gardens', for example, Arnold set out to locate a margin at the centre of London:

> In this lone, open glad I lie,
> Screen'd by deep boughs on either hand;
> And at its end, to stay the eye,
> Those black-crown'd, red-boled pine trees stand!

The uniform stress of that last line virtually palisades the ear, for Arnold wanted to locate a margin which was also an enclosure:

> In the huge world, which roars hard by,
> Be others happy if they can!
> But in my helpless cradle I
> Was breathed on by the rural Pan.

Here Arnold can become like a being recently formed from the hands of nature. Here he can glimpse an essential, generic human bond:

> The will to neither strive nor cry,
> The power to feel with others give!

It is not an auspicious poem, but revealing.

Such defensive margins proliferated in contemporary thinking, the most notable being the Victorian home; 'when we come home,' wrote J. A. Froude, 'we lay aside our mask and drop our tools, and are no longer lawyers, sailors, soldiers, statesmen, clergymen, but only men.' There we forget status and self-esteem, Frederic Harrison claimed, and learn to 'live for humanity'. Arnold himself, while no doubt appreciating these pieties, yearned also for more distant margins, of the kind opened by Rousseau's *Rêveries d'un promeneur solitaire*. Indeed, wanderers fascinated him, as his interest in a passage from the journals of Maurice de Guérin shows:

> The longer I live, and the clearer I discern between true and false in society, the more does the inclination to live, not as a savage or misanthrope, but as a solitary man on the frontiers of society, on the outskirts of the world, gain strength and grow in me.

Such a solitary man could free himself from the distorting impositions of society and become once again like a being recently formed; he could live out a perpetual rite of passage. On the outskirts of the world, nobody would interfere with him, except perhaps the occasional gipsy. For Arnold gipsies also represented liminal entities, although his use of hybrid terms like 'scholar-gipsy' and 'gipsy-child' indicates a half-measure: the gipsy-element proposing distance and freedom, the scholar – or child-element drawing the figure back into the realm of more gentlemanly preoccupations.

Like Wordsworth, Arnold was worried that his readers might not share his enthusiasm for marginals, and he took steps to ensure that they would. His poems do not simply describe gipsies and wanderers; they tell us how to associate ourselves with these figures, how to enter into what the figures represent. And they do so by means of a single poetic device, the simile. Similes become the primary mode of the 'power to feel with others' celebrated by 'Kensington Gardens' and embodied by all liminal entities. Arnold's most interesting poem from this point of view is 'Stanzas from the Grande Chartreuse', published in 1855, which identifies the Carthusian monastery as a sacred margin:

Take, me cowl'd forms, and fence me round,
Till I possess my soul again;
Till free my thoughts before me roll,
Not chafed by hourly false control!

Unfortunately, there can be no escaping the fact that the
monastery is a *Catholic* margin. Arnold's rite of passage has been
cast in religious terms, but it is Romantic in its sense of having
come to the wrong place; to a place whose sanctity no universal
faith or culture underwrites. His 'rigorous teachers' whisper
accusations of infidelity. Should the Protestant Arnold and his
presumably Protestant readers acknowledge a papist shrine?

Well, yes, by means of a simile:

Wandering between two worlds, one dead,
The other powerless to be born,
With nowhere yet to rest my head,
Like these, on earth I wait forlorn.

Arnold shares the situation of the Carthusian monks, if not their
faith. 'Simile,' wrote the critic E. S. Dallas in 1852, 'is the
comparison of like with like, not forgetting that they are only like;
metaphor is the employment of like for like, not doubting that
they are one and the same.' Arnold's choice of simile rather than
metaphor was exact, for it announces an essential and generic
human bond while at the same time preserving distinctions. 'To
like,' Dallas concluded, 'impels us to liken . . . Our liking
determines the likeness.' A similar liking determined, in other
poems, the likeness of the Scholar Gipsy to a Tyrian trader, and
the likeness of the modern world to a battle on a darkling plain.
The formal device encodes a moral stance.

Arnold's similes create the space and the terms in which the
secret complement of his poems is to operate. Those who read for
the right reasons will do what the similes say, and allow the
likeness to become a liking, comparison on specified grounds to
become sympathy. In doing so they will identify themselves as a
minority whose respect for an essential and generic human bond
is greater than self-interest or dogmatic scruple. As Ruskin put it,
the finest description can be appreciated by everyone, but the
finest expression 'can only be met and understood by persons
having some sort of sympathy with the high and solitary minds

which produced it – sympathy only to be felt by minds in some degree high and solitary themselves'.

* * *

Arnold's similes are of course a special case, and we need terms which will describe similar effects in a wider range of writing. Various conventions regulate the appearance of a poem's secret complement, including metaphor and simile and other devices such as prosody ('the system of rhythmic organization that governs the construction and reading of a poem', in Charles Hartman's recent definition). Here I want to examine the function in poetic language of what are usually called 'reference items'. These are words – possessives, demonstratives, comparatives – which instead of being interpreted in their own right, refer to something else for their interpretation. ('These', in the sentence I have just written, does not mean anything itself, but rather refers back to 'reference items' in the previous sentence.) Such words direct the reader to look elsewhere for the information needed to identify them.

There are two types of reference, which I shall call internal and external. An item can refer backward or forward to other parts of the utterance which contains it, as in the example I have just given, providing cohesion and enabling the addressee to conceive of the utterance as a unity rather than a random assortment of phrases. Or it can refer outside, to an object or person or event in the environment of the utterance. Suppose I say to you 'Pick up that pencil'. The reference item 'that' tells you to refer to an earlier phase of the conversation or to the environment in which it is taking place. If neither of us has yet mentioned any pencil, then you must assume that my reference is external, and you will have to look around until you see the pencil I am referring to. In such cases the reference item gives an effect of unfulfilled specificity: you are told that the object in question is specific (*that* pencil, not this one), but you will have to supply its exact identity yourself.

If I really wanted you to pick up the right pencil, I would probably point to it. Poems, of course, cannot point and any use they make of external reference will establish a particular and very interesting relation to the reader. Roughly speaking, they will call upon the reader to supply information from his or her own experience, while to some extent determining by the reference items they use *how* the information will be supplied.

They will keep the reader's imagination busy, while at the same time hoping to dictate the form of the business. Here, perhaps, we have a way of analysing how Valéry's blocks of print shape the handwriting which surrounds them. For I believe that external reference has proved an effect of language vital to poets who have not known for whom they were writing, poets who have had somehow to draw out an identifiable readership from the promiscuous herd. These poets could expect that the true reader would demonstrate his or her competence by supplying the information which their poems gestured at but finally withheld.

Let us return to the problem of Wordsworth's old men. If the Cumberland Beggar constantly reminds us that 'man is dear to man', why does everyone seem so keen to lock him up in the workhouse? How can Wordsworth persuade his 'few and scattered hearers' of something which the world has chosen to ignore, without lecturing them? 'Old Man Travelling; Animal Tranquillity and Decay' provides an answer to the second, if not the first, of these questions. Published in *Lyrical Ballads,* the poem subsequently underwent a series of revisions and eventually lost its last six lines. Although the revisions show the anxiety Wordsworth felt in attributing significance to the old man, the final version does in fact resolve his dilemma brilliantly:

> The little hedge-row birds
> That peck along the road, regard him not.
> He travels on, and in his face, his step,
> His gait, is one expression: every limb,
> His look and bending figure, all bespeak
> A man who does not move with pain, but moves
> With thought. – He is insensibly subdued
> To settled quiet: he is one by whom
> All effort seems forgotten; one to whom
> Long patience hath such mild composure given,
> That patience now doth seem a thing of which
> He hath no need. He is by nature led
> To peace so perfect that the young behold
> With envy, what the Old Man hardly feels.

The dash marks the shift from description to interpretation on which 'The Old Cumberland Beggar' had foundered. But this time Wordsworth carefully withholds the identity of the protagonist: a chain of pronomial items (him, he, his, etc.) leads across the transition, but it is not until the last line that we are given a noun phrase (Old Man) to substitute for them. Instead of describing the old man, and then proclaiming his sanctity in a loud voice, Wordsworth holds his identity open long enough for us to acknowledge him as a silent monitor. (Compare the similar introduction of Beaupuis in *The Prelude*, IX, 403–30.) We know him at the same time as figure in the landscape and ritual function; here there is no dangerous lag between the two recognitions.

But what transforms an itinerant into a liminal entity? No so much a statement as a particular reference item: 'he is *one* by whom . . . *one* to whom . . . ' Here, 'one' has a powerfully generalising effect. While 'he' and 'his' refer forward to 'Old Man', 'one' works slightly across that chain, referring to a category whose definition lies beyond the scope of the poem. We know that it means 'a person', but it doesn't refer to an occurrence of the word 'person' anywhere in the text. *We* supply, from our own experience or imagination, the definition of the category referred to. Wordsworth once said that the poet's aim was to arouse a 'co-operating *power* in the mind of the Reader'. In this case, we cooperate by identifying something the poem itself declines to identify. At the same time, the scope of our 'co-operating power' (the sense of universality we bring to our notion of the old man) has been determined by Wordsworth's choice of reference item.

So it is also in another, slightly later poem, 'Resolution and Independence', where the narrator actually addresses the itinerant, making some remark about the weather:

> A gentle answer did the Old Man make,
> In courteous speech which forth he slowly drew:
> And him with further words I thus bespake,
> 'What occupation do you there pursue?
> This is a lonesome place for one like you.'
> Ere he replied, a flash of mild surprise
> Broke from the sable orbs of his yet-vivid eyes.

Why is the old man surprised by such an obvious question? Could it be that the phrase 'one like you' implies a rather intimidating knowledge about the kind of person he is? The narrator has already begun to assimilate him to a category larger than any he can himself recognise. We do not find out that he is a leech-gatherer until thirty lines later, by which time he has achieved the status of a liminal entity:

> The Old Man still stood talking by my side:
> But now his voice to me was like a stream
> Scarce heard; nor word from word could I divide;
> And the whole body of the Man did seem
> Like one whom I had met with in a dream;
> Or like a man from some far region sent,
> To give me human strength, by apt admonishment.

By the end of the stanza the old man has become a silent monitor, a shaman returning from some far region to admonish the living. It is our cooperating power, as much as any effort on the part of the narrator, which transforms him; our cooperating power which supplies a meaning for 'one'.

It is important to realise that we are dealing with a particular and comparatively uncommon use of the word, whose various functions can be illustrated from Ford Madox Ford's account of D. H. Lawrence:

> It was quite obvious to me that here was a young fellow who ought to write, who indeed would write, so the sooner he got to it the better. One would have to find some way for him. I was never one to be afraid of taking on responsibilities.
>
> He shied a bit at that, plunging away, as if he had been a startled colt, from a too attractive novelty. It wasn't that the two thousand a year and establishment and titled company were not as real to him as his life in the cage. He felt himself as sure of the one as of the other.

In the last sentence, 'the one' is a substitute for 'the two thousand a year and establishment and titled company'; unlike the two other instances in the passage, it refers internally and is accompanied by a modifier ('*the* one'). Both the other instances refer externally: the first is a pronoun, and always likely to include the speaker among those it refers to ('One would have to . . . '); the second is what Halliday and Hasan call a pronoun, and quite likely to exclude the speaker from those it refers to ('I was never one to . . .'). I have argued for the importance of the latter, a comparatively rare usage, in poems by Wordsworth. It contrasts with the substitute in that it always refers outside the text, and with the pronoun in that the category it refers to is less likely to include the speaker.

Because the pronoun has such a distinctive function, we can follow its career in modern poetry quite closely. What interests me is that it seems consistently to have marked the place in discourse of a particular social role: that of 'silent monitor'. Indeed, it serves as a kind of radioactive tracer, by which we can follow the passage of such figures through English poetry since Wordsworth. It has served other purposes, of course, but the coincidence between it and the representation of marginal figures is none the less striking.

Wordsworth's beggars had become silent monitors by virtue of the physical and social condition to which they had been subdued. But later poets were drawn instead to those who deliberately marginalised themselves, by flouting the conventions of the age. The shift is apparent in Arnold's preference for Rousseauesque wanderers, and in Thomas Hardy's poem 'A Man', which concerns the demolition of a fine old building:

> Among the hired dismantlers entered there
> One till the moment of his task untold.
> When charged therewith he gazed, and answered bold:
>   'Be needy I or no,
> I will not help lay low a house so fair!'

As I read it, 'one' is ambiguous: it could refer back to the word 'dismantlers', or it could refer outside the text and mean 'a person'; it could be a substitute or a pronoun. The ambiguity may be deliberate, for we do not at this stage know whether the man will count himself among the dismantlers, or by opting out become a silent monitor whose identity must be supplied by the reader. Then the man speaks, choosing unemployment rather than complicity with the age, and is made to pay for his boldness:

> Dismissed with sneers he packed his tools and went,
> And wandered workless; for it seemed unwise
> To close with one who dared to criticize
>   And carp on points of taste:
> Rude men should work where placed, and be content.

This time 'one' definitely refers outside the text, for the protagonist has separated himself from the dismantlers and become 'a man' in the true sense. He has turned his back on social custom and decided to live for humanity; the poem celebrates his decision.

Thus the pronoun continued to guard the identity of beggars and tramps, in Hardy's 'I Am the One' and Edward Thomas's 'Lob' and William Plomer's 'John Drew', but came increasingly to stand in for those whose dissent was conscious, and probably intellectual. Artists have always featured prominently in this latter tradition, as poets from Hardy to Auden sought to identify 'fellow-citizens of the independent gypsy land of Bohemia'. Most striking of all is the ghost encountered in Eliot's 'Little Gidding', at the end of an air-raid:

> After the dark dove with the flickering tongue
>> Had passed below the horizon of his homing
>> While the dead leaves still rattled on like tin
> Over the asphalt where no other sound was
>> Between three districts whence the smoke arose
> I met one walking . . .

Like Wordsworth's old men, like Hardy's dissident, the ghost is a creature apart. Like them, he is made into a 'silent monitor' by our willingness to identify the category he belongs to ('I met one walking'). For this is the first apparition in the *Four Quartets* not to be pressed back out of sight among rustling shrubbery or *corps de ballet*. It speaks with great authority, indeed with a kind of collective authority, because it is a 'compound' ghost ('one and many'). Another monitor, then, but emphatically not silent, since it abides by a mischievous protocol in Eliot's poetry, whereby the less there is of you, the more you have to say for yourself (compare the spry assortment of bones in 'Ash-Wednesday'). Being both 'intimate' and 'unidentifiable', it achieves the effect of unfulfilled specificity which characterises the use of external reference items in much modern poetry.

Artists were not the only entities to seem attractively liminal. Auden's 'In Memory of Sigmund Freud' used the pronoun to offer the founder of psychoanalysis, then still a scandalous figure, as a kind of silent monitor:

If some traces of the autocratic pose,
the paternal strictness he distrusted, still
    clung to his utterance and features,
  it was a protective coloration

for one who'd lived among enemies so long:
if often he was wrong and, at times, absurd,
    to us he is no more a person
  now but a whole climate of opinion

under whom we conduct our different lives . . .

Freud's passage from a distant and defensive autocrat to a whole climate of opinion is negotiated by the pronoun, which works here exactly as it had in 'Animal Tranquillity and Decay' and 'A Man' and 'Little Gidding'.

Those who supply the information demanded by the pronouns, and thus attribute a liminal status and a certain universality to the old men and the dissidents, will thereby identify themselves as readers. They will busy themselves as Tristram would have liked them to, but in a manner prescribed by the poem; their 'handwriting' will occupy the space left by the 'blocks of print'. And the poet will once again know for whom he is writing.

Such enticing and cajoling of the secret complement of the text by thematic and rhetorical strategies has played an important part in American, English and Irish poetry from the time of the French Revolution to the time of the Second World War. Since then, I believe, new factors have entered into the equation, factors which I shall consider in Chapter 9. But my next seven chapters will attempt to define some of those thematic and rhetorical strategies in writing from the first half of the century.

2 The duration of mortmain

Wordsworth's itinerant old men seem to have passed through the distractions of subjectivity and come out the other side into a biological adventure, a drama of genetic coding. This ability to subsist, to keep going, is a tribute to their *stamina* (threads spun by the Fates at birth and therefore the measure of a person's vital impulse). What they have come to after a lifetime is what they were originally allotted, a purely generic identity.

Tennyson's old men would like to come to that. They would like to embark on a rite of passage, or complete what they imagine to be a rite of passage. But they have no stamina. They cannot empty themselves of distracting self-consciousness so as to recover a generic identity. We see them at a standstill: locked in perpetual embrace, or waiting for the tide to change, or stuck up a very tall pole.

Tennyson's Ulysses has returned to Ithaca, but is not enjoying the comforts of home and reputation. The disadvantages of a life in the public eye strike him forcibly. He sits by a 'still hearth' with his wife, dealing 'unequal laws' to an idle and resentful populace, playing a role: 'I am become a name.' Hierarchy inhibits and falsifies his relationships with other people. So he decides to travel again, leaving his son – prudent, respectful, 'centred in the sphere Of common duties' – to take over. Once on board ship, he will rediscover the liminal qualities to be found only among 'an equal temper of heroic hearts'. His voyage will represent a rite of passage lasting until he dies.

But the poem ends with Ulysses still on the dockside, forever about to embark, and this hiatus allows us to ask why he wants to do it. We can weigh his sprightly charm against his irresponsibility. Is not his way of living for humanity really rather absurd, a fantasy inspired by some regimental reunion and vivid with gout? Tennyson does not openly question the validity of the

rite, but he encourages scepticism by leaving Ulysses on the
threshold, at the point of entry. Tennyson's thresholds are ghastly
pauses, moments when there seems no defence against the
thought that the whole thing may be a waste of time.

If such a thought did not occur to St Simeon Stylites, it
certainly ought to have done. For thirty years he has lived at the
top of a pillar (a 'sign betwixt the meadow and the cloud'), and
his rite of passage should therefore be nearing its conclusion – if,
that is, it counts as a rite of passage at all. So he prays, anxiously,
that the experience will turn out to have eroded his human
identity and equipped him for the company of saints:

> Courage, St. Simeon! This dull chrysalis
> Cracks into shining wings, and hope ere death
> Spreads more and more, that God hath now
> Sponged and made blank of crimeful record all
> My mortal archives.

Simeon hesitates between metaphors of archive and chrysalis,
between painstakingly accumulated social identity and sudden
absolving nature. But the flaring self-consciousness of his
monologue adds to the mortal archives which should by now have
been made blank. The more he talks, the less we trust him.

It is not far, as Robert Langbaum has pointed out, from
'Ulysses' to 'Gerontion'. But Eliot's old man driven by the
Trades to a sleepy corner seems an even less likely candidate for
liminal status than Ulysses or Simeon Stylites. Their fanaticism
had at least demonstrated an appetite for regeneration, whether
by sainthood or homoerotic adventure. Simeon's sojourn on the
pillar has been attended by miracles, while Ulysses seems to have
learnt something on the playing-fields of Eton. Their dreams may
be perverse, but at least it is a determined perversity. Gerontion,
on the other hand, has no determination and no vestige of
stamina. He never stood at the 'hot gates', never heaved a cutlass
(a Highland sport?), and his sceptical account of the opportunities
afforded by history makes it clear that he will venture nothing; at
the same time he can only conceive spiritual regeneration as a
violent and arbitrary force from outside, a tiger springing at his
throat. Eliot appears to drain off the significance that Wordsworth
and even Tennyson had invested in old men.

If so, he was responding to a fairly widespread sentiment. The old men who had led Europe and America into the First World War remained obstinately alive, unlike many of those they had led. Or so it seemed to the young American writer Robert McAlmon, visiting his English in-laws in the year 'Gerontion' was published, 1920:

> Having the young man's resentful belief that the war had killed off, in Europe and England, the best of my generation for moralizing hacks and elders, most worm-eaten old men with a patronizing attitude gave me the creeps.

No doubt the worm-eaten and patronising Gerontion, like the old men who discuss Helen's fate in Ezra Pound's Canto 2, had a similar effect. Pound was recreating an episode in the *Iliad,* but his portrayal of the anxious elders echoed (as Ronald Bush has shown) a general contempt for the negotiators at the Paris Peace Conference of 1919. Keynes, for example, remembered Clemenceau as 'silent and aloof' on the outskirts of the debate, 'throned, in his gray gloves, on the brocade chair, dry in soul and empty of hope, very old and tired, but surveying the scene with a cynical and almost impish air;' while President Wilson seemed to him to be in the grip of mental paralysis, utterly rigid in his preconceptions. Eliot and his readers would have had every reason to distrust a man like Gerontion, very old and tired, dry in soul.

Pound was later to describe government by such men as 'the duration of mortmain'. 'How long shall the dead hand rule,' he was to ask, 'and to what extent?' To many it seemed that the dead hand ruled not only over politics, but over the entire regenerative capacity of Western civilisation. As the old men lost their stamina, so the margins they inhabited became – literally, in some cases – a no-man's-land, a waste land. What would Eliot and Pound have made of the solace Wordsworth had enjoyed in graveyards?

> It is such a happiness to have, in an unkind World, one Enclosure where the voice of detraction is not heard; where the traces of evil inclinations are unknown; where contentment prevails, and there is no jarring tone in the peaceful Concert of amity and gratitude.

Like the beggar's stated round, the inscriptions on gravestones asserted a generic human bond; they were 'acknowledgements to our common nature'. Wordsworth was most deeply moved by the stone on a child's grave which simply bore a name and the date of birth and death. This inscription prompted by its very sparseness 'awful thoughts of rights conferred, of hopes awakened, of remembrances stealing away or vanishing'. It became for him an image of subsistence and generic identity as powerful as the stamina of the old men. 'Origin and tendency,' Wordsworth concluded, 'are notions inseparably co-relative.' The liminal figures demonstrated this correlation between what we are given at birth and what we come to; the sanctuaries encouraged him, and through him his readers, to recognise its validity.

But urban development was threatening the sanctuaries as well as the beggar's way of life. Wordsworth felt that their remoteness was crucial to their purpose, and that they lost much of their 'monitory virtue' when 'obtruded upon the notice of men occupied with the cares of the world, and too often sullied and defiled by those cares'. Dickens' novels told much the same story. Henry James thought that London was a bad place to die in, not on account of the perversity of its inhabitants, but on account of 'the awful doom of general dishumanisation'.

By Hardy's time there were still plenty of secluded graveyards, but it was not easy to regard them as 'acknowledgements to our common nature'. His 'Paying Calls' describes a walk out of town to one such sanctuary – 'Beyond where bustle ends' – whose graves have little to offer by way of monitory virtue: 'they spoke not to me'. Indeed, evil thoughts and vitriolic discourses seem commonplace in Hardy's graveyards. *Satires of Circumstance,* published in November 1914, is full of talkative corpses; so full that it might be, as Paul Fussell suggests, 'a medium for perceiving the events of the war just beginning'.

The young men killed off for 'moralizing hacks and elders' died on an almost unprecedented scale and in peculiarly horrible ways. Sigmund Freud, like Eliot and Pound a non-combatant living in the capital of a nation at war, thought that the 'conventional treatment' of death had been rendered obsolete by the carnage. Not even the most secluded sanctuary was safe any more, as Edmund Blunden realised when contemplating the mess made of a graveyard close to the front line. Apparently the litter of bones and the pools of stagnant water fascinated the front-line troops.

How, Blunden asks, could men who saw death every day 'find the strange and the remote in these corpses?' The strange and the remote had perhaps been reduced from their ritual function to a protective irony, a numbing *frisson*.

So it was for Leopold Bloom, at Paddy Dignam's funeral:

> I daresay the soil would be quite fat with corpse manure, bones, flesh, nails, charnelhouses. Dreadful. Turning green and pink, decomposing. Rot quick in damp earth. The lean old ones tougher. Then a kind of a tallowy kind of a cheesy. Then begin to get black, treacle oozing out of them.

Nor did the epitaphs inspire awful thoughts of remembrances stealing away:

> Mr. Bloom walked unheeded along his grove by saddened angels, crosses, broken pillars, family vaults, stone hopes praying with upcast eyes, old Ireland's hearts and hands. More sensible to spend the money on some charity for the living. Pray for the repose of the soul of. Does anybody really? Plant him and have done with him. Like down a coalshoot. Then lump them together to save time . . . Who passed away. Who departed this life. As if they did it of their own accord. Got the shove, all of them. Who kicked the bucket. More interesting if they told you what they were. So and so, wheelwright. I travelled for cork lino. I paid five shillings in the pound. Or a woman's with her saucepan. I cooked good Irish stew. Eulogy in a country churchyard it ought to be that poem of whose is it Wordsworth or Thomas Campbell.

Bloom declines the eulogy in the country churchyard, the 'peaceful Concert of amity and gratitude'. He would rather hear about the occupations and eccentricities of the people buried there than about the generic human bond their deaths asserted.

Eliot published the early chapters of *Ulysses* in the *Egoist* in 1919, and read the rest in manuscripts two years later. Echoes of the Dublin graveyard survive in *The Waste Land*, where a corpse is planted and the twilight of ritual practice announced. Eliot said that anyone who has read Frazer's *Adonis, Attis, Osiris* will recognise in the poem references to 'vegetation ceremonies'. Such ceremonies are not rites of passage; they have to do with the renewal of the earth, rather than with a change of state among human beings. Nevertheless, Frazer considered Osiris a god not only of fertility but also of the dead, a god whose office was to ensure the safe passage of the human spirit into eternal life:

> We may assume that in the faith of his worshippers the two provinces of the god were intimately connected. In laying their dead in the grave they committed them to his keeping who could raise them from the dust to life eternal, even as he caused the seed to spring from the ground. Of that faith the corn-stuffed effigies of Osiris found in Egyptian tombs furnish an eloquent and unequivocal testimony. They were at once an emblem and an instrument of resurrection. Thus from the sprouting of the grain the ancient Egyptians drew an augury of human immortality.

It was this aspect of the ceremony that Eliot chose to caricature in the opening section of *The Waste Land*:

> 'That corpse you planted last year in your garden,
> 'Has it begun to sprout? Will it bloom this year?'

The ancient Egyptians, Frazer continued, were not the only people to have

> built the same far-reaching hopes on the same fragile foundation. 'Thou fool, that which thou sowest, thou sowest not that body that shall be, but bare grain, it may chance of wheat, or of some other grain: but God giveth it a body as it hath pleased him, and to every seed his own body. So also is the resurrection of the dead. It is sown in corruption; it is raised in incorruption; it is sown in weakness; it is raised in power; it is sown in a natural body; it is raised in a spiritual body.'

Frazer's quotation from 1 Corinthians 15 forms part of the Order for the Burial of the Dead in the *Book of Common Prayer*. When Eliot entitled the opening section of his poem 'The Burial of the Dead', he may have meant (like Frazer) to draw attention to the persistence of rites of passage in modern societies. But it is more likely that he meant to ask whether such ceremonies could serve any purpose at all in the world of Stetson and Madame Sosostris, and in a city where death had 'undone so many'.

Ritual remained throughout Eliot's career the proper means for correlating origin and tendency. He searched the writings of the anthropologists for evidence, and concluded that they did not lay enough stress on the importance of ritual for all known societies. In Josiah Royce's similar at Harvard in December 1913, he criticised them for failing to explain ritual in terms of *need*. I shall have more to say in my next chapter about the place of ceremony in Eliot's thinking, but I want first to give some idea of the world which ceremony was supposed to stabilise and renew. For it was not a world devoid of ceremony, but a world full of endlessly parodied ceremony. The problem was not to create what had been lacking, but to distinguish between true and false.

On one hand, there was a panoply of official ceremonies and official observances which had lost their meaning but which still survived: the duration of mortmain. On the other, there was a panoply of private and secular acts which had somehow come to be invested by their protagonists with what would normally be thought a ritual impulse. It was to behaviour of the second kind that Freud addressed himself in papers from 'Obsessive Acts and Religious Practices' (1907) to *Beyond the Pleasure Principle* (1920). Freud was the supreme archivist of defective meaning: meaning which is faulty (that is, unintelligible) because it has defected, come over from somewhere else, and now appears where it is least expected – in dreams, parapraxes, jokes, afterthoughts, obsessive acts. Eliot's work up to and including 'The Hollow Men' was beset, in its attempt at a rite of passage, by the failure of public rites and by an increasing familiarity with what Freud termed 'neurotic ceremonial'. Thus Eliot became the poet of the time between the disappearance of ceremony and its return under the guise of neurosis.

* * *

I think that if we can establish the sense in which Freud and Eliot might be thought to share certain preoccupations, we can then use Freud's more conceptualised procedures to throw some light on Eliot's poems. We might begin with Freud's account of neurotic ceremonial. This, he explained, consists in 'making small adjustments to particular everyday actions, small additions or restrictions or arrangements, which have always to be carried out in the same, or in a methodically varied, manner'. Such rites are clearly significant, because the patient proves incapable of renouncing them and is punished by intolerable anxiety if he fails to perform them. But their meaning remains obscure, not least to the patient himself.

Freud came across many examples in his clinical practice. He often returned to the case of a woman in her late twenties, who would run compulsively from one room in her house to another, stand beside a table there, summon her maid, dismiss the maid, and then run back into the other room. Freud explained this apparently meaningless behaviour as an attempt to exonerate her husband, whom she had left but still loved. On their wedding night, the husband had proved impotent and had run backwards and forwards between his own room and hers to make fresh attempts. Next morning, he had said that he would feel ashamed in front of the chambermaid, and poured a bottle of red ink on to the sheets, although in the wrong place. (One remembers the couple in Eliot's 'Death of the Duchess', who wonder whether they will be able to face the chambermaid when she opens the door next morning.) In her neurotic ceremony, the wife was restaging her bridal night, but making sure that everything would be done properly this time. So when she summoned her maid, she stood in such a position that the maid could not fail to see a large stain on the table-cloth in front of her.

Freud concluded that a ceremonial begins as an act of defence or security, as 'a *protective measure*': in this case, the woman was defending herself against the knowledge that her husband was impotent. A neurotic rite reenacts the very trauma it is meant to control, just as a religious rite (in Freud's view) summons the asocial instincts it is designed to master. For him, the latter resembles the former in everything except its public content, and even that can often be analysed in sexual or familial terms: 'the puberty rites of savages, which represent a rebirth, have the sense of releasing the boy from his incestuous bond with his mother and of reconciling him with his father'.

Eliot was uncomfortably aware of the proximity of religious to neurotic ceremonial, but he would have disputed Freud's assimilation of one to the other. His aim was to discover a rite which would correlate origin and tendency, and thus reconstitute subjectivity in a realm beyond the neurosis bred by modern life. Desperate to be somewhere else, to escape the smug decorum of Boston and Paris and London, he might well have echoed what

Henry Adams said in 1906: 'I yearn for St. Simeon Stylites or sin.'

But Tennyson had already done for the saint what Baudelaire had done for the sin. Liminal status of any kind was hard to envisage, and relentlessly shadowed by its neurotic counterpart. So Eliot found when, in late 1914 or early 1915, he came to write a remarkable if rather desperate poem, 'The Death of Saint Narcissus'. Narcissus was a Bishop of Jerusalem who, at the end of the second century, hid himself in the desert for several years; his retreat was to be a rite of passage fitting him for the company of saints. But the central figure of Eliot's poem owes as much to Ovid's Narcissus as to any bishop.

Freud, too, was following up the Ovidian tale, in his paper 'On Narcissism: An Introduction', published in 1914. If we are to understand what he meant by narcissism, we must refer first to the earlier concept of auto-erotism, adapted from Havelock Ellis in *Three Essays on the Theory of Sexuality* (1905). Auto-erotism describes a state of the organism where each instinct seeks gratification on its own account, without reference to any object or to any overall organisation of the ego. It may involve contact between one part of the body and another (thumb-sucking, masturbation), but its ideal prototype is the action of lips kissing themselves. Narcissism develops out of this state by what Freud calls 'a new psychical action': the hitherto isolated sexual instincts come together into a whole and find an object. That object is the ego in its entirety, an image acquired by observing and then internalising the image of another. So narcissism, unlike auto-erotic activity, depends on relationship, on an identification with someone else formed and then abandoned as the subject discovers in his own now unified image what he had loved in another. Identification with the unified image of another must precede identification with the unified image of oneself.

The distinction between auto-erotism and narcissism suggests that, in Freud's words, 'a unity comparable to the ego cannot exist in the individual from the start; the ego has to be developed'. The ego develops by perceiving the unities which other people (or its own bodily image in the mirror) represent, and by itself emulating those unities. Identity is not given from the outset, but made; and what has been made can be taken apart, or doubled. Freud's theory of narcissism thus proposed that there is no essential self, but only the putting together of selves through a new psychical action.

The theory played an important part in his tracing of the connections between religious and neurotic ceremonial, because it allowed him to argue that idealism serves to produce an acceptable psychic unity rather than a self-less state of grace. The idealist may internalise the image of a loved one in the form of an ideal version of himself, and so love himself as the ideal unity he *might* represent rather than the disunity he *does* represent; 'and in general,' Freud added, 'it is harder to convince an idealist of the inexpedient location of his libido than a plain man whose pretensions have remained more moderate'. Instead of an essential and generic human bond uncovered during a rite of passage, we find defective libido.

It is an eventuality which haunts the spiritual progress of Eliot's Saint Narcissus. In the first stanza of the poem, a narrator contracts to tell us the story of the saint's martyrdom, which begins with what one can only call an experience of auto-erotism. Walking by the sea, Narcissus becomes aware of his limbs 'smoothly passing each other'. His hands feel the tips of his fingers, and he is stifled and soothed by 'his own rhythm'. Each part of his body derives independent gratification from itself, without reference to any object or to an image of the unified self.

Appalled by the experience, Narcissus decides to separate himself from the ways of men and to become a dancer 'before God'. This retreat to the margin will, he hopes, strip away his old identity and make him anew. Indeed, some strange things happen to him. He becomes a tree caught in its own branches, a fish writhing in its own clutch, a young girl raped by an old man and discovering the taste of her own whiteness and smoothness. These experiences differ from the earlier one in that they involve the unified image of another being or an object: tree, fish, young girl. Yet each image is grasped in a moment of self-gratification: it is himself as a young girl that Narcissus perceives through the eyes of an old man. He has passed from auto-erotism to narcissism. A self has been made.

It is of course a somewhat defective self, incapable of relationship. Coming into it, Narcissus merely feels drunken and old. This might recall another of Tennyson's old men, Tithonous, who was granted immortality so that he could lie for ever with the goddess of dawn: 'I wither slowly in thine arms, / Here at the quiet limit of the world.' Marginal status has clearly become something of a strain for Tithonous. He speaks of it not as a reward but as a punishment for his desire to 'pass beyond the goal of ordinance / Where all should pause.' He too, having tasted whiteness, feels drunken and old. Both men have transgressed the goal of ordinance, but Narcissus's punishment is to wither slowly in *his own* arms, in neurotic ceremony.

He decides to try something else. He will become a dancer 'to' God rather than a dancer 'before' God. He will commit himself to martyrdom, speaking more directly through his death than through his self-involved apartness. But he cannot shake off his narcissism, and this ideal version of himself turns out to be yet another hiding-place for libido. The arrows which puncture his skin gratify him by allowing him to surrender to the redness of his own blood. Martyrdom seems like a continuation of narcissism by other means, a different and more ingenious way of tasting oneself. The martyr is no better than the sensualist, because both selves have been produced out of an original auto-erotism; both selves have been made rather than given.

Each of Freud's new psychical actions has the effect of multiplying rather than uniting the selfhood of the subject. Our behaviour will inevitably fall short of any ideal image we may have internalised, and we must therefore always contend with the difference between ourselves as we are and ourselves as we ought to be. At this point a third factor comes into play, a 'special psychical agency' which seeks to ensure that narcissistic gratification is derived from the ego-ideal and which 'constantly watches the actual ego and measures it by that ideal'. This special agency – conscience – urges most of us to martyrdom of one kind or another. We respond to it like paranoiacs, Freud said, feeling that we are being watched and that our most secret thoughts are known. He remarked that paranoiacs are also made aware of the demands of conscience by 'voices which characteristically speak to them in the third person (''Now she's thinking of that again'' . . . ''now he's going out'')'. Is this eye which watches us and voice which speaks of us in the third person our essential self, or just another fiction?

Eliot described the artist as 'an Eye curiously, patiently watching himself as a man'; and his poems of this period echo with unattributable voices. J. Alfred Prufrock, in part Eliot himself and in part a man of about forty, urges an expedition: 'Let us go, then, you and I . . .' The 'you' addressed is his timid, conformist self, whom he proceeds to talk about in the third person: 'They will say: ''How his hair is growing thin!'' ' The 'I' is the voice of conscience which observes this conformist self and measures it against an ideal image of the self as a solitary thinker given to apocalyptic visions. Yet the voice does not seem particularly authoritative, and it fails to establish the ideal ego in a realm beyond narcissism.

'The Death of Saint Narcissus' opens in a rather similar fashion:

> Come under the shadow of this gray rock –
> Come in under the shadow of this gray rock,
> And I will show you something different from either
> Your shadow sprawling over the sand at daybreak, or
> Your shadow leaping behind the fire against the red rock:
> I will show you his bloody cloth and limbs
> And the gray shadow on his lips.

From this point on Narcissus is described in the third person, until the poem concludes at the rock where 'you' and 'I' shelter, and where he now lies with the shadow in his mouth. Are we hearing the voice of a narrator, or the voice of a conscience which wants to observe its empirical self in action and to see how far short of an ideal image that self has fallen? It may be the latter, I think, judging by the way the stanza parodies a moment in *Paradise Lost* (Book 4, 465–71). Eve describes how a mysterious voice advised her to stop staring at herself in a lake and search for Adam:

> . . . there had I fixed
> Mine eyes till now, and pined with vain desire,
> Had not a voice thus warned me, What thou seest,
> What there thou seest fair creature is thyself,
> With thee it came and goes: but follow me,
> And I will bring thee where no shadow stays
> Thy coming, and thy soft embrace . . .

Follow me, both voices say, and I will show you something different from your own shadow. In *Paradise Lost* the voice speaks with divine authority; it offers relationship and true identity. But the outcome of Eliot's poem mocks this happy tale. It suggests that what lies beyond your shadow is another shadow, and that the voice which urges you to abandon one for the other may be a delusion.

Of course, Eliot did not rejoice in this state of affairs. He was envying rather than mocking Milton. As his search for a rite of passage which would reconstitute subjectivity intensified, so did his attempts to enhance the voice of conscience. In 1917 he told Bertrand Russell that he wanted to give new expression to Authority and Reverence. When a revised version of the opening stanza of 'Saint Narcissus' appeared in *The Waste Land* (lines 24–9), the shadowy voice which spoke it had been properly identified. 'Son of man,' the voice intones; God, as the reference to Ezekiel makes clear, is talking to his prophet. This voice is to all appearances as unambiguously authorised as its original in *Paradise Lost*.

However, it took some time for Eliot to arrive at any expression of Authority and Reverence. His self-disgust during this period was, Lyndall Gordon says, 'in a class of its own' and 'quite uncompassionate'; it would not yield anything to revere. Before it did, Eliot would have to work through Gerontion, whose loss of passion was yet another narcissism.

Freud tackled an aspect of uncompassionate self-disgust in his 1917 paper 'Mourning and Melancholia', where he returned to the connections between a socially validated rite (mourning) and an obsessive state of mind (melancholia). He drew on his theory of narcissism to explain melancholia, which he thought a disease of the psyche turned in on itself; 'In mourning it is the world which has become poor and empty; in melancholia it is the ego itself.' The patient again internalises an identification, coming to love in himself what he had loved in another. But this time the person he loves has abandoned him, and all the resentment he feels against that person is transferred on to a part of himself. He talks about himself endlessly, as though his own depravity was the only object in the world, and his perpetually active conscience should thus be considered a means of gratifying his self-love. His sense of spiritual poverty caricatures the grief of the mourner.

Henry James's story 'The Beast in the Jungle' turns on a similar distinction between mourning and melancholia. John Marcher has lived his life in anticipation of the decisive experience which might transform or overwhelm it; he waits to be made anew, or to be broken. But so self-obsessed is he that he does not even notice the event which might have ended his waiting: May Bartram's love for him. He will not allow her to redeem him from his destiny, which is to be 'the man in the world

to whom nothing whatever was to happen'. By the end of the
story all he has acknowledged is his own emptiness: 'the things he
saw couldn't help being common when he had become common
to look at them'. But the damage done by his melancholia is only
brought home to him in the final scene, when he visits May
Bartram's grave. He meets another mourner, a man whose grief
is overt and unmistakable: 'The stranger passed, but the raw
glare of his grief remained, making our friend wonder in pity
what wrong, what wound it expressed, what injury not to be
healed. What had the man *had*, to make him by the loss of it so
bleed and yet live?' For this man the *world* is – justifiably – empty.
His grief is objective and worldly, because the relationship he
mourns had its existence in the world and not just in his own
head. Marcher realises that his feelings have never had such
validity, since he never loved May for herself:

> No passion had ever touched him, for this was what passion
> meant; he had survived and maundered and pined, but where
> had been *his* deep ravage? . . . He had seen *outside* of his life,
> not learned it within, the way a woman was mourned when she
> had been loved for herself: such was the force of his conviction
> of the meaning of the stranger's face, which still flared for him
> as a smoky torch.

The stranger mourns; Marcher has never known anything except
melancholia, the caricature of mourning.

Lyndall Gordon points out that Gerontion's self-absorption
and anxiety for experience 'recall Henry James's late tales of the
unlived life: middle-aged gentlemen who crave and shrink from a
tremendous experience, like the leap of a beast in the jungle.'
Gerontion's self-abasement is to Christian humility what
Marcher's melancholia was to the stranger's mourning. He draws
a 'lurid comfort', as Hugh Kenner has said, from reiterating his
loss of passion and from imagining the tigerish Christ who will
judge him. He savours 'the ascription to himself of conspicuous
honesty at the moment (he rather likes to suppose) of damnation'.

Where 'Prufrock' and 'Saint Narcissus' had considered
personal dilemmas in personal terms, 'Gerontion' alludes to the
failures of history: the old men at the Paris Peace Conference, the
hollowness of public ceremonial, the duration of mortmain. Even
so it turns finally, like the other poems, on a narcissism which has

substituted a self-image for the world; the house and its tenants are phantoms, barren thoughts. Eliot's attempts to discern a rite of passage for himself and for his readers may have been hampered by the duration of mortmain, but they were damaged even more by the very facility with which he struck off versions of neurotic ceremonial.

3 In the cage

The work of Eliot, Joyce and Pound is often taken to represent a moment when, in Eliot's words, 'Psychology (such as it is, and whether our reaction to it be comic or serious), ethnology, and *The Golden Bough* have concurred to make possible what was impossible even a few years ago.' Psychology, ethnology, *The Golden Bough*: these, Eliot thought, were the frames of reference or the vocabularies which might be expected to accommodate literary innovation.

One or two of the terms used by the literary innovators did derive from psychology. Pound borrowed the term 'complex' from Bernard Hart's *Psychology of Insanity*, an enormously popular vade-mecum, in order to define an image as 'that which presents an intellectual and emotional complex in an instant of time'. Elsewhere in Hart's book we find an account of 'dissociation of consciousness', a state in which unrelated thoughts (a mathematical problem, holiday plans) jostle for attention. 'The patient's mind seems, in fact, to be split into two smaller minds, engaged in two different occupations, making use of two distinct sets of memories, and without any relation whatever one to the other.' Eliot's reaction to Hart's book, if he read it at all, may well have been comic rather than serious. Even so, he did come to talk of a 'dissociation of sensibility' in the seventeenth century, and of how the fragments of an ordinary person's experience – Spinoza, falling in love, the noise of the typewriter, the smell of cooking – fail to cohere.

Eliot, of course, had good reason to know about dissociations of consciousness. On 12 October 1921 he was granted three months' sick leave from the bank where he worked, and during his recuperation in Margate and Lausanne he wrote a large part of *The Waste Land*. He went to Lausanne to consult the psychiatrist Roger Vittoz, who had been recommended by Julian Huxley and Ottoline Morrell, and whose book on *Treatment of Neurasthenia by Means of Brain Control* had been translated into English in 1911. Vittoz assumed that the brain has two 'working centres', subjective and objective: 'the subjective brain is in a general way the source of the ideas and sensations, and . . . the objective brain in a sense "focusses" them.' Neurasthenia occurs when one working centre fails to focus the ideas and sensations produced by the other. Vittoz described its symptoms as 'apathy, fatigue, and want of interest in life'. The patient feels 'only half awake and in a sort of half-dreamy state from which he cannot escape'; he loses all interest in the world and 'has no feeling except for his own personality, which he often detests'. The clinic in Lausanne must have seemed to Eliot like a rest-home for Gerontions.

The psychology of Hart and Vittoz was little more than common sense spiced with technical terms, and we must assume that Eliot remained pretty sceptical about it. His interest in ethnology and anthropology, on the other hand, seems to have been more serious. If psychology helped to *define* the dilemma of modern society, ethnology and anthropology, offered a method for *resolving* it, or at least for writing poems about it: Eliot's 'mythical method', a 'continuous parallel between contemporaneity and antiquity'. However, before taking him at his word and rushing to designate this a *Golden Bough* era (or even a Schliemann era), we should take note of differences of emphasis between those writers who were attracted to mythic expression and those who were attracted to ritual expression.

In the final volume of *Mythologiques*, Claude Lévi-Strauss distinguishes firmly between myth and ritual. He identifies the former with the mediating and differentiating powers of language and thought, and the latter with a nostalgia for immediacy, a futile attempt 'to re-establish the unbrokenness of a reality dismantled by the schematism which mythic speculation has substituted for it'. Ritual is a 'debasement' of thought, a wilful regression, an enemy to difference and change. Myth is 'essentially transformative', a triumph of the powers of language, a discourse modified and extended by each successive narration.

Lévi-Strauss's disdain for ritual seems rather gratuitous, but there may be some justice in his distinction. The purpose of the liminal phase in a rite of passage, for example, is clearly to suspend the schematism imposed on individuals by social structure and so to reassert the strength of a generic human bond; in so far as language and thought articulate that schematism, they also must be suspended. Following Lévi-Strauss's distinction, we can suggest that a writer drawn to the regenerative effect of such rites is indulging a nostalgia for immediacy, even if we regard his indulgence as something less than a mortal sin.

Pound and Joyce, rewriting the *Odyssey* in Anglo-Saxon rhythms or Dublin argot, celebrated mythic expression (the power of language and thought to transform what has already been transformed). Eliot was more interested in a rite which would conclusively dissolve the schematism of modern life. He admired Lucien Lévy-Bruhl's attempt, in *Les fonctions mentales dans les sociétés inférieures,* to posit a pre-logical mentality which does not rely on the kind of classifications we take for granted. For example, the Bororo who has a parrot for a totem does not confuse himself with a parrot. But he is nevertheless, Eliot wrote,

> capable of a state of mind into which we cannot put ourselves, in which he *is* a parrot, while being at the same time a man. In other words, the mystical mentality, though at a low level, plays a much greater part in the daily life of the savage than in that of the civilised man.

When this 'mystical mentality' does enter into the life of a 'civilised man', it might well be considered a nostalgia for immediacy.

By founding *The Waste Land* on ritual rather than myth, Eliot sought to describe and affirm the mystical mentality. To that extent Jessie Weston's *From Ritual to Romance* does indeed shadow the poem. For Weston argued that events which survive as legend were in the first instance ceremonies. 'The Grail romances repose eventually,' she claimed, 'not upon a poet's imagination, but upon the ruins of an august and ancient ritual, a ritual which once claimed to be the accredited guardian of the deepest secrets of Life.' They bear witness not so much to the transformative power of poetic imagination as to the enduring and stabilising power of ceremony. Weston filleted the Grail romances, separating out for Eliot those parts which connected back most stirringly to august and ancient ritual: the Perilous Chapel, a 'reminiscence' of some initiation ceremony; the Fisher King, who 'corresponds with remarkable exactitude to the central figure of a well-recognized Nature ritual'.

The Waste Land attempts a rite of passage, a rite which will reconstitute subjectivity in a realm beyond social structure. It is dogged by an awareness that little separates religious from neurotic ceremonial, and that the schematisms imposed on us by society run deep and dividingly. For Eliot's thinking had by this time become genuinely social in scope, even if its codes and gestures remained defiantly personal. I want now to draw attention to that scope.

The second section of the poem, 'A Game of Chess', is as confessional as anything Eliot ever wrote. It alludes to his disastrous first marriage, and he gave it the interim title of 'In the Cage'. But cages often have people outside them looking in, and anyone peering through these particular bars in 1922 might well have recognised the captives.

For Eliot certainly wasn't the only writer to deplore the neurotic behaviour of society-women like the one portrayed in the opening passage of 'A Game of Chess'. Julien Benda's *Belphégor* (1918), which Eliot considered a model of the new 'classical' consciousness, managed to reveal an entire Decline of the West in their seductive languor. Benda thought that there were two types of sensibility, 'plastic' and 'musical', the one poised and compact, the other dizzy and diffuse. Women, it turns out, were mostly 'musical', and Benda cited the example of a young countess whose 'whole process of thought is an orgy of disconnected somersaults, her reasoning a cyclone of impressions, her opinion a jingle of images'. But even this jingling somersaulting cyclone was outshone by a formidable creature who once summoned the unfortunate Benda to her drawing-room:

> Looking round the room, I noticed that everything – the materials and colour of the hangings, the carpet, the cushions, the ornaments, the shape of the furniture, the lighting system – had been arranged with a view to flattering the senses, and avoiding any impression of severity.

It all proved too much for the philosopher, who withdrew to steady himself, and then to formulate his view that the civilisation of the West had been taken over by dizzy women.

Max Nordau was another pundit who wandered through fashionable boudoirs denouncing them for their lack of severity. His book, robustly entitled *Degeneration,* caused quite a stir on publication; it was translated into English in 1895, and read by Eliot at Harvard some time between 1908 and 1914. Nordau claimed to hear a 'sound of rending' in the fabric of tradition: 'Things as they are totter and plunge.' Things as they are apparently tottered and plunged most alarmingly in fashionable mansions, where the tireless Nordau was often to be found:

> Everything in these houses aims at exciting the nerves and dazzling the senses. The disconnected and antithetical effects in all arrangements, the constant contradiction between form and purpose, the outlandishness of most objects, is intended to be bewildering. There must be no sentiment of repose, such as is felt at any composition, the plan of which is easily taken in, nor of the comfort attending a prompt comprehension of all the details of one's environment. He who enters here must not doze, but be thrilled.

Such 'effects' could not be comprehended from or held within a single point of view; indeed, they were meant to destroy the unified and stable point of view (the repose) of anyone who observed them. It seemed to Nordau that modern culture had created a class of people who actually revelled in such disorientation. On the few occasions when these people left their antithetical lounges and bathrooms, it was to visit art galleries where they would twitter at revolting portraits of women with 'grass-green hair, faces of sulphur-yellow or fiery-red, and arms spotted in violet and pink'.

Eliot, who returned from Paris in 1911 with a copy of Gauguin's 'Yellow Christ', was certainly no enemy of the modern aesthetic. Attending a performance of Stravinsky's *Le Sacre du Printemps,* he became so angry when the audience burst out laughing that he started to poke his neighbours with the tip of his umbrella (a singularly Eliotic mode of retribution). But the luxurious interiors which so upset Benda and Nordau were not all that far from the one described in 'A Game of Chess', with its picture of rape, its jewels pouring from satin cases, its synthetic perfumes which trouble and confuse. Nor was there much difference between the occupants of these various boudoirs.

Society-women had menaced before in Eliot's poetry, in 'Prufrock' and 'Portrait of a Lady'. There they had tried to coax the poet into some kind of intimacy; casual remarks and gestures (settling a pillow, throwing off a shawl, twisting a lilac stem) were hints he could neither ignore nor resolve. It was a world of Proustian codes.

But by the time of *The Waste Land* these women had come to seem a threat to society as well as to the stripling philosopher; their sexuality had acquired a desperate and violent edge. The neophyte now found himself confronted not by an occasional escape of scent, but by a hearty female stench. That last phrase comes from the description of Fresca which Pound edited out of 'The Fire Sermon'. Fresca is a jingling somersaulting cyclone in direct line of descent from Benda's countess, entirely made up of cultural odds and ends. She denies repose, threatening not so much the virginity of occasional Prufrocks – although there is that danger – as the very principle of a poised and compact sensibility.

The opening line of 'A Game of Chess' alludes to *Antony and Cleopatra,* partly because the woman whose hair spreads out in fiery points is a caricature Cleopatra, but also perhaps because Shakespeare's play had recently got caught up in the struggle between 'plastic' and 'musical' sensibilities. Eliot began his 1920 essay 'The Perfect Critic' with some remarks about Arthur Symons, 'the critical successor of Pater'. Symons seemed to him the type of critic who 'reacts in excess of the stimulus', altering the object of his criticism without ever transforming it. He cited a gushing commentary on *Antony and Cleopatra* from Symon's *Studies in Elizabethan Drama* as evidence: 'What, we ask, is this for? as a page on Cleopatra, and on her possible origin in the dark lady of the Sonnets, unfolds itself.' The commentary is indeed rhapsodic, dilating on the 'boundless empire' of Cleopatra's caprice, on the 'incalculable instability of her moods', and on her sexual expertise: 'She knows how to interest him, to be to him everything he would have in a woman, to change with or before every mood of his as it changes.' Symons, the representative of 'musical' sensibility, had made a Fresca out of Shakespeare's Queen; as, with ironic intent, did Eliot himself.

Eliot describes Fresca awakening from pleasant dreams of love and rape to summon a maid whose hand is coarsened and whose tread is plebeian. The social implications of her sexuality only become evident when it is framed by the plebeian hand and tread. Sexuality, which might have been thought a realm outside or prior to social structure, and perhaps even the ground of a reconstituted subjectivity, proves as schematised an experience as any other. Different classes, that is to say, entertain and abide by different representations of sexuality. In 'A Game of Chess' the behaviour of the woman whose hair spreads in fiery points contrasts sharply with the bluntness and the scarred fertility of the women in the pub.

By 1921 an issue which sharpened the contrast even further – birth control – had become a topic of widespread concern and debate. Two clinics were opened in that year, one by Marie Stopes, the other by the Malthusian League. In October the King's Physician, Lord Dawson of Penn, addressed the Church Congress in Birmingham and caused a great stir by advocating birth control. Next year the Malthusians published the proceedings of a conference on the subject which had attracted a large number of delegates from Britain and from abroad. In July 1923 one of the leading medical journals, the *Practitioner,* produced a special number on birth control. 'The subject of contraceptives,' its editor reported, 'has now become a commonplace of conversation at women's clubs and mixed tea-tables.'

The debate revealed that in one respect at least the nation's sexual conduct differed according to social status. The enlightened and responsible classes used contraceptives, the rest did not. As the *Practitioner* put it, 'limitation is now practised by the classes from which it is desirable that the community should be recruited, and is not practised by the undesirables'. Clearly this had important social and political consequences. 'To attempt,' one contributor said, 'to lower the number of the efficient while the inefficient multiply spells disaster in the future.' Eliot's juxtaposition of a childless and frustrated middle – or upper – class couple with a recklessly fertile working-class woman followed the line of a real social fissure which was asserting itself in terms of sexual conduct.

Some doctors felt that birth control might induce neurosis. Professor Knight Dunlap, from Johns Hopkins University, told the Malthusians that all known contraceptive measures were 'psychologically objectionable': they produced frigidity in women, impotence in men and 'disintegration of the family relationship'. In the *Practitioner,* Louise McIlroy complained that 'what should be an almost unconscious spontaneous impulse is forced into a mechanical one by preparing for it by means of chemical or rubber appliances'. (Anyone who has had to wrestle with such appliances in the heat of the moment will know there's some truth in that.) McIlroy provided a case history:

Patient, aet. 30. Married one year. Could not permit

intercourse because her nerves were so upset after it. Interrupted intercourse had been practised from the beginning of married life, because the husband said it was 'the usual thing to do'. The patient was on the verge of a serious mental breakdown, and there was also the danger of domestic estrangement. Both individuals were perfectly normal when marriage was undertaken.

Henry Corby argued in the same journal that birth control (like masturbation) would result in madness: if it became widespread, the nation would be 'cumbered by a weakly degenerated race of neurasthenics and hypochondriacs, not a small percentage of whom will drift into lunatic asylums where, poor creatures, they will be in the midst of their fellow-masturbators.'

But the mental state of the enlightened classes, though worrying, finally mattered less than the proliferation of those who did not practise birth control at all. 'The question of sterilizing degenerates,' reported the *Practitioner*, 'has been seriously advocated and discussed in very influential quarters.' And at this point the argument took a eugenicist turn. 'To-day,' said Professor MacBride,

clerical families consist of one or two; and the same is true of doctors' families. Whilst, however, the birth rate as a whole has fallen, the birth rate of the lowest strata of the community has not appreciably diminished. Road sweepers, dock labourers, and people of that class still indulge in large families, and one of the Labour Members of Parliament was congratulated a short time ago on the birth of the thirteenth child.

The 'better strain' of the population, he concluded, was diminishing, while the irresponsible and degenerate (road sweepers, dockers and Labour MPs) had more and more children. Sterilisation was the only way to deal with the 'residuum of people so utterly careless of the welfare of the State or of their prosperity as to breed recklessly'. MacBride continued to say this in the country's most prestigious scientific journal, *Nature*. On 10 May 1924 he argued that the 'lowest stratum of utterly reckless and vicious people' should be sterilised. 'These people', he added on May 31, 'are lacking not only in intelligence but also in self-control, which is the basis of morality.'

The debate about contraception revealed the depth of class-division in post-war Britain. Sexual and reproductive behaviour seemed to vary according to social status, taking the form of neurotic inhibition among the bourgeoisie and of reckless breeding among the proletariat. Eliot's juxtaposition of scenes in 'A Game of Chess' reproduced exactly the difference between these two worlds.

He even found a separate idiom for each world, devising modes of speech which would render meticulously the 'social tone' of the people who used them, or had become implicated in them. (His efforts recall Ezra Pound's contemporary interest in novelists who seemed able to catch the tone of minds immured in cliché.) Thus the disorientation one might feel in the lady's antithetical boudoir is rendered by what Donald Davie calls a 'sustained ambiguity' between past participle, past indicative and adjectival participle. The language tells us that we must not doze, but be thrilled.

By contrast the speech of the working-class women in the pub reveals a kind of vacancy. They constantly talk around the subject; or, to be more precise, around the reference item 'it'. We can guess what 'it' refers to in each case, but the women refuse, or are unable, to give 'it' a name. Perhaps they know each other so well (unlike the husband and wife in the previous episode) that they don't need to specify. At any rate their speech defines their 'social tone' and separates them effectively from the clotted luxury of the bourgeois temperament. For all their talking around the point, they recognise what is at issue; whereas the portrayal of the neurotic couple owes more to the indirect representation of sexuality in the novel from Austen to James.

When even such natural processes as sexuality and reproduction are constituted differently for different groups of society, we are faced by a truly formidable schematism. The caricature rites of 'The Burial of the Dead' had failed to restore wholeness and immediacy to this divided society. So Eliot turned to fiercer remedies.

* * *

He sought the most ancient remedies: purgation by fire, pilgrimage, quest, initiation, revelation. But he had to bring them home to readers who had grown sceptical of ancient remedies. He had to revive in those readers who did not merely 'snatch a glance' perceptions of wholeness and immediacy (and thus learn for whom he was writing). To that end, he made use of a particular form of what I have called 'external reference', one involving the demonstratives 'this' and 'that' and their respective plurals. These are specifying agents, which serve to identify the individual or sub-class within the class designated by the noun they precede. (If I talk about 'this pencil', I am referring to a particular, identifiable specimen.) As with all reference items, the information they presuppose can be retrieved either from another part of the text or from the situation of its utterance. In *The Waste Land* it is the use of demonstratives to refer outside the text which is the more interesting. For example, when Eliot talks about 'this red rock' and 'that noise', we know he means a particular rock and a particular noise, but the poem does not supply the information needed to identify them. We will have to supply the information ourselves, from our knowledge or imagining of the situation in which the rock and the noise occur.

But poems do not have situations. We know that we will never gain access to the full identity of the rock and the noise. The referential function of the demonstratives cannot be fulfilled. This being the case, their relation to one another within language comes to the fore. In English 'this' and 'that' are ranged along a scale of proximity. The former refers to things which are close (in time or space) to the speaker, which bear some relation to him or her; the latter refers to things which are distant from and bear no relation to the speaker. (I talk about 'this' table if I happen to be leaning on it at the time, and 'that' table if it stands at the far end of the room.) 'This' has associations of intimacy and relatedness built into it, while 'that' tends to suggest distance and strangeness. These associations are so powerful that they survive even where we can not identify the object referred to, as is often the case in *The Waste Land*. It was in such terms that Eliot revived for his readers a perception of wholeness and immediacy.

After the rendering of Marie's 'social tone' in 'The Burial of the Dead', an authoritative voice beckons a prophet in under the shadow of 'this red rock'. The rock is indicated firmly – *this* one, not that uninspiring lump of sandstone over there – but we learn nothing about it except its colour. For what matters is that it has been identified by the demonstrative as lying close to the speaker. We feel that we are in the vicinity of or the approaches to a source of redeeming knowledge; the closeness matters more than the nature of the object we are close to, because what is intimate is more real. If we obey the associations of relatedness embedded in the demonstrative, we can perceive something which the poem itself will not name. The allusion to Ecclesiastes suggests an end to mortmain, an apocalyptic return to wholeness and immediacy. However, Ecclesiastes also recommends, as Frazer's mentor Robertson Smith pointed out, 'extreme scepticism towards all religious speculation'. The shrine proves to be empty. There have surely been more encouraging revelations than 'fear in a handful of dust'.

The aridity of this scene, and of the knowledge which greets the Jewish prophet, requires some comment. Eliot had previously associated a Jewish figure with images of aridity in 'Gerontion': the old man's dry thoughts in a dry month circulate through a house where 'the Jew squats on the window sill'. But the environment described in 'The Burial of the Dead' is even more barren, a dry and stony waste which in some ways recalls the account of Judaea given in George Adam Smith's *Historical Geography of the Holy Land,* published in 1894 and reprinted several times. 'But the prevailing impression of Judaea,' Smith wrote,

> is of stone – the torrent-beds, the paths that are no better, the heaps and heaps of stones gathered from the fields, the fields as stony still, the moors strewn with boulders, the obtrusive scalps and ribs of the hills. In the more desolate parts, which had otherwise been covered with scrub, this impression is increased by the ruins of ancient cultivation – cairns, terrace-walls, and vineyard towers.

He reported that the 'dreariness' of the landscape was accentuated by lack of water – 'at noon the cattle go down by dusty paths to some shadowless gorge, where the glare is only broken by the black mouth of a cistern with troughs around it' – and lack of contour: 'The horizon has no character or edge.' A wilderness encroaches on one side: 'The desert is always in face of the prophets, and its howling of beasts and its dry sand blow mournfully across their pages the foreboding of judgement.'

Eliot's contemporaries did not hesitate to ascribe various psychological effects to such barrenness. An entry in the *Encyclopaedia of Religion and Ethics* suggested that the 'peculiarly sterile cradleland of the Semites' had always encouraged the habit of matriarchy and 'barbarous sexual customs'. In 1916 Eliot reviewed a book whose purpose was to survey the available theories concerning the psychological effect of environment. One theory surveyed by the book, and judged 'highly satisfactory', was that of an American sociologist called Ellen Churchill Semple. This is what she had to say about desert peoples such as the Jews:

> The dry, pure air stimulates the faculties of the desert-dweller, but the featureless, monotonous surroundings furnish them with little to work upon. The mind, finding scant material for sustained logical deduction, falls back upon contemplation. Intellectual activity is therefore restricted, narrow, unproductive; while the imagination is unfettered but also unfed.

A nomadic people, she thought, being rootless, 'originates nothing'. Eliot's linking of Jews with images of sterility mobilised the same suspicion. What could a prophet in the desert, an imagination unfettered but unfed, hope to see except 'fear in a handful of dust'? We are in the presence not of truth but of empty religious speculation.

A few lines later we encounter Madame Sosostris, with a snuffle, fortune-telling. The cards she interprets for us seem cryptic enough: drowned sailor, Lady of the Rocks. But worse follows:

> Here is the man with three staves and here the Wheel,
> And here is the one-eyed merchant, and this card,
> Which is blank, is something he carries on his back,
> Which I am forbidden to see.

'Here', the adverbial equivalent of 'this', establishes an atmosphere of intimacy, a sense of crowding round the source of knowledge. But again all that emerges is an empty speculation, a blank, an icon as unforthcoming as the red rock: 'this card'. Like the voice in the desert, Madame Sosostris can only show us part of what we would like to see: 'something different', 'something he carries on his back'. She really does play her cards close to her chest.

These episodes represent abortive struggles against mortmain,

deluded attempts to initiate a purging rite. But they also bring
into play a relation between knowledge and intimacy which was
to prove crucial to Eliot's quest for ritual immediacy. To know
something is to come into its presence, probably alone and
probably at the end of a perilous journey. Fragments from the
manuscript use the demonstrative to posit a moment of intimate
awareness which can be lackadaisical or transforming, indifferent
of redemptive. The poem itself had somehow to twist from one
kind of intimacy to another, from neurotic to religious
ceremonial.

Eliot's interest in philisophy, and particularly his work on F.
H. Bradley at Oxford, tended to confirm the dilemma. Bradley's
theory of knowledge, developed in *Appearance and Reality* (1893)
and *Essays on Truth and Reality* (1914), held a precarious balance
between the validity of an immediate apprehension of experience
and the need for more objective and abstracted modes of enquiry.
He stated that the truth of a proposition depended on its
coherence and comprehensiveness, but one feels the presence in
his work of an alternative criterion, a valuing of the intimate and
immediate. The alternative criterion emerges as much in his
terminology as in the progress of his argument. For the terms he
used to characterise an intimate and immediate apprehension of
experience were 'the *this*' and 'the *mine*': two specifying agents, a
demonstrative and a possessive, both invested with associations of
relatedness. Whatever we perceive in an immediate way
convinces by its sheer closeness, its appearance of speaking to us
alone. Bradley believed that the *this* is 'real for us in a sense in
which nothing else is real'. Indeed, the forms are so powerfully
marked off within language (this/that, mine/yours) that no appeal
to coherence and comprehensiveness will integrate the criterion
they represent into a community of knowledge.

Eliot placed even greater emphasis than Bradley on this
criterion: 'All significant truths are private truths.' Nothing can
be said about such truths except that they happen to you alone:
'And if anyone assert that immediate experience, at either the
beginning or end of our journey, is annihilation and utter night, I
cordially agree.' So it is at the beginning and end of the journey
proposed by *The Waste Land*: annihilation and utter night,
otherwise known as the *this*.

* * *

If the first section of the poem sets up small but futile movements in the direction of a saving knowledge, the second puts us back in the cage and slams the door. Not only is its description of social and personal dividedness particularly harsh, as I have shown, but its demonstratives posit a place stranger and more sinister than the red rock or the blank card, a place at the far end of the scale of proximity stretching between 'this' and 'that'. We find ourselves in an enclosed room, listening to 'that noise', which may or may not be the wind under the door, but which is in any case nothing. The wind's nothing seems more terrible than the something revealed to us by the voice in the desert or by Madame Sosostris. Knowing what caused the noise would not erase the mark left by the demonstrative 'that', the mark of a distant and hostile exterior.

In the first section of the poem, we edge towards a tantalising but ultimately sterile knowledge; here, we edge away from a threat to the very possibility of knowledge. Such is the span of consciousness allocated to the inhabitants of the waste land, a narrow wavering between credulity and oblivion. The next section of the poem, 'The Fire Sermon', binds these two tendencies into a defensive strategy, a neurotic ceremonial. Tiresias presides over it, a 'mere spectator', Eliot said, although what he sees is in fact 'the substance of the poem'. Tiresias is the authoritative voice sought by earlier poems, the observing eye which utterly possesses the significance of what it observes. (According to a draft of 'The Fire Sermon', people in London do not in any case know what they think or feel, but exist only for the observing eye.) Unlike Prufrock or Narcissus or Gerontion, Tiresias is master of 'the *this*'. He presides over a moment of annihilation and utter night, when a young clerk visits and seduces a typist:

> (And I Tiresias have foresuffered all
> Enacted on this same divan or bed;
> I who have sat by Thebes below the wall
> And walked among the lowest of the dead.)

The clerk leaves, groping his way down unlit stairs. Unlike the protagonists of Eliot's early poems, who used to worry about getting up stairs, he has trouble getting down them. He has already scaled his summit, and what was once anticipated nervously has become predictable. His acts have meaning not for himself but for the observing eye, whose world-weary parenthesis makes out of them a site of intimate if unsavoury knowledge: *this* same divan or bed.

What Tiresias holds to himself, the typist pushes away, thus completing the neurotic ceremony:

Her brain allows one half-formed thought to pass:
'Well now that's done: and I'm glad it's over.'

What was 'this' to him is 'that' to her, already distant and somehow unrelated. What she pushes away from her Tiresias will presumably gather in to himself once more; so the ceremony goes on. In this respect we might compare the episode with Freud's attempts, in *Beyond the Pleasure Principle* (1920), to theorise something he had already noted as a clinical phenomenon, the 'compulsion to repeat'. Freud noted that the recent war had provided all too many examples of traumatic neurosis, in which the patient was brought back repeatedly to the situation of his original accident; since this process was extremely painful, the force which compelled him to it must be stronger than the pleasure principle.

Freud's efforts to define this force led him to a game played by his young grandson. The boy had a wooden reel attached to a piece of string. Holding the end of the string, he would repeatedly throw the reel away from him into his cot, and then draw it back towards him. As he threw it away from him, he would utter a sound which Freud interpreted as 'fort', meaning away or gone; as he pulled it back towards him, he would say 'da', meaning there or present.

According to Freud, the boy was compensating himself for the absence of his mother by 'staging the disappearance and return of the objects within his reach'. He was repeating an unpleasant experience in play so as to master the pain it caused him. 'At the outset he was in a *passive* situation – he was overpowered by the experience; but, by repeating it, unpleasurable though it was, as a game, he took on an *active* part.' The content of the experience remained unpleasant; but by staging it over and over again in play, and in language, he put himself in a different relation to it, although the process was of course compulsive and therefore a rather uncertain kind of mastery. We do not really know whether the child is playing the game, or the game playing the child.

Eliot's poem also engages in a compulsive repetition, a drawing close and pushing away, as Tiresias gathers in what the typist has renounced. The two elements of the earlier poems, observing eye and empirical self, have been replaced by a neurotic ceremony, a play within language between 'this' and 'that'. And the trauma against which the ceremony has been erected is the young clerk, a figure of social and personal division.

The clerk is a petty-bourgeois, caught between the class from which he is trying to escape and the class he wishes to enter. Hugh Kenner remarks that his language is remote from the way a clerk might actually speak, but not from the way he might *aspire* to speak or write; and Kenner quotes Eliot's comment that 'an artisan who can talk the English language beautifully while about his work or in a public bar, may compose a letter painfully written in a dead language bearing some resemblance to a newspaper leader and decorated with words like ''maelstrom'' and ''pandemonium''.' What fascinated Eliot about such people (here an artisan, more often a petty-bourgeois) was the way that uncertainty about their social status had produced an inner division between speech and identity. They hoped to raise themselves by aping bourgeois dress and speech and manners, and so their behaviour was inevitably at odds with their class origins.

The figure of the parvenu clerk had a long and totally inglorious history. An article in the *Cornhill Magazine* in 1862 made the point Eliot was to make sixty years later:

> A gentleman and a labouring man would tell the same story in nearly the same words, differently pronounced, of course, and arranged in the one case grammatically, and in the other not. In either case the words themselves would be plain, racy, and smacking of the soil from which they grow. The language of the commercial clerk, and the manner in which he brings it out, are both formed on quite a different model. He thinks about himself, and constantly tries to talk fine. He calls a school an academy, speaks of proceeding when he means going, and talks, in short, much in the style in which the members of his own class write police reports and accounts of appalling catastrophes for the newspapers.

The speech of the labourer is as transparent as that of the gentleman, and distinguished only by its lack of grammar; the social position of both shines unambiguously through every word they say. The clerk, on the other hand, tries to behave like somebody he is not and to obscure his class-origins. His words smack of a soil from which they did *not* grow. As a result we no longer know who we are talking to, and a society where speech does not match identity must be considered dangerously unstable.

George Eliot's Felix Holt, whose aim is to secure national unity by reconciling gentleman and labourer, refuses to take a position as a clerk:

> I'll take no employment that obliges me to prop up my chin with a high cravat, and wear straps, and pass the live-long day with a set of fellows who spend their spare money on shirt-pins . . . I mean to stick to the class I belong to – people who don't follow the fashions.

To assume a 'clerkly gentility' would be to obscure his true nature and so become divided against himself. Someone who did assume a clerkly gentility was the magnificent Mr. Guppy, in *Bleak House*. Someone who tried but failed was Leonard Bast in Forster's *Howards End* (1910). Bast always felt obliged, Forster says, 'to assert gentility, lest he slipped into the abyss where nothing counts'; the Schlegel sisters see in him a terrible reminder of the trauma which might overwhelm them too, were they less well off.

The hero of Wyndham Lewis's 1917 story, 'Cantleman's Spring Mate', finds himself billeted with four other officers, one of whom stinks of 'Jack London, Summer Numbers of Magazines, bad flabby Suburban Tennis, flabby clerkship in inert, though still prosperous, city offices'. This man brings a 'demoralizing dullness' into the room and is unwise enough to own a copy of *The Trumpet Major*, which Cantleman promptly steals, thinking it too good for him. Lewis's routine brutality found an echo in Eliot, who was no less savage about the clerk in 'The Fire Sermon', commenting with asperity on his dandruff. Pound, however, managed to edit out some of the cruder insults. Still, it is clear that Eliot felt himself to be staring into a suddenly opened abyss when he contemplated the young man. It was both a social and psychic abyss, a gap between classes which fractured and tormented the subjectivity of those who tried to cross it.

Eliot's clerk stood at the point where *The Diary of a Nobody* turns into its grim parody, the *Diaries* of Joseph Goebbels.

Indeed, this whole section of a supremely class-conscious poem belongs to the petty-bourgeoisie. Even the class origins of the girl seduced in a boat on the Thames are patiently explained in a draft version. Her parents were humble people, and conservative in a way unfamiliar either to the rich or to the poor. They owned a small business, an anxious business, but one providing enough for a house in Highbury and three weeks at Bognor. In the minds of those excluded on one side from what the rich know and on the other side from what the working classes know, life is indeed an anxious business. Eliot's ceremony tries to master the anxiety these minds give off by compulsive repetition.

* * *

But Eliot could not let matters rest there. He had to find some way of transforming neurotic into religious ceremonial. He had to purge the divisiveness of social structure by stepping beyond into some regenerative margin. It would not prove easy, because his representation of an anxiety about divisiveness had been chillingly exact and immutable. Even so, he tried. 'From the close of "The Fire Sermon",' Lyndall Gordon writes, 'the sordid city is blotted out by exemplary characters who escape contamination either by the practice of asceticism – like the Buddha or St. Augustine – or by dreams of a voyage, a journey, a pilgrimage, the metaphoric clichés of spiritual autobiography.' Suddenly the rites of passage are in business again, although it may still be an anxious business.

The concluding section of the poem, 'What the Thunder Said', involves a journey to a regenerative margin. But as important as the metaphor is a subtle revision of the terms of neurotic ceremonial. In 'The Fire Sermon', Tiresias had drawn to himself an experience which the typist rejected, endlessly foresuffering what she wishes to forget. But only reverse the terms, and the circuit is broken. For a pilgrim may wish to forget the boredom and terror of the life he is leaving behind, but he can regard them as the means to an end, as something he must endure in order to separate himself from one world and become fit for another. The significance of his actions does not belong to a perceiving eye, but to the shrine he approaches. The menace surrounding Eliot's pilgrims is a phase through which they must pass on their journey to the source of truth:

> What is that sound high in the air
> Murmur of maternal lamentation
> Who are those hordes swarming
> Over endless plains . . .

The demonstratives 'that' and 'those' pick out a sequence of threats equivalent to 'that noise' in 'A Game of Chess' and 'that' seduction in 'The Fire Sermon'. They are superseded, the moment we arrive at the Perilous Chapel, by a welcoming 'this':

> In this decayed hole among the mountains
> In the faint moonlight, the grass is singing . . .

The chapel seems singularly without amenities, and there is no guarantee that we will catch a glimpse of anything more fruitful than fear in a handful of dust. But now the aura of intimacy and relatedness bestowed by the demonstrative comes as a reward for surviving the boredom and terror of the world. The scale of proximity stretching between 'that' and 'this' has been transformed into a spiritual progress, a route-map of our quest. We are closer to the source than we have ever been before.

It is from the chapel that the thunder speaks. What it says is what Freud's grandson had said: a solemn and emphatic DA. And they were not the only ones. A few years previously Hugo Ball and Richard Huelsenbeck, in search of a name for their literary journal, had chanced on the word 'dada', a word which changed a group of émigré artists notable chiefly for their drunkenness into an international movement. At the same time, 'da' – and the noun derived from it, 'Dasein' – acquired a mystical intensity in the work of Rilke. During the twenties, Martin Heidegger elaborated a whole philosophy of 'Dasein'. The primary meaning of 'da' in German is 'there': 'hier and da' means 'here and there'. But it can also mean 'here' ('da bin ich' = 'here I am'). So it includes associations of closeness (like 'this' and 'here') and associations of distance (like 'that' and 'there'), uniting what in Eliot's rhetoric had remained separate. For Rilke and Heidegger, to be distant from oneself was to enter into a truer relation with one's being. 'Dasein' is sometimes translated as 'being-here' and sometimes as 'being-there'.

Eliot's thunder may or may not speak German. It speaks from afar, but echoes in the pilgrim's skull. It introduces into the defensive ceremonies of the poem a relation to others: give, sympathise, control. For arrival at the Perilous Chapel has not only revised those ceremonies, but transcended them. The thunder speaks a foreign word which is also a root-word, a margin which is also a beginning-again.

But it is an anxious business, this rite of passage. What the thunder says, once it has spat out its root-word, sounds remarkably like what has already been said by the voice in the desert and by Madame Sosostris and by Tiresias:

> The awful daring of a moment's surrender
> Which an age of prudence can never retract
> By this, and this only, we have existed . . .

By this and this only: privately, defensively, secretively, under the shadow of a red rock, on the same divan or bed. What we have given is investment in the *this*. Who is to say whether we have taken part in a neurotic or a religious ceremony? The poem ends with the Fisher King, most ritual of mythic figures, but it is not certain that he has been made anew by the voice of the thunder. 'These fragments,' he says, 'I have shored against my ruin.' These fragments, not those.

One might argue that things have changed, to the extent that the poem at last supplies the information needed to identify what the demonstrative refers to. 'These fragments' are quotations from Dante and Nerval and Kyd. Like Madame Sosostris the Fisher King plays his cards close to his chest, but at least we can see what is written on them. And yet quotations cannot be all that a man in such extremity would shore against his ruin. We are free to suppose that he would assemble everything that was most dear to him, all those perceptions which are 'real for us in a sense in which nothing else is real'. Even here the associations of intimacy and relatedness built into the demonstrative outlast, as they do more obviously in other parts of the poem, the identity of what it refers to. The passage from Bradley cited in the notes reinforces this impression:

> My external sensations are no less private to my self than are my thoughts or my feelings. In either case my experience falls

within my own circle, a circle closed on the outside; and, with all its elements alike, every sphere is opaque to the others which surround it . . . In brief, regarded as an existence which appears in a soul, the whole world for each is peculiar and private to that soul.

Eliot's thunder was surely meant to break down the opacity of those spheres. But it ended up illuminating from the inside a circle still closed on the outside. Eliot could not find the ritual immediacy that would transform neurotic into religious observance. 'At the outset he was in a *passive* situation – he was overpowered by the experience; but, by repeating it, un-pleasurable though it was, as a game, he took on an *active* part.' Did the child play the game, or the game play the child?

* * *

The game was so compulsive that it more or less generated Eliot's next poem, 'The Hollow Men', which sets out as the limits of its scale of proximity a near place and a far place: death's dream kingdom, a limbo full of hollow men, and death's other kingdom, which the hollow men aspire to because the people there seem properly and ceremonially dead. Familiar reference items – 'this' and 'that', 'here' and 'there' – space the two kingdoms; but their values have been reversed, so that redemption now lies at the far end of the scale while everything close to hand is corrupt. The hollow men share the predicament of Milton's Satan, in *Paradise Lost*, arriving at the 'dreary plain' of hell:

> Is this the region, this the soil, the clime,
> Said then the lost archangel, this the seat
> That we must change for heaven, this mournful gloom
> For that celestial light?

They too have their minds on the celestial light of a distant kingdom, a world preferable to the world they already know:

> This is the dead land
> This is cactus land
> Here the stone images
> Are raised, here they receive

The supplication of a dead man's hand
Under the twinkle of a fading star.

The dead man's hand is just about the most lively thing around,
in the cheerless vicinity of 'this' hollow valley, 'this' last meeting-
place. Mournful gloom, indeed. But there is an important
difference between the regions inhabited by the hollow men and
by Satan's army. For the cosmos which Milton's demonstratives
point to is described elsewhere in *Paradise Lost* in considerable
detail. If we want to know more about it we can find out from the
poem. Eliot is not nearly so forthcoming, and his reliance on
unfulfilled specificity should remind us that we are dealing with a
particular rhetoric, a particular relation to the reader. The
sparseness of 'The Hollow Men' gives the demonstratives a
prominence which they had not been granted by *The Waste Land*.
But in each case it is our acceptance of the challenge they throw
down which helps to make us as readers: the challenge to enter
our own rite of passage or neurotic ceremony, our own span of
consciousness sealed eternally on the outside.

But that is not the only challenge to which readers have
responded. Many have interpreted the two poems as critiques of
society, despite Eliot's appeals to the contrary. And the titles of
the poems, unlike their rhetoric, do encourage such an
interpretation. It is after all *the* Waste Land, *the* Hollow Men; not
'this' or 'these'. The identity of the waste land and the hollow
men is less carefully screened than that of Tiresias's divan or the
decayed hole among the mountains. For although the definite
article is a specifying agent, it has no semantic content. It tells us
that the information needed to identify the object in question is
available, but it does not say where – does not itself point in a
particular direction, as demonstratives and possessives do. It
signals definiteness, without in any way contributing to the
definition, and so offers a more positive encouragement to the
reader or listener to do the defining himself. Had Eliot spoken
about 'this waste land' or 'these hollow men', he would have
meant a waste land and a group of men characterised by their
relation to him rather than by any quality that we might attribute
to them. In fact he spoke about 'the waste land' and 'the hollow
men', and the relative neutrality of the definite article allows us to
recognise features of our world in his. Few other major poems in
the language can have been read to such an extent, with or
without the author's compliance, through their titles.

4 Words full of far-off suggestion

Eliot was not the only poet to hold carbuncular young men responsible for the decline of the West. In 'At Galway Races', Yeats declared that all had been well before merchant and clerk turned their 'timid breath' on society. This timid breath may not have been directed into a typist's ear, but it was none the less noxious for that. Yeats blamed it for the eclipse of a truly popular literature. Like Eliot, only more fervently, he played off both ends of the social spectrum against the vulgar and shifting middle. Like Eliot, he hoped that schematism could be dissolved through ritual; or, failing that, through the allegiance of enlightened readers to a ritualistic poetry and drama.

In his essay 'What is "Popular Poetry"?', published in 1901, he argued that the poetry of the sophisticated coteries and the poetry of the people both differ from the 'popular' poetry sponsored by merchant and clerk in their reliance on a certain opacity. Both are 'alike strange and obscure, and unreal to all who have not understanding'; both avoid the 'clear rhetoric' of popular poetry, conceiving of art as 'a cult with ancient technicalities and mysteries':

> Indeed, it is certain that before the counting-house had created a new class and a new art without breeding and without ancestry, and set this art and this class between the hut and the cloister, the art of the people was as closely mingled with the art of the coteries as was the speech of the people that delighted in rhythmical animation, in idiom, in images, in words full of far-off suggestion, with the unchanging speech of the poets.

The counting-house has so thoroughly extinguished the common values and memories (the Common Readership) on which a genuinely popular poetry might rely that we do not even know 'what it is to be disinherited'.

In Yeats's eyes, the new poetry of the new class sinned by its 'clear rhetoric'. He came closest to defining that rhetoric when discussing Longfellow, whom he considered the representative of a falsely popular art. 'Longfellow,' he wrote, 'has his popularity, in the main, because he tells his story or his idea so that one needs nothing but his verses to understand it.' Such verses did not rely on the kind of external reference I have described in the work of Wordsworth and Eliot. All the information needed to identify story or idea was available from the text itself, and did not have to be supplied by the reader. Yeats thought that by contrast a genuinely popular poetry 'presupposes . . . more than it says', relying on the reader to track down the far-off suggestions sown by its words and thus incorporate it into a commonly held set of values and memories.

One way of upsetting the new art of the new class would be to cultivate a rhetoric based on far-off suggestions, a rhetoric which presupposed more than it said. Those who expected the verses themselves to identify story and idea would be discouraged, while those willing and able to complete the poem's meaning from the testimony of their own experience would constitute a proper and identifiable readership. 'I had not wanted a large audience,' Yeats wrote in 1906, 'certainly not what is called a national audience, but enough people for what is accidental and temporary to lose itself in the lump.' Like Wordsworth, he wanted to feel that there were some who read him for the right reasons, rather than merely snatching a glance.

By 1914 'enough people' were reading Yeats' poetry for a rather more aggressive attitude towards the accidental and temporary to make sense. The volume he published in that year, *Responsibilities*, is thought to have been his first advance into modernity. 'Then,' Eliot concluded, 'Mr. Yeats began to write and is still writing some of the most beautiful poetry in the language'; while Pound applauded him for describing himself as a post the passing dogs defile. This advance involved a more confident selection among readers, by means of a particular use of external reference.

The means of selection became apparent in a group of poems in *Responsibilities* whose theme is the poverty of modern culture: 'To a Wealthy Man', 'September 1913', 'To a Friend whose Work

Has Come to Nothing', 'Paudeen', 'To a Shade'. Against the
power of the counting-house, Yeats said in a note to these poems,

> we have but a few educated men and the remnants of an old
> traditional culture among the poor. Both were stronger forty
> years ago, before the rise of our new middle class which made
> its first public display during the nine years of the Parnellite
> split, showing how base at moments of excitement are minds
> without culture.

The poems set out to restore the memory of the culture which
once, supposedly, united aristocrat and beggar. But they did so in
such a way as to make the reader participate fully in the work of
restoration, as 'September 1913' shows:

> Was it for this the wild geese spread
> The grey wing upon every tide:
> For this that all that blood was shed,
> For this Edward Fitzgerald died,
> And Robert Emmet and Wolfe Tone,
> All that delirium of the brave?
> Romantic Ireland's dead and gone,
> It's with O'Leary in the grave.

The demonstratives 'this' and 'that' function rather as in 'The
Hollow Men': one indicating the depraved present, the other a
different and better world. Neither reference is fulfilled by the text
itself. In order to understand what is depraved about 'this' world
or heroic about 'that' one, we must either know already or want
badly to find out; we must either share Yeats' assumptions, or
train ourselves to share them. Accidental and temporary readers
will lose interest, leaving those who remain in the hunt surer of
their identity as the enlightened few. Pound remarked that these
poems show Yeats 'at *prise* with things as they are', and so likely
to disappoint many of his readers: 'That is always a gain for a
poet, for his admirers nearly always want him to "stay put", and
they resent any signs of stirring, of new curiosity or of intellectual
uneasiness.' Pound thus rationalised the bafflement of some
admirers as the price to be paid for modernity.

But there is another aspect to Yeats' use of external reference
which distinguishes it from Eliot's. The stanza talks of '*all* that
blood', '*all* that delirium'. Yeats took pains to identify his heroes,

but he also wanted to indicate the sheer immensity of what had been lost by their eclipse. Just as Wordsworth's old men were assimilated to a universal category, so Fitzgerald and the rest became part of an unspecifiably grand heroism, a quite unparalleled magnanimity. Yeats referred to particular events ('*that* delirium'), but it was their grandeur rather than their particularity which fascinated him, and so he built into the reference a kind of disclaimer: 'all that delirium'. The 'all' deflects attention from the 'that', diffusing or numbing the curiosity of the reader. Eliot's poetry challenges us with the uniqueness of particular experiences, particular terrors and revelations: that noise, this card. Yeats's poetry challenges us to refrain from specificity and to acknowledge the grandeur of something which exceeds us by far. His use of external reference dissolves our expectation of a clear rhetoric adapted to the counting-house, and so restores the ritual immediacy of a delirium which might have dissolved the schematism of Irish society.

The prominence of 'all' in 'The Magi', also from *Responsibilities*, hardly needs underlining:

> Now as at all times I can see in the mind's eye,
> In their stiff, painted clothes, the pale unsatisfied ones
> Appear and disappear in the blue depth of the sky
> With all their ancient faces like rain-beaten stones,
> And all their helms of silver hovering side by side,
> And all their eyes still fixed, hoping to find once more,
> Being by Calvary's turbulence unsatisfied,
> The uncontrollable mystery on the bestial floor.

The potency of the crucifixion has been damaged by its diffusion in mythic form, its endless transformation into tale and commentary. Yeats's nostalgia for immediacy demands something more elemental still, an as yet unrecorded rite available only to 'the mind's eye', to the mind's eye of a reader goaded by the reiteration of 'all' into dispensing with detail.

A similar largesse was required of the audience for Yeats's imaginings of Maud Gonne in *Responsibilities* and *The Wild Swans at Coole*, this time prompted by the reference item 'some'. In 'Fallen Majesty', Yeats casts himself as the only surviving witness of a vanished splendour:

> Although crowds gathered once if she but showed her face,
> And even old men's eyes grew dim, this hand alone,
> Like some last courtier at a gypsy camping-place
> Babbling of fallen majesty, records what's gone.

The courtier is as specific as the poet ('this hand'), but impossible to identify ('*some* last courtier'). An indefinite article would have been possible here, but more neutral. 'Some', on the other hand, tells us that the information needed to identify the courtier might be available, but that it should not be sought because it is unimportant. The vanished splendour matters more than the identity of those who witnessed it. Similarly, in 'Her Praise', the poet seeks out 'some beggar' sheltering from the wind, some outcast who will remember Maud Gonne. In 'Broken Dreams' he records her fading beauty and hopes that 'some old gaffer' will mutter a blessing as she passes. Courtier, beggar and old gaffer are necessary mediators, necessary witnesses to her original majesty. But they must not be allowed to become mythologists rather than ritualists, to transform or diffuse the immediacy of that splendour, to intrude their own imaginations. They are summoned and then disowned: *some* last courtier, *some* beggar, *some* old gaffer. 'Some' disables the transformative power of these men's speech, permitting them to bear babbling or muttering witness but not to narrate. It challenges us to acknowledge that their identity and narrative skill matter less than the once unmediated splendour of what has been lost. We participate in these poems under very strict instructions as to what we should and should not imagine. If 'all' awakens us to a scarcely conceivable grandeur, 'some' discourages any attempt we might make to press for details.

* * *

In the year Pound reviewed *Responsibilities* for *Poetry*, he also praised in the same magazine a collection by Robert Frost, *North of Boston*. Frost's themes were pastoral – 'I know more of farm life,' Pound confided, 'than I did before I had read his poems' – and he was not having great success in finding a readership. No American publisher would take *A Boy's Will* or *North of Boston*, and according to Pound an American editor had refused to print

'Death of the Hired Man': 'why, in heaven's name, is this book
of New England eclogues given us under a foreign imprint?'
When he called the Noh plays which so fascinated Yeats and
himself 'eclogues', he was perhaps glancing at the derivation of
the term from the Greek verb meaning 'to choose'. Such plays
were made, he said, 'only for the few', for 'those trained to catch
the allusion'; and Yeats described them as 'an aristocratic form'
distinguished by its indirectness. Frost's eclogues may have been
selective by consequence rather than by design, but they did
incorporate a use of external reference which bears comparison
with Yeats's.

Three of the most famous eclogues in *North of Boston* –
'Mending Wall', 'Death of the Hired Man', 'Home Burial' –
provide good examples. In the first, the prim and property-
conscious assumption that good fences make good neighbours is
set against the poet's more generous attitude to natural process, to
the 'Something there is that doesn't love a wall'. The phrasing of
this tag – 'Something there is that . . . ' – is as important as its
content, and is held to later in the poem. It tells us that we need to
recognise a process beyond our control, without enquiring too
closely into its constitution. We should not schematise a process
whose function is to resolve differences, to erase boundaries and
all that people make of them. By designating it as some-thing,
Frost states that his poem will not offer any identification, and
thereby discourages us from attempting to do so.

Frost's eclogues are narrative poems, but they tell of mysteries
or crises which can only be resolved outside narration, by a rite
they themselves can circle around but never perform. So it is with
the famous exchange between husband and wife in 'Death of the
Hired Man', where she concludes that home is something you
somehow don't have to deserve. So it is, more poignantly, in
'Home Burial', at the moment when the woman looks out
through the window of the house at her child's grave. Just as the
grave lies outside the house, so identification of the fear it arouses
lies beyond the scope of the poem. The fear has to do with her
husband's indifference to the death of their child, but he cannot
even conceive the rite which would atone for his behaviour. He
tries to open the way: 'There's something I should like to ask you,
dear.' But he will never get round to it. As his wife points out, he
does not really know how to ask. So it is with the narrator of 'For

Once, Then, Something', a poem published in *New Hampshire* (1923). Looking into a well, he thinks he sees something below the surface, something in the depths. The opening lines redistribute the elements of the title (once, then, something) into a narrative: 'once' and 'then' become adverbs of time; they promise a myth, a once-upon-a-time which will reveal the identity of the something. But the something could only be known through ritual, never through mere narrative. Like Yeats's babbling or muttering witnesses, the elements of narrative are summoned and then disowned. They circle around a rite they can never perform, a depth they can never penetrate. The concluding phrase of the poem simply recomposes its title. Like Yeats, Frost does not want to identify the delirium, the lost splendour. He declines to anatomise the mystery in the depths of life: the something that does not love a wall, the something that home somehow is, the something that should be asked.

*   *   *

Frost never showed any great desire to ignore the temporary and accidental among his readers, and his use of external reference was a matter of sly goading rather than imperiousness. Yeats, on the other hand, did not mellow. After his Abbey Theatre audience had declined to acknowledge a common inheritance of values and memories, he worked in his later plays to 'create for myself an unpopular theatre and an audience like a secret society where admission is by favour and never to many'. (When Eliot wrote *Sweeney Agonistes* he intended to have 'one character whose sensibility and intelligence should be on the plane of the most sensitive and intelligent members of the audience;' the other personages in the play – 'material, literal-minded and visionless' – and the rest of the audience would not be expected to grasp what this character had to say.) Yeats's use of external reference remained intemperate.

In 'The Second Coming' the specificities of the first stanza – the falcon, the falconer, the centre, the world, and so on – give way in the second to a spate of indefinite articles:

> Surely some revelation is at hand;
> Surely the Second Coming is at hand.
> The Second Coming! Hardly are those words out

When a vast image out of *Spiritus Mundi*
Troubles my sight: somewhere in the sands of the desert
A shape with lion body and the head of a man,
A gaze blank and pitiless as the sun,
Is moving its slow thighs, while all about it
Reel shadows of the indignant desert birds.

Occasionally, though, the indefiniteness is willed rather than
neutral: 'Surely *some* revelation is at hand.' That is a challenge, I
think. The poem is mobilising its secret complement, asking
whether we are sufficiently repelled by mortmain to accept a
revelation whose content may well be bloody. The vision itself
demands an abstention from detail: '*some*where in the sands of the
desert'.

Like the druids imagined in 'The Magi', Yeats cannot rest
satisfied with Christian myth (Calvary or Bethlehem). In this
respect, he emulates a passage in the *Prelude* (XIII, 312–35),
where Wordsworth had drawn strength from 'a source of
untaught things':

> To a hope
> Not less ambitious once among the wilds
> Of Sarum's Plain, my youthful spirit was raised;
> There, as I ranged at will the pastoral downs
> Trackless and smooth, or paced the bare white roads
> Lengthening in solitude their dreary line,
> Time with his retinue of ages fled
> Backwards, nor checked his flight until I saw
> Our dim ancestral Past in vision clear;
> Saw multitudes of men, and, here and there,
> A single Briton clothed in wolf-skin vest,
> With shield and stone-axe, stride across the wold;
> The voice of spears was heard, the rattling spear
> Shaken by arms of mighty bone, in strength,
> Long mouldered, of barbaric majesty.
> I called on Darkness – but before the word
> Was uttered, midnight darkness seemed to take
> All objects from my sight; and lo! again
> The Desert visible by dismal flames;
> It is the sacrificial altar, fed
> With living men – how deep the groans! the voice

Of those that crowd the giant wicker thrills
The monumental hillocks, and the pomp
Is for both worlds, the living and the dead.

In each case a preliminary intimation, an attempt to record or speak or name, is brusquely superseded by the event itself, unmediated perception ('but before the word/Was uttered'; 'Hardly are those words out / When'). Mere narrative gives way to 'vision clear', and the vision articulates a rite of unambiguous immediacy prior to and more permanent than myth: a pomp for both worlds.

The pomp is also for both worlds in one of Yeats' poems in memory of Robert Gregory, 'An Irish Airman Foresees His Death':

I know that I shall meet my fate
Somewhere among the clouds above;
Those that I fight I do not hate,
Those that I guard I do not love;
My country is Kiltartan Cross,
My countrymen Kiltartan's poor,
No likely end could bring them loss
Or leave them happier than before.
Nor law, nor duty bade me fight,
Nor public men, nor cheering crowds,
A lonely impulse of delight
Drove to this tumult in the clouds;
I balanced all, brought all to mind,
The years to come seemed waste of breath,
A waste of breath the years behind
In balance with this life, this death.

Like the pilgrims in *The Waste Land,* Gregory passes by a distantly menacing crowd ('Those that I fight . . . Those that I guard . . .') and hurries on to an intimate encounter: this tumult, this life, this death. Yeats represents him as a true marginal who by renouncing mortmain in favour of a motiveless delight may come to embody the generic bond uniting aristocrat and beggar.

Yet like Maud Gonne Gregory must be protected from the transformative power of the mythic imagination. Fortunately, the circumstances of his death remain uncertain. Although he was a skilled and successful fighter-pilot, he was not killed in battle.

'What brought him to his end is not known,' Yeats told John Quinn in February 1918:

> He seems to have fainted while flying at a great height, on his return from a scouting expedition. They judge this from his not having stopped his machine as a man does when he is wounded.

It is not a question, as it was with Maud Gonne, of summoning witnesses whose ability to specify and transform what they have seen must then be disowned. We know that Gregory died in his plane, but we will never know how: nobody can specify or transform. This uncertainty is exploited to the full in the poem, where he dies a spectacularly motiveless – and therefore ritual – death. The airman predicts that he will meet his fate *some*where among the clouds above, after having 'balanced all, brought all to mind'. So his rite of passage, his arrival at this life and this death, is negotiated by the terms of Yeats's consistent refusal to specify: 'some' and 'all'.

*   *   *

This chapter would not be complete without further reference to a poet who has so far only appeared in the role of impresario, Ezra Pound. I have placed him with Joyce among the mythologists, and there can be little doubt that he relished the transformative power of language and thought: the *Odyssey* recreated in Latin paraphrase and then in Anglo-Saxon rhythm. Yet his sense of that poem was based on an episode, Odysseus's encounter with the spirits of the dead, which he regarded as a survival from some awesomely archaic culture: 'The Nekuia shouts aloud that it is *older* than the rest, all that island, Cretan, etc., hinter-time, that is *not* Praxiteles, not Athens of Pericles, but Odysseus.' Pound's versions of the Nekuia, both in the Ur-Cantos and in Canto 1, dwelt unmistakably on its ritual aspect. He wanted to found his own epic on hinter-time, on an age steeped in the immediacy of pomp. Bloom's musings at Paddy Dignam's funeral also remembered the Nekuia, but there it was by contrast the audacity of the transposition, the sheer distance from any origin, which told.

Pound's use of mythic resources in the early Cantos is curtailed by external references which posit a ritual immediacy. Canto 4, a kaleidoscope of mythic event, nevertheless concludes with a gesture at what can never be narrated:

> And we sit here . . .
>> there in the arena . . .

Narrative itself fades out. The reference items 'here' and 'there' are never fulfilled and their relation to each other within language supervenes, initiating a to and fro between the observing eye on the terraces and the arena of some unspecifiable ceremony. We must imagine a proximity and a remoteness which we can never articulate.

Pound's description of Venice in Canto 25 achieves a similar effect:

> Which is to say: they built out over the arches
> and the palace hangs there in the dawn, the mist,
> in that dimness,
> or as one rows in from past the murazzi
> the barge slow after moon-rise
> and the voice sounding under the sail.

This passage occurs at the mid-point of the Canto and at the transition from a series of documents concerning medieval Venice to personal reflection ('Which is to say . . . '). The second part of the passage ('or as one rows') makes an accommodating place for the reader, a place from which to see the city. But the external references in the first part ('there' and 'that') have already determined the kind of palace and the kind of dimness 'one' is to imagine. These terms extend the Canto's emphasis on law, its reiteration of the tag 'be it enacted', into the realm of personal reflection. Love and art, like government, must answer to and act from unidentifiable verities. The Canto seeks to protect these verities from contemporary mortmain ('The dead concepts, never the solid, the blood rite'). Here, as elsewhere in the early Cantos, it is external reference which sustains the blood rite.

The demonstratives keep history at arm's length, neither abolishing nor identifying it:

> I sat on the Dogana's steps
> For the gondolas cost too much, that year . . .   (Canto 3)

And that year they fought in the streets,
And that year he got out to Cesena
    And brought back the levies,
And that year he crossed by night over Foglia . . . (Canto 8)

And that year I went up to Frieburg,
And Rennert had said . . .   (Canto 20)

There is an atmosphere of narration, but little story and virtually no identification at all. Whether public or private, the years are equalised to a lost immediacy. More alarmingly, perhaps, Pound's many adversaries come to be characterised less by their actual shortcomings than by a uniform distance from the speaker: 'that pot-scraping little runt'; 'that monstruous swollen, swelling s.o.b.'; 'that squirt of an Ausstrrian'. These figures seem to invite our contempt by their expulsion into unrelatedness.

Altogether, Pound was at this stage as committed to ritual immediacy and the self-evident authority of 'I have seen what I have seen' (Canto 2) as Yeats or Frost. Three poets faced by three different problems – launching an epic, a new style, a career – all managed to extend ritual into rhetoric by different used of external reference. By acknowledging what they specify but omit to name, we shed our accidental and temporary status, and become the readers they were writing for.

5 The spirit of anti-pathos

In the spring of 1921, Eliot planned for restless Marie an evocative stay at a lake seventeen miles south-west of Munich –

> Summer surprised us, coming over the Starnbergersee
> With a shower of rain

– and Bertolt Brecht sat in a hut beside the same lake, dodging a hailstorm. Marie seems to have enjoyed a coffee and an hour's conversation. Brecht thought the event worth remembering because his girlfriend was also inside the hut, while her clothes were outside.

Still, he wasn't feeling all that cheerful:

> How this Germany bores me! It's a good middling country, with lovely pale colours and wide landscapes: but what inhabitants! A degraded peasantry whose crudeness however doesn't give birth to any fabulous monsters, just a quiet decline into the animal kingdom; a middle class run to fat; and drab intellectuals.

And surly adolescents. However, Brecht's fantasy of escape from mortmain was more interesting than his resentment. 'The answer: America . . . '

His fantasy was not Coleridge's, for by this time America had become a twice-promised land. America had been promised to Europeans once in the realm of nature, by God; and it was now being promised a second time in the realm of culture, by Henry Ford. Thus where Coleridge had seen an empty space, Brecht saw a production-line. And Ford had gone one better than God in claiming that his promise would travel to meet the pilgrim, that his methods could be seen as 'something in the nature of a universal code'. The answer, then: Americanism . . .

That universal code could, like Coleridge's empty space, be

seen as the catalyst of regeneration. 'In America,' wrote the Italian Marxist Antonio Gramsci, 'rationalisation has determined the need to elaborate a new type of man suited to the new type of work and productive process.' Gramsci thought that technology would purge the old type of man, the 'sedimentations of idle and useless masses living on "their ancestral patrimony", pensioners of economic history'. Capital and labour would then stand clear in binary splendour, and a new type of man would be shaped by the struggle between them.

It was an extreme vision, and horrifying to some. Rilke felt that Ford's universal code had obliterated the 'morsel of humanity' which used to inhere in every object (a trace of work or affection or use); while in Yeats's eyes technology had so cauterised experience that people no longer knew what it meant to be disinherited. But there were writers who made out of Americanism, broadly understood, a metaphor for regeneration; or, with less ambitious but more enduring effect, a metaphor for immunity to mortmain.

Let us start with Americanism in its technological aspect. Gramsci wrote well on the way mechanisation had affected 'the professions connected with the reproduction of texts': compositors, linotype operators, stenographers, typists. He pointed out that any interest shown by such workers in the texts they were reproducing would hinder speed and accuracy, and that every effort was therefore made to isolate the intellectual content of the texts from their written symbolisation. Gramsci asked whether this would mean the 'spiritual death' of the workers concerned, and it is a sign of his determination to adopt and master Ford's universal code that he should think not:

> Once the process of adaptation has been completed, what really happens is that the brain of the worker, far from being mummified, reaches a state of complete freedom. The only thing that is completely mechanicised is the physical gesture; the memory of the trade, reduced to simple gestures repeated at an intense rhythm, 'nestles' in the muscular and nervous centres and leaves the brain free and unencumbered for other occupations.

The requirement now was that people should *not* find any 'morsel of humanity', any trace of human labour and care, in the material they were working; so far from worrying about this, as Rilke and Yeats had, Gramsci rejoiced in the opportunities it afforded. For him, alienation was not an effect of the Fall, but an armature of the new type of man.

More orthodox economists concurred, although they rather hoped that the workers might be given something other than political debate to sharpen their newly autonomous minds on. As Dexter Kimball put it:

> Repetitive work that requires little mental effort is not necessarily deadening to the intellect. In most work of this character, the manual operations become almost automatic upon the part of the worker, leaving his mind more or less free. Thus, cigar makers, whose work is highly repetitive, can perform the necessary operations almost automatically and at the same time listen to readers who are hired for the purpose of providing mental entertainment while they work.

Pound incorporated the remark about the cigar makers into Canto 38 without any obvious sign of disapproval. Here was an alteration in human behaviour which the writer should observe impartially.

Even more interesting was the way this armature of the new type of man became a literary principle: Brecht's *Verfremdungseffekt*, which encouraged the actor to distance himself from the role he was playing, so that the audience might appraise rather than identify with that role. The system allowed an actor to separate himself from the gestures nestling in his muscular and nervous centres, the memory of his trade, and to exploit the resulting freedom. 'The alienation effect intervenes,' Brecht wrote, 'not in the form of absence of emotion, but in the form of emotions which need not correspond to those of the character portrayed.' He and Gramsci celebrated this duality, this refusal to allow mind to flow into labour and labour to flow into mind.

Of course, few writers were as interested in technological progress as Brecht and Gramsci and Pound. For most people Americanism was an atmosphere or a style. To the satirist Georg Grosz it meant movies and efficiency and advertising as well as production lines. 'Even I,' he reported, 'got a suit in which I felt quite ''American'', with extremely broad shoulders, leather belt and narrow-bottomed trousers.' Oskar Schlemmer, painter and director of the stage workshop at the Bauhaus, noted a more extreme version of the same mood:

> The artistic climate here cannot support anything that is not the latest, the most modern, up-to-the-minute. Dadaism, circus, *variété*, jazz, hectic pace, movies, America, airplanes, the automobile. Those are the terms in which people here think.

Schlemmer defined the terms in which people thought as a 'spirit of anti-pathos'. It was not considered chic to show or to respond to pathos, to excite or to be excited by pity and sadness. People at the Bauhaus cut themselves off from the impulses which 'nestled' in their muscular and nervous centres as effectively as Gramsci's typists and Brecht's actors.

This immunity from the conventions of a moribund bourgeois world was a European phenomenon, even though its exponents saw America as the promised land. Marcel Duchamp, arriving in New York in 1915, praised the city as a technological wonderland, an arsenal of mechanical obsessions; but he had so intensely imagined the place before he ever set foot in it that no amount of power-cuts and defective elevators would have made him change his mind. Americanism was a European need, an anarchic response to mortmain. It was exported back to Europe at the end of the First World War, when Duchamp and Picabia and Man Ray returned to Paris. After them came the next wave of visitors, as much Americanists as Americans, living an image: in Hemingway's *Movable Feast,* McAlmon's *Being Geniuses Together,* Ford Madox Ford's account of the founding of the *transatlantic review.*

The difference between Americans and Americanists can be seen in Wyndham Lewis's impressions of Ezra Pound before and after the War. When Pound first arrived in London, he seemed to Lewis a bit too much of the 'singing cowboy', rushing 'with all the raw solemnity of the classic Middle West into a sophisticated post-Nineties society dreaming of the Eighteenth century'. But Lewis saw him again after the War, in Paris, and he seemed rather different:

> Having found his abode, I rang the bell. A good deal of noise was to be heard but no one answered: therefore I pushed the

door, which opened practically into the studio. A splendidly built young man, stripped to the waist, and with a torso of dazzling white, was standing not far from me. He was tall, handsome, and serene, and was repelling with his boxing gloves a hectic assault of Ezra's. After a final swing at the dazzling solar plexus Pound fell back upon his settee. The young man was Hemingway.

The young man was also the very embodiment of Americanism, not least in his obsession with sport (an obsession shared by Brecht). Pound himself, Hemingway reported to Sherwood Anderson, was willing but short-winded: 'Going over there this afternoon for another session but there ain't much job in it as I have to shadow box between rounds to get up a sweat.'

Others had plenty to sweat out. 'Why do American artists go to France,' demanded William Carlos Williams, 'and continue to do so and when there to drink, if they are wise, heavily?' Williams thought that it was because Paris offered them the opportunity to 'awaken' from the dead hand of convention: 'Drink breaks the savage spell of nonentity, or equality as they call it, which chokes them in the great western republic.' Everywhere, apparently, has its own version of mortmain, and he himself projected an apocalyptic release in *Spring and All,* a collection of prose and verse published in Paris in 1923: 'The imagination, intoxicated by prohibitions, rises to drunken heights to destroy the world.' This was the 'secret project' of *his* anti-pathos: 'Imagine the monster project of the moment! Tomorrow we the people of the United States are going to Europe armed to kill every man, woman and child in the area west of the Carpathian mountains (also east) sparing none. Imagine the sensation it will cause.'

The insouciance, which Williams cannot quite handle, undoubtedly derives from a perception of technological process:

> In passing with my mind
> on nothing in the world
>
> but the right of way
> I enjoy on the road by
>
> virtue of the law –
> I saw . . .

Feckless rhyming proclaims that we should enjoy whatever rights of way we enjoy: that is the only 'virtue' of the law which frames them. Driving along, Williams sees an elderly man, a woman in blue, a boy, the man's belly, a watch-chain. Motoring parlance – to go for a spin – becomes wonderfully literal, as attention ricochets from one object to the next. It engenders a kind of anti-pathos, a refusal to let perception flow into meaning and meaning into perception: 'Why bother where I went?' Why bother where the line, or the poem, should end? Poetry, Williams claimed, liberates words from their 'emotional implications', from the 'usual quality' of their meaning; it grants them the kind of autonomy from the memory of their trade which Gramsci had seen in his typists and Brecht in his actors.

The sports arena provided a favourite metaphor for that autonomy, and for the response it might hope to excite. The spectators at a ball game are moved uniformly, he says, as though by a kind of liminal experience; but it is an experience which makes them conscious of pleasure, or of a spirit of uselessness, rather than of a generic human bond. They respond anti-pathetically to a display of anti-pathos. Brecht, too, valued the knowledgeable and unsentimental response of the audience for professional sport. At the beginning of *In the Jungle of the Cities*, a play first performed in 1923, he announced that he was about to present 'an inexplicable wrestling match between two men'. 'Don't worry your heads about the motives for the fight,' he counselled the audience, 'concentrate on the stakes. Judge impartially the technique of the contenders, and keep your eyes fixed on the finish.'

That final remark reveals that what Brecht and his contemporaries saw in professional sport was anti-pathos skilfully handled. Spectators may applaud a graceful flourish, but they are brought 'uniformly' to their feet by moments of absolute, controlled aggression: the knock-out punch, the goal scored, the volley put away. Such moments leave an opponent outwitted and humiliated; they are perfect not because of their finesse, but because of their triumphant ruthlessness. (They represent what the amateur – who wants desperately to win, but cannot control his desperation – will never achieve.) Professional sportsmen had perfected the armature of the new type of man; professional writers could only admire them, and envy the admiration they provoked.

The writer who came closest to finding a language for the spirit of anti-pathos represented by the sportsmen was Wyndham Lewis, who vigorously pursued his task in works like *The Enemy of the Stars, The Ideal Giant,* 'Cantleman's Spring Mate', *Tarr, The Wild Body* and *The Apes of God.* Motiveless conflicts spark all through these works, as their alarming protagonists manoeuvre for the knock-out punch, the moment of triumphant aggression. In *The Wild Body,* a collection of stories published in 1927 but written during the previous fifteen years, Lewis found one of his most striking metaphysicians of violence, the narrator Kerr-Orr: 'I am a large blond clown, ever so vaguely reminiscent (in person) of William Blake, and some great American boxer whose name I forget.' Kerr-Orr perfects the spirit of anti-pathos by laughing rather than by fighting:

> My body is large, white and savage. But all the fierceness has become transformed into *laughter.* It still looks like a visi-gothic fighting-machine, but it is in reality a *laughing* machine . . . Everywhere where formerly I would fly at throats, I now howl with laughter.

By transforming fierceness into laughter, he hopes to work off his alarm at himself (at the sadistic and anti-pathetic element in human behaviour).

Lewis added to *The Wild Body* an essay, 'Inferior Religions', which goes some way towards expounding his perception of that element: 'Within five yards of another man's eyes we are on a little crater, which, if it erupted, would split up as would a cocoa-tin of nitrogen.' His memories of the 'motiveless conflict' exemplified by trench warfare came into play alongside the sporting metaphors of a Brecht or a Hemingway.

> The opposing armies in the early days in Flanders stuck up dummy-men on poles for their enemies to pot at, in a spirit of ferocious banter. It is only a shell of that description that is engaged in the sphere of laughter.

The spirit of ferocious banter involved detachment from other people and a refusal to acknowledge the pathos of their predicament, but also detachment from oneself (from the pathos of one's own predicament). Here again technology gave the lead, demonstrating as clearly to Lewis as it had to Gramsci and Brecht that the mind could float free of the gestures embedded in the muscular and nervous centres of the body. Kerr-Orr sees himself as hanging somewhere in the midst of his visigothic fighting-machine, quite separate from its lungings and grimaces. Our own predicament, like that of most other people, constantly leaks pathos and the spirit of ferocious banter demands nothing less than cautery: the cautery of the knock-out punch or the shell fired at dummy-men, an extinction of feeling. Only if we obey that spirit, as Lewis's fiction did, can we find language for an element in human behaviour which would otherwise remain unspoken (but always pressing).

* * *

I believe the voicing of a spirit of anti-pathos in the fiction of the twenties to be a fascinating and important subject, but not one for a book concerned with modern poetry. Even so, the spirit did move poets as well as novelists, and it did produce at least one anti-pathetic successor to Eliot's caricature marginals. The development from caricature to ferocious banter may appear slight, but it helps to explain the manner of a poem in a book published in the same year as *Spring and All* and *The Waste Land,* Wallace Stevens's *Harmonium.*

'The Comedian as the Letter C' certainly hustles its protagonist into a rite of passage:

> Just so an ancient Crispin was dissolved.
> The valet in the tempest was annulled.
> Bordeaux to Yucatan, Havana next,
> And then to Carolina. Simple jaunt.

The simple jaunt annuls Crispin's stale European identity and exposes him to the 'elemental potencies and pangs' of barbarous margins, Yucatan and Havana. Surviving the 'hubbub of his pilgrimage' and 'made desperately clear', he settles to a new life in Carolina. And yet as much suspicion attaches to this regeneration as to the martyrdom of Saint Narcissus. For what is not made desperately clear is the validity of the margin opened by the hubbub of pilgrimage:

> Here was prose
> More exquisite than any tumbling verse:
> A still new continent on which to dwell.

The prose of this world is not only delicate, but consciously sought-out (the root meaning of 'exquisite'), and perhaps falsified by the search. Crispin, we have already been told, is 'aware of exquisite thought'. Furthermore, the 'still new continent' has the ambiguous status of the 'still unravished bride' of Keats' 'Ode on a Grecian Urn'. It is both still (calm) and still new (as yet unknown). However many times we return, the bride will still be unravished, the land still new; our interpretative or colonising zeal cannot disclose the true nature of either. Just as Narcissus's rite of passage does not deliver him into the company of the blessed, so Crispin's does not deliver him into the company of Pantisocrats and Aspheterists. In this sense 'The Comedian as the Letter C' represents, as Harold Bloom has pointed out, 'the satyr-poem or parody that culminates and almost undoes the tradition of the High Romantic quest-poem'. Childe Roland to the guzzly fruit came.

Crispin certainly culminates, and maybe undoes, Eliot's series of caricature marginals. Like Narcissus, he has a third-century saint for a namesake. Like Prufrock, he plays, 'at times, the Fool': 'A clown, perhaps, but an aspiring clown.' He has been identified with the valet Crispin of late seventeenth-century French comedy, the Pierrot of Laforgue and the harlequin of the *Commedia del'Arte*. Indeed, the harlequin's motley seems to have become the official uniform of caricature marginals. Conrad's Marlow encounters on his 'weary pilgrimage among hints for nightmares' a bizarre Russian who had set off into the African interior with no aim in mind, met up with Kurtz and enlisted as a disciple:

> His aspect reminded me of something I had seen – something funny I had seen somewhere. As I manoeuvred to get alongside, I was asking myself, 'What does this fellow look like?' Suddenly I got it. He looked like a harlequin. His clothes had been made of some stuff that was brown holland probably, but it was covered with patches all over, with bright patches, blue, red, and yellow . . .

The Russian serves as a silent monitor, an eccentric – 'There he was before me, in motley, as though he had absconded from a troupe of mimes, enthusiastic, fabulous' – whose apartness rebukes more worldly people: 'If the absolutely pure, uncalculating, unpractical spirit of adventure had ever ruled a human being, it ruled this be-patched youth.'

For Rilke, the harlequinade represented an equally eccentric but less pure marginality. Picasso, too, began to edge clear of Cubist preoccupations and assorted bric-à-brac by way of the harlequin motif. His *Saltimbanques*, which shows a group of six travelling acrobats (one dressed as a harlequin) against an indeterminate background, inspired the fifth of the *Duino Elegies*. Rilke told Lou Andreas-Salomé that the memory of such acrobats had lain on him 'like a task' since his early days in Paris; he thought them even more transient than most people, even more thoroughly condemned to routine. The 'Fifth Elegy' sites them in the margin, the place marked in his poems by 'da':

> Und Kaum dort,
> aufrecht, da und gezeigt: des Dastehns
> grosser Anfangbuchstab . . .

> (And hardly there,
> upright, shown us: the great initial
> letter of Thereness . . .)

Five of the figures in Picasso's painting could be contained in a large capital D, the capital letter of *Dastehn,* or 'thereness'. But they do not deserve to be identified with the ground of being, because their acrobatics represent a false and sterile freedom. These, too, are caricature marginals: the comedian as the letter D.

However, neither Conrad's Russian nor Rilke's acrobats are portrayed in a spirit of ferocious banter: they leak pathos insistently. For some truly anti-pathetic acrobats one has to look to Lewis's short story 'The Cornac and His Wife', included in *The Wild Body* and originally entitled 'Les Saltimbanques'. Kerr-Orr uses the intimate but essentially hostile relations between a group of Breton acrobats and their peasant audience to illustrate his theory of humour:

Violence is of the essence of *laughter* (as distinguished of course from smiling wit): it is merely the inversion or failure of *force* . . .
It must be extremely primitive in origin, though of course its function in civilized life is to keep the primitive at bay. But it hoists the primitive with its own explosive. It is a realistic firework, reminiscent of war.

Examples of such inversions of force are provided, Kerr-Orr says, by the modern circus, the *Commedia del'Arte,* Punch and Judy shows, and by the Breton peasants and their strolling players:

With their grins and quips they are like armed men who never meet without clashing their weapons together. Were my circus-proprietor and his kind not so tough, this continual howl or disquieting explosion of what is scarcely mirth would shatter them.

These people are not poignant after the fashion of Conrad's Russian or Rilke's acrobats; they exemplify the spirit of anti-pathos that Lewis tried so hard to define both in his art and in his writing.

If one wanted to determine the exact sense in which Kerr-Orr's body could be considered 'wild', one might compare it with the varieties of wildness catalogued and savoured in Yeats' letters. Yeats did speak of *The Player Queen* as a 'wild' comedy and of writing a poem with a 'wild comedy setting', but for him wildness usually involved an excess of emotion. He talked about 'wild people' or 'rhapsodical persons'; about Maud Gonne doing something 'wild' in an ecstacy of political hatred; about the 'wild men' of the IRA and the 'wild regrets' of old age. Emotion has blinded these people to prudence and common sense, and therefore suffused them with pathos (even though it may have led them to hate and kill); they have become, in their wildness, paradigms of feeling. Lewis's characters, on the other hand, cauterise the springs of rhapsody and detach themselves coldly from their own extravagance and from the folly of others.

Conrad's Russian, Rilke's acrobats, Eliot's saint and lover and wise old man: these were improbable or caricature marginals, barren and absurd but all the same pathetic. Lewis's sal-timbanques and soldiers of humour are creatures of a different stamp, and it is with them that Crispin must be ranged. The evidence for this assertion lies not so much in anything he does, as in the spirit of ferocious banter which the poem subjects him to. Its manner is, as Frank Kermode remarks, 'a sustained nightmare of unexpected diction, so that one sometimes thinks of it less as a poem than as a remarkable physical feat'. Stevens directs this nightmare of unexpected diction against Crispin's wild body, a visigothic quest-machine launched upon pilgrimage. One need think only of the epithets he finds for the valet: this nincompated pedagogue, this short-shanks, this auditor of insects, this odd discoverer, this connoisseur of elemental fate. The harshness becomes evident not so much in the epithets themselves, as in the demonstrative which introduces them, a more intimate and self-lacerating version of the extrovert belligerence of the *Cantos* ('that squirt', 'that pot-scraping little runt'). Stevens allows the inverted force of laughter to break in upon the most intimate communing and cherishing. We await the knock-out punch or the shell that will explode the dummy-man, Crispin. For this is a High Romantic quest-poem revised by the spirit of ferocious banter, or anti-pathos.

6 Form-sense and dictator-sense

Whatever else the spirit of anti-pathos may have achieved (and I shall argue that it plays an important part in contemporary writing), it certainly hastened the demise of the marginals. Their supply of pathos cut off, the old men and the wanderers and the artists could not so obviously serve as beacons of a dissent which was both cultural and social. But anti-pathos made few readers for Lewis and Stevens and Williams; so few, in fact, that the subsequent discovery of politics in the thirties proved virtually irresistible; here at last, it seemed to many writers, was a way of identifying those readers who could be relied upon to pick up a book for the right reasons. New criteria for the identification of readers and new rhetorics began to appear. 'Only from about the year 1926,' Eliot later claimed,

> did the features of the post-war world begin clearly to emerge –
> and not only in the sphere of politics. From about that date one
> began slowly to realize that the intellectual and artistic output
> of the previous seven years had been rather the last efforts of an
> old world, than the struggles of a new.

He was offering, in 1939, his 'Last Words' as editor of the *Criterion*, terminating not only a magazine but also a specific phase in literary history.

The years 1926–8 certainly witnessed some defiant conversions among literary men: Eliot's to Christianity and Brecht's to Marxism being the most notorious. Pound produced the apt formula for these changes of heart:

> Form-sense 1910 to 1914. 15 or so years later Lewis discovered
> Hitler. I hand it to him as a superior perception. Superior in
> relation to my own 'discovery' of Mussolini.

One can imagine Lewis's response to this courtesy: thanks a lot, Ezra. But it would have been hard to deny Pound's perception of a development, in the late twenties, from form-sense to dictator-sense. By 1939 the scramble for dictators had become sufficiently hectic to discompose Eliot himself. 'If you will not have God (and He is a jealous God),' he wrote, 'you should pay your respects to Hitler or Stalin.' It is the conventions of readership produced by that development which will interest me here.

Pound's own dictator-sense catalysed his enthusiasm for Italian Fascism, while remaining to some extent distinct from it. 'Never in Italy,' he remarked in 1936, 'have I heard one word against Lenin or Stalin. I have heard many tributes, and I once heard a responsible official "blow up" a journalist who wanted to support Trotsky *against* Stalin, in order to weaken Russia.' It seems to me that this fascination with the principle of absolute and singular authority, whether of Right or of Left, had greater consequences for Pound's work than anything he might have learnt (or gained) from the Italian system of government.

Those consequences were produced by a tension between the essentially nostalgic cast of his politics and his preference for innovatory rhetorics. Many of his political attitudes stem, as William Chace has shown, from a tradition of American nativism (or agrarian dissent, or populism) which reaches back to Thomas Jefferson. The tradition defended the interests of primary producers against those of the middlemen who live off wealth created by others. The primary producer could be a pioneer, a farmer, an entrepreneur, or (in Pound's eyes) an artist: he had to act vigorously and work directly on the material world. Pioneers and farmers had of course been more prominent in the settling and building of America than they were in its industrial triumph, as Pound well knew. 'I remain a Jeffersonian republican,' he said in 1933, adding the proviso that 1930 was not 1820 and that – as Jefferson had foreseen – the primary producer was now more likely to be a manufacturer than a farmer.

Still, even these Mark II primary producers had something to show the writer. 'Ole Henry Ford,' Pound declared in 1928, 'has seen several points that wd. be useful in la vie littéraire. I.e. anteriority of production to blurb.' Ford himself was a nativist, defending the interests of 'creative Industry' against those of 'international Finance' in his journal, *The Dearborn Independent*. His autobiography called for 'artists in industrial relationship':

'We want those who can mould the political, social, industrial and moral mass into a sound and shapely whole.' Another commentator, Hamilton Yorke, took up the theme of entrepreneurial creativity. The 'Nordic capitalist', he claimed, 'plays the game not so much for money as he does for the joy of constructing, the satisfaction of accomplishment'. We might compare this with Pound's upstaging of C. H. Douglas, some time in the early twenties;

> Over a decade ago, Major Douglas admitted that I had made a contribution to the subject (economics) when I pointed out that my grand-father had built a railroad probably less from a desire to make money or an illusion that he could make more that way than some other, than from inherent activity, artist's desire to MAKE something, the fun of constructing and the play of outwitting and overcoming obstruction.

The criterion of 'inherent activity' was Pound's greatest intellectual debt to American nativism.

It became increasingly apparent that the only politicians fuelled by this mysterious substance were the dictators. Mussolini was on the whole popular with Americans to the extent that he embodied the virtues, and furthered the interests, of the primary producer. He was acclaimed for getting things done. 'In the end,' John Diggins concludes, 'America's apologia for Fascism would betray an inevitable desire to see the Americanization of Italy.' Here is one business editor's view of the Mussolini style:

> Executive actions, not conferences and talk . . . He cuts through. No idle words . . . Accomplishment! Not fine-spoken theories; not plans; not speeches he is going to make. Things done! And this is your successful American executive.

Ford had established a factory in Italy, and Mussolini was using his doctrines to foster industrial peace and smooth over class-conflict. No wonder we find Pound praising Ford and Mussolini in the same breath, in a letter written to Harriet Monroe on 30 November 1926. His most concise endorsement of Mussolini, given nine years later, made much of the Duce's abundance of 'inherent activity':

I don't believe any estimate of Mussolini will be valid unless it *starts* from his passion for construction. Take him as *artifex* and all the details fall into place. Take him as anything save the artist and you will get muddled with contradictions.

For Pound, primed as he was by nativist thinking, the details fell into place only too easily.

But the 'inherent activity' of the entrepreneur and the politician had always met with an 'obstruction' greater and more insidious than that offered by the block of stone to the Vorticist's chisel. By the beginning of the twentieth century, populism had been deflected into anxiety about the power of financiers and immigrants and other 'parasites'. From this point of view, Fascism could be seen as a necessary purging of the Italian character: 'common sense applied to the problems of a fool-ridden nation,' in the words of the bellicose popular novelist and opponent of immigration, Kenneth Roberts. Pre-Fascist Italy had been a chaos of unemployment, disorder and class-hatred. Then, according to Roberts, came 'The Salvage of a Nation'; and he went on to describe in a jocular manner how peasant agitators had been 'perforated' and 'ventilated' by Fascist gunmen. After sorting that lot out, Mussolini turned his attention to another breeding-ground of parasites, the bureaucracy, which proved no match for his ventilating talents: 'he is probably the most persistent, effervescent and successful comer-into-contact ever known outside of machinery circles'.

Whether practised inside or outside machinery circles, 'inherent activity' had come to depend – dangerously – on the exercise not only of talent but also of *will*. Pound admired Ford and Mussolini for asserting the anteriority of production to blurb, and for maintaining it in the face of a host of sinister enemies. Mussolini had always seemed, to his disciples and to his opponents alike, an embodiment of will; as a speaker in a parliamentary debate of 16 November 1922 informed him, 'the will for you is everything'. Four years later, Mussolini demonstrated this quality in a particularly flambouyant way. At the end of July 1926 the lira stood at 153 to the £. The bankers advised a revaluation to 120 or even 150. Mussolini, however, insisted on 'quota 90': the rate of exchange when he had come to power. It was the exercise of political will against the bankers, as much as any theoretical nicety, which attracted Pound to Fascist

economic policy. In November of the same year he wrote to
Harriet Monroe, praising Mussolini; in 1933, he published a
'concise introduction to "volitionist economics"', and declared
that the science would fail unless it granted 'the existence of will
as a "component"'. Two years later, in 1935, he was still
celebrating the Duce's act of will: 'This possibility to eat, sleep
and keep warm at home without invading foreign markets,
conduces to that sanity which Mussolini has obtained largely by
force of character, aided by control of his banking system, the
checking of foreign devils who wanted to sink the value of the lira,
etc.'

1930 was not 1820, both in the sense that the industrialist had
taken the place of the farmer and the pioneer, and in the sense
that the odds facing the primary producer now seemed
overwhelming. As a result the temptation to acclaim 'force of
character' and to justify ruthlessness became harder to resist.
Pound did not resist. It was not so much his reverence for
'inherent activity' as his fears for the very survival of such activity
in the modern world which led him to Mussolini – a man whose
innovatory politics admitted no hiatus between will and deed, and
who was thus able to destroy the conspiracies levelled at the
primary producer. 'The real views of the "Duce",' wrote
Giovanni Gentile, 'are those which he formulates and executes at
one and the same time.' Pound's writing in the thirties never
resolved the tension between nostalgia for a lost world governed
by the spirit of 'inherent activity' and envy of a politician who
seemed to have succeeded by doing things in a new way. He may
have hoped that the innovating politician would restore the lost
world, but the qualities of both continued to fascinate him.

* * *

This was not simply the tension between conservatism and
innovation found in all millennial politics, but a tension between
different imaginings of the audience to which Pound could
address his literary and political message. For he had an
extremely well developed sense of his own public role and of the
ways in which his views (and subsequently, perhaps, his poems)
might be aired.

As early as 1911, while he was travelling in Italy, the
Philadelphia Evening Herald devoted some space to his exploits:

Philadelphian Wins Renown With Verse. It assured its readers of his reputation abroad and his increasing fame at home ('Pound, however, cares nothing for that, he declares'). When he moved to Rapallo in the twenties he became a popular subject with the gossip columns, and serviced this interest by writing frequently to the newspapers. Indeed, he never wavered from a resolute and almost morbid courtship of a newspaper-audience. Romano Bilenchi recalls a visit to his house in the winter of 1941–2:

> Sometimes, when I made a remark, he would take off running toward the oval door at the back of the sitting room. For ten minutes or so I would hear the loud noises of paper tearing and wood sliding, as if a dog had gotten into a chicken coop. Then Pound would re-emerge with a bundle of five- and ten-year-old American newspapers. He showed me articles and interviews with four- and five-column headlines: 'Ezra Pound, disembarking in San Francisco, says that in case of war, the Japenese would overcome the US in a few months.'

Pound knew that the newspapers would give space even to a poet, providing the poet's manner and opinions were sufficiently larger-than-life.

There were other kinds of celebrity, too. In November 1933 a small magazine called *Outrider* introduced a selection of Pound's work with the remark that 'if America generally does not know him we can only refer to the English *Who's Who,* where the recital of his attainments runs over a solid column of agate type'. Those Americans who did turn to the *Who's Who* of, say, 1930 would have seen that Pound bulked larger than Eliot, Forster, Galsworthy, Graves, Joyce, Lawrence, Middleton Murry, Harold Monro, I. A. Richards, Russell, Sassoon, Osbert Sitwell, Arthur Symons and Virginia Woolf; that he merited as much space as Arnold Bennett, Edgar Wallace and W. B. Yeats; and that he was beaten out of sight only by panjandrums such as Sir Henry Newbolt, Rudyard Kipling, H. G. Wells and John Buchan. Of course, these entries registered neither talent nor influence; but Pound seems nevertheless to have taken the exercise seriously. Thus while Buchan's favourite recreation was listed as deer-stalking, Joyce's as singing and Sitwell's as 'regretting the Bourbons', Pound laid claim to 'the Public taste'. Eliot did not admit to any recreation at all.

However, by the early thirties Pound was beginning to consider even this degree of celebrity restrictive. He had talked to the newspapers and conquered *Who's Who*, he had filled the columns of type – but all to very little political effect. At the same time, he knew that the newspapers were being outstripped as a medium of mass communication by the radio, and that the new medium was essential to the innovatory politics of the dictators. In 1928 the fourth and final issue of Pound's magazine *The Exile* had celebrated Lenin and Mussolini primarily as technicians of utterance, exponents of a new form of communication. Lenin, he claimed, 'never wrote a sentence that has any interest in itself, but he evolved almost a new medium, a sort of expression half way between writing and action'. Pound added that any writer who thought himself modern should observe with interest, and perhaps a little professional jealousy, the development of this new sort of expression, this unity of will and deed.

Mussolini's political style depended even more on exploitation of the media. Whereas Jefferson had, as Pound noted, 'guided a limited electorate by what he wrote and said more or less privately,' Mussolini ruled by mass-rally and newsreel and radio broadcast. In 1922, when he came to power, there was no radio, no large audience for film and no newspaper with a circulation over 500 000; ten years later, he was ruling by mass media. 'From sheer force,' Pound wrote to *Guide to Kulchur*, 'physical prowess, craft, jaw-house, money-pull, press to radio, government has undergone revolutions of modus and instrument.' Lenin, he thought, had 'won by Radio'. In Italy, radio had become by 1934 the chief modus and instrument of Fascist propaganda, due to a great increase in the ownership of sets. As Adrian Lyttelton points out, it made possible a new atmosphere: 'the range and constancy of the charismatic relationship between the Duce and his audience could be immensely extended'.

Beyond the readers of the *Chicago Tribune* and the *Philadelphia Evening Herald* lay the radio-audience of millions, engrossed by Mussolini's oratory. Here was a new and enticingly immediate relation to an audience, and a new sort of expression which dwarfed the achievements of the most experimental writer. Pound himself did not know the blessings of such immediacy until 1941, when he finally got to broadcast for Rome Radio. But he felt its lure throughout the thirties. In terms of his relation to an audience as well as in terms of his politics, the innovatory form which he thought might return him and his readers to an older and more immediate knowledge ended up by becoming its own justification. With this is mind, we might turn to the poems he wrote during the thirties. There, too, nostalgia conflicts with the bravado of experiment, old rhetorics with new.

* * *

Pound sometimes spoke of the successive issues of the *Cantos* as 'books', and we can best follow the passing of form-sense into dictator-sense if we concentrate on a particular one: *Eleven New Cantos* (numbers 31 to 41), published by Farrar and Rhinehart on 8 October 1934 and by Faber the following March.

The most striking thing about the new book was its ambitious incorporation of historical documents, and consequent reliance on the editorial eye and ear of the poet rather than on his lyric and narrative skills. These documents were for real; they had not been chosen for their ability to flesh out a 'factive personality', or to provide atmosphere, like the material relating to Malatesta in Canto 9. They were wise sayings, self-evident truths whose identity ought not to depend on the vigour of their secret complement or on the vagaries and nuances of individual perception. For if the dictators did not employ demonstrative reference, nor should the poet who admired their new sort of expression half-way between writing and action. Something would have to be done about the obliquity of the conventions which had sponsored the early Cantos, about the rhetoric of unfulfilled specificity.

Pound was fond of Mussolini's observation that nobody any more wanted a government in which there was no responsible person having a hind-name, a front-name and an address. In *Eleven New Cantos* he hurried, as he might not have done before, to supply information presupposed by reference items and so to identify the people and places mentioned in his sources. Canto 33 reprints the following from *Das Kapital*:

Rogier (minister) told me that this government (Brussels) had been intending to introduce such a law but found itself (re/child labour not limited to 12 hours per day) always blocked by the jealous uneasiness that met any law tampering with the absolute freedom of labour.

Lord H. de Walden from Brussels. 1862

The phrase 'this government' does not appear in the original. But
having introduced it in order to make De Walden's report more
vivid, Pound feels obliged to tell us which government is being
referred to; he gives the demonstrative an address. There are
other examples of such solicitude in Canto 34:

> Ney to be here (Paris) tomorrow, because it is the
> King of Rome's birthday . . .
>
> This has been (May 26th) a harassing day
> but I perceived a tamarind heaving up the earth
> in tumbler number 2, and in tumbler number 1, planted . . .

Pound no longer wants us to marvel at the special truth of
perceptions whose identity is available only to the speaker, an
identity which the reader must guess at. For he was becoming
interested in the kind of truth which should appear immediately
self-evident to all, without prompting or coaxing.

Of course, a lyric and narrative voice does recur in *Eleven New
Cantos,* and it invariably marks its presence by a trail of unfulfilled
reference items. Canto 35 includes some of Pound's distancing
demonstratives: 'that ass Natannovitch', and so on. Canto 38
fixes his memories of the War in similar fashion: 'An' that year
Metevsky . . . And that year Mr Whitney . . . And that year Mr
Wilson . . . ' It also suggests that self-evident economic truths
have in these degenerate times achieved the status of Eleusinian
mystery:

> and the light became so bright and so blindin'
> in *this* layer of paradise
> that the mind of man was bewildered.

> (my emphasis)

In such times, according to Canto 39, illumination reverts to the
most shrouded of intimacies: 'Discuss this in bed said the lady.'
Yet Pound had to find more than a name and address for his view
of history, more than editorial competence. He had to present it
to readers in usable form, as something which would not bewilder
the mind of man or turn the mind of woman towards bed. His
efforts to do so foreshadowed a later and more public disaster. For

just as a fantasy of the instant communication of ideas by radio was to unsettle his real but painfully limited *rapport* with newspaper-readers, so a fantasy of new sorts of expression unsettled the viable but nostalgic view of history familiar to him from modern literature. In each case, a convention he could handle gave way to one he wanted to handle, but could not.

That view of history, although scarcely invented by 'Modernism', was probably enhanced by the resort to fragmentary forms. In order to understand how the fragmentation came to articulate a view of history, we need to define its logic: the logic of works which proceed by way of discrete tableaux, works in which the 'burden of meaning and pleasure' (as Roland Barthes has described it) does not depend on any single unifying convention. Here (Barthes is thinking of Brecht and Eisenstein) each tableau or pregnant moment is a hieroglyph in which past and present and future can be read at a glance; each one of them possesses 'demonstrative power', but they do not add up to a final or matured meaning. Barthes argues that a film by Eisenstein involves a 'contiguity of episodes', and that the result is

> a cinema by vocation anthological, itself holding out to the fetishist, with dotted lines, the piece for him to cut out and take away to enjoy (isn't it said that in some *cinémathèque* or other a piece of film is missing from the copy of *Battleship Potemkin* – the scene with the baby's pram, of course – it having been cut off and stolen lovingly like a lock of hair, a glove or an item of women's underwear).

Anthological texts do not prescribe the burden of meaning and pleasure to be attached to each tableau; but they do prescribe the 'dotted lines' around it. So those 'dotted lines' might be considered their logic, the convention which enables us to make sense of them.

Like Eisenstein, Brecht and Pound anthologised. Walter Benjamin spoke of the 'strict, frame-like, enclosed nature' of the epic tableaux around which Brecht's plays were built; and the same might be said about the statements Pound extracted from *The Writings of Thomas Jefferson*. For example, Jefferson wrote to George Washington as follows:

Dear Sir, – I am happy to find, by the letter of August the 1st,

1786, which you did me the honor to write to me, that the modern dress for your statue would meet your approbation. I found it strongly the sentiment of West, Coply, Trumbull, and Brown, in London; after which, it would be rediculous to add, that it was my own. I think a modern in an antique dress as just an object of ridicule as a Hercules or a Marius with a periwig and a chapeau bras.

I remember having written to you while Congress sat at Annapolis, on the water communication between ours and the western country, and to have mentioned particularly the information I had received of the plain face of the country between the source of Big Beaver and Cayohoga, which made me hope that a canal of no great expense might unite the navigation of Lake Erie and the Ohio. You must since have had occasion of getting better information on this subject, and if you have, you would oblige me by a communication of it. I consider this canal, if practicable, as a very important work.

In Canto 31 only fragments of the letter survive:

> 'modern dress for your statue . . .
> 'I remember having written you while Congress sat at Annapolis,
> 'on water communication between ours and the western country,
> 'particularly the information . . . of the plain between
> 'Big Beaver and Cayohoga, which made me hope that a canal
>   . . . navigation of Lake Erie
> and the Ohio. You must have had
> 'occasion of getting better information of this subject
> 'and if you have you wd. oblige me
> 'by a communication of it. I consider this canal,
> 'if practicable, as a very important work.
>   T. J. to General Washington, 1787.

By omitting crucial verbs, Pound has broken the ligatures of Jefferson's argument, and disarmed it as an act of communication. Details stand out as events in their own right, rather than contributing to the utterance as a whole. Each one possesses 'demonstrative power' of a kind, but they do not amount to anything. Freed from narrative and logical convention, the 'tableaux' are up for grabs. All in all *Eleven New Cantos* seems a more overtly anthological text than anything produced by Eisenstein or Brecht: the dotted lines are there for everyone to see.

But what principle guided the selection and arrangement of these pregnant details? Stephen Fender has pointed out to me that Canto 31, the first in the sequence, might be said to offer an elliptic statement of method. Its subject, Jefferson was also an anthologist. 'I, too,' he wrote to Charles Thomson in 1816,

> have made a wee-little book from the same materials, which I call the Philosophy of Jesus; it is a paradigm of His doctrines, made by cutting the texts out of the book, in a certain order of time or subject . . . And I wish I could subjoin a translation of Gosindi's Syntagma of the doctrine of Epicurus, which, notwithstanding the calumnies of the Stoics and caricatures of Cicero, is the most rational system remaining of the philosophy of the ancients.

Pound quotes part of this in Canto 31:

> ' . . . wish that I cd. subjoin Gosindi's Syntagma
> 'of the doctrines of Epicurus.

What Pierre Gassendi had done to Epicurus, Jefferson did to Jesus Christ, and Pound was doing to Jefferson himself. But Jefferson's syntagma, like Gassendi's, was clearly arranged so as to present the most important tenets and the overall coherence of the philosophy from which it derived. Pound, on the other hand, can hardly be said to have presented the most important tenets and the overall coherence of Jefferson's thinking: the details he chose were neither momentous nor orderly. He may have told Mrs. Scratton that this section of the poem was to be devoted to just men and law-givers, but it does not contain much justice and law-giving of the 'Kung said' variety. Indeed, his own selection from Jefferson's letter to Charles Thomson very carefully excludes the remark about the 'certain order of time or subject' which should govern the cutting of texts out of books. Canto 31 is a syntagma of a distinctly odd kind.

Perhaps it is not a syntagma at all, but an anthology of fetish-objects: texts held out to us not as essential tenets of a coherent system, but as a substitute or defence. I would like to pursue this hypothesis, again using Freud's conceptualised account of a psychic defence to comment on poetic process. (I shall be offering a less sophisticated and more localised description of the fetishism of the *Cantos* than that recently proposed by Alan Durant.)

Freud's 1927 paper on fetishism asked why the libido of certain of his patients should have come to rest on objects unrelated to the sexual act. Since the objects themselves seemed insignificant, Freud claimed that the fetishist treasures a moment rather than an object. What determines the significance of (say) a piece of clothing has less to do with its nature than with its place in a sequence of events. The fetishist embarks on a course of action, but his interest 'comes to a halt half-way,' as he anticipates some awful consequence. Thereafter that half-way moment, the 'last impression before the uncanny and traumatic one', will absorb his libido. Thus fur and velvet

> are a fixation of the sight of the pubic hair, which should have been followed by the longed-for sight of the female member; pieces of underclothing, which are so often chosen as a fetish, crystallize the moment of undressing, the last moment in which the woman could still be regarded as phallic.

The fetishist's quest stops short of the terrible revelation that a woman does not have a penis, and that castration is therefore possible. So the 'logic' of his defence against trauma might be said to involve the cunning interruption of the sequence of events on which he is embarked.

Freud was prepared to acknowledge other traumas: 'In later life a grown man may perhaps experience a similar panic when the cry goes up that Throne and Altar are in danger, and similar illogical consequences will ensue.' Those illogical consequences would presumably involve the treasuring of the last impression before an uncanny and traumatic awareness of the fallibility of Throne and Altar. They would produce a view of history based on the preservation of last moments rather than the designing of first ones.

In the *Prelude* (VI, 425–9), Wordsworth described how he had approached the monastery of the Grande Chartreuse at the same time as

        riotous men commissioned to expel
    The blameless inmates, and belike subvert
    That frame of social being, which so long
    Had bodied forth the ghostliness of things
    In silence visible and perpetual calm.

Although Wordsworth recognises the value of this 'frame of social being', he has to admit that it is something of an anachronism, and he weighs up the conflicting claims of monastic piety and revolutionary secularism. But Matthew Arnold, whose affection for the place I have already alluded to, clearly flinched from acknowledging the danger in which it had once stood and might stand again. He copied into his notebook the last three lines of the passage, thus preserving an image of the monastery in its perfection and blocking off the awareness of catastrophe instilled by the earlier part of the sentence. One could say that he interrupted Wordsworth's narrative in such a way as to isolate the last impression before the uncanny and traumatic one.

Trauma, in this case, involves a knowledge of political rather than sexual difference, a knowledge of the 'castrating' power of modern secularism. It was a feeling which took root in the melancholy nineties, and then evolved into a specific rewriting of the past. While Ernest Dowson's 'Carthusians' was echoing Arnold's love of monastic calm, Lionel Johnson applauded the victims of historical progress for the manner of their defeat. His 1895 *Poems* included a meditation 'By the Statue of King Charles at Charing Cross':

        Vanquished in life, his death
        By beauty made amends:
        The passing of his breath
        Won his defeated ends.

        Brief life, and hapless? Nay:
        Through death, life grew sublime.
        Speak after sentence? Yea:
        And to the end of time.

Yeats, too, celebrated the beauty of defeat, although he declared it to be a prerogative of the Irish. Addressing the Academy of Music in New York on 28 February 1904, he honoured the

memory of the patriot Robert Emmet, who had hoped to give
Ireland the gift of a 'victorious life' and 'accomplished purpose',
but gave her instead his 'heroic death': 'England celebrates her
successes. She celebrates her victorious generals . . . In Ireland
we sing the men who fell nobly and thereby made an idea
mighty.' Generalising this doctrine, Yeats told Sturge Moore that
the one 'heroic sanction' was 'that of the last battle of the Norse
Gods, of a gay struggle without hope. Long ago I used to puzzle
Maud Gonne by always avowing ultimate defeat as a test.' A
reasonable puzzlement, one might suppose, but Yeats did not
waver. In *A Vision,* Michael Robartes suggests that we should
always 'test art, morality, custom, thought, by Thermopylae'.

Yeats's historical sense, like that of Johnson and Dowson,
halted half-way, at the last impression before the uncanny and
traumatic one: the last flourish of an ancient way of life before its
extinction by the march of 'progress'. T. S. Eliot, a fervent
defender of Throne and Altar, also tried to defend the reverence
we feel for those who finished up on the losing side. In a verse
draft of the third section of 'Little Gidding', Richard III suddenly
appears, mysteriously accompanied by the Duke of Wellington.
Mysteriously, that is, until one realises that both figures represent
a dying social order (feudalism, aristocracy). Eliot always wore a
white rose on the anniversary of the Battle of Bosworth, in
memory of 'the last English King', and his draft imagines
Wellington sheltering behind iron shutters closed against the
London mob. He remembers them at the moment before they
were overwhelmed by history, the moment when they made an
idea mighty:

> Whatever we inherit from the fortunate
> We have taken from the defeated
> What they had to leave us – a symbol:
> A symbol perfected in death.

By interrupting an imagined sequence of events – at the moment
before the demise of feudalism or the dissociation of sensibility or
the triumph of democracy – Eliot was able to derive meaning from
historical process without acknowledging the direction it
subsequently took. His 'libido' was arrested not by the fulfilment
of a course of action, but by a symbol, an idea tested by
Thermopylae: or, we might say, a fetish-object.

In Eliot's case, the fetishism was textual. For his refusal to admit the sentimentality of celebrating defeat –

> It is not to ring the bell backward
> Nor is it an incantation
> To summon the spectre of a Rose

– itself incorporates a talisman from an earlier 'last impression' text. In speaking of the bell he was presumably after a term for the reversal of time, a metaphor equivalent to 'turn the clock back'. But you cannot in fact ring a single bell backwards. The association between bell-ringing and reversal of the course of history derives not from customary usage, but (as Helen Gardner has shown) from an imperfectly remembered song by Walter Scott:

> Dundee he is mounted, he rides up the street,
> The bells are rung backward, the drums they are beat . . .

The bells were rung backwards – beginning with the bass rather than the treble – to call out the citizenry; Dundee was calling them out because he intended to set up the standard for James II at Stirling, and so reverse the Glorious Revolution of 1689. Dundee was a classic representative of a dying order, stubborn against progress and democracy, and the ringing of the bells represents an idea made mighty in the moment before its inevitable defeat. So powerful was this idea that it forced its way into Eliot's poem, despite being translated into a form which did not make sense and despite all his attempts to contradict it.

That such a view of history pervaded Pound's literary milieu does not mean that it pervaded Pound. His Jefferson was a rather different figure from Dowson's Charles I or Yeats's Robert Emmet or Eliot's Richard III, different in that he might be supposed to represent a first rather than a last impression, a beginning rather than an ending. Yet Pound believed that Jefferson's republicanism had been betrayed by the course of American history, just as Eliot believed that Wellington had been betrayed by the London mob. The whole subsequent catastrophe of banks and cartels and machine-guns was something he could refuse to acknowledge by dwelling on a half-way moment, a republicanism tested by Thermopylae. Thus the fragments cut out of Jefferson's correspondence don't show a law-giver, or a politician engaged in establishing the identity of America by the exercise of power; they are not usable. Instead we see a man at ease, in control of the situation and unruffled by responsibility: public and private reflections mingle happily, thoughts about slavery and thoughts about flowers which vegetate when suspended in the air. This is a last impression of how things might have been, before it all went wrong. Canto 31 holds out, with dotted lines, the pieces we are to excise and take away. The dotted lines are the convention according to which we read the poem.

*   *   *

However, it seems to me that Pound could not rest contented with this nostalgic view of history and its fetishising rhetoric. He placed more trust than any of his contemporaries in the dictators' ability to sustain a new politics and new sorts of expression, and he had somehow to bring his poem into line with that trust. We must therefore recognise the importance of his interview with Mussolini on 30 January 1933. The Duce's presence and style had enthralled many people before Pound; he was personable – the 'despot with a dimple', an American journalist called him – and seemed to embody power. Mussolini, another commentator wrote, 'is built like a steel spring (Stalin is a rock of granite, by comparison, and Hitler a blob of ectoplasm)'; he had the fitness and temperament of the professional sportsman, the controlled aggression so painfully lacking in democratic politicians. Pound, at any rate, was impressed (or confirmed in his faith). In February he started work on *An ABC of Economics* and *Jefferson and/or Mussolini*: by now the emphasis was shifting from 'and' to 'or'. He also began Canto 37, having bought a copy of Martin Van Buren's *Autobiography* towards the end of 1932.

This brief encounter with power in the flesh seems to have at least dented his nostalgic habit. Instead of presenting extracts from historical documents and leaving us to cut along the dotted lines, he modified and rewrote – as he had already begun to do in Canto 33. Consider what happened to the following passage from *Das Kapital,* where Marx was citing a report on child-labour:

Now, the same children and young persons were shifted from the spinning-room to the weaving room, now, during 15 hours,

from the factory to another. How was it possible to control a
system which, 'under the guise of relays, is some one of the
many plans shuffling "the hands" about in endless variety,
and shifting the hours of work and of rest for different
individuals throughout the day, so that you may never have
one complete set of hands working together in the same room at
the same time'.

Marx tended to use not only the content but also the ponderous
phrasing of government reports, in order to guarantee the
authenticity of his evidence. Pound, while recognising the
provenance of the statement he quotes, nevertheless alters its
mode of address completely:

> And if the same small boys are merely shifted from
>   the spinning room to the weaving room or from
>   one factory to another, how can the inspector
>   verify the number of hours they are worked?
>   (1849, Leonard Horner).

Pound is not after ponderous authenticity. He simplifies the
structure of the passage (if . . . how . . .), transforming it into as
direct a mode of address as possible.

I believe that the meeting with Mussolini, and the renewal of
his faith in dictatorial style, strengthened this tendency in
Pound's writing. The principle guiding his method of revision
found an ideal in the utterances of Lenin and Mussolini, and
might have found a parallel in the poetry of Brecht. Brecht freed
his verse from regular rhyme and rhythm so that it might enact
more forcefully the attitudes it was expressing; it was to be coded
by some principle other than poetic convention. 'A language is
gestic,' he wrote, 'when it is grounded in a gest and conveys
particular attitudes adopted by the speaker towards other men.'
The term 'gest' included the senses of 'gist' and 'gesture': it is a
gesture whose structure and pacing convey the gist of the
speaker's attitude. An example would be the biblical injunction 'if
thine eye offend thee, pluck it out'. The definition and
arrangement of clauses, each of them a gest, make this a more
emphatic utterance than possible alternatives such as 'pluck out
the eye which offends thee'.

What Brecht called a gest, J. L. Austin, in an analysis also begun during the late thirties, called a 'performative utterance'. In certain cases, Austin argued, 'the issuing of the utterance is the performing of an action – it is not normally thought of as just saying something'. When bride and bridegroom say 'I will', they are not reporting on an act, but indulging in it. Such gests interested Pound as well as Brecht, although both men turned their attention to a particular variety: gests which performed a social or political attitude, or which performed the contradictions shaping an attitude.

In *Guide to Kulchur* Pound declared his preference for the ancient and strong 'I know not' over the weaker modern 'I do not know'. The words were virtually identical, but he felt that the construction of the older version had made it more emphatic, more gestic. What he wanted his own gests to convey above all was authority. Brecht, on the other hand, had shown more interest in collective and demotic speech: advertising slogans, the 'rhythmical cries' of newspaper-vendors, the 'short shouted choruses' at workers' demonstrations. 'These experiences,' he claimed, 'were applied to the development of irregular rhythms.' An example would be the 'German Satires', written for the German Freedom Radio. 'It was a matter of projecting single sentences to a distant, artificially scattered audience. They had to be cut down to the most concise form possible and to be reasonably invulnerable to interruptions (by jamming).' Thus Pound and Brecht, in their contrasting predicaments, responded to different models for an utterance which would perform what it stated.

Pound hoped to move from 1820 to 1930, from Jefferson to Mussolini, by finding a language as performative as the new politics. Canto 31 had consisted largely of extracts from correspondence, much of it private (Jefferson writes to Joel Barlow: '. . . care of the letters now enclosed. Most of them are / of a complexion not proper for the eye of the police'). But Canto 37 shifts the emphasis on to public utterance: speeches in the Senate, remarks made in a public context, a newspaper headline ('Peggy Eaton's own story'), an election slogan ('Tip an' Tyler / We'll bust Van's biler'). A world ruled by radio was different from a world ruled by the effect of composure on a limited electorate.

So Canto 37 did not offer itself to the fetishist's scissors; it transformed document into gest. Van Buren, speaking in the Senate in 1826, had said:

I believe the judges of the Supreme Court (great and good men as I cheerfully concede them to be) are subject to the same infirmities, influenced by the same passions, and operated upon by the same causes that good and great men are in other situations. I believe they have as much of the *esprit de corps* as other men.

Pound rescued the essential theme of this ponderous rumination by separating and transposing its elements:

High judges? Are, I suppose, subject to passions
as have affected other great and good men, also
subject to esprit de corps.

The high judges now head the sentence, suitably furnished with an arresting tone-marker, while the speaker has been relegated to a parenthesis ('I suppose'). Indeed, the entire disposition of Van Buren's remark has been altered, so that the same information is conveyed, but more effectively.

The same thing happens to a speech by James Kent, recorded over two pages in Bancroft's biography of Van Buren:

If we are like other races of men, with similar follies and vices, then I greatly fear that our posterity will have reason to deplore in sackcloth and ashes the delusion of the day . . . I wish to preserve our Senate as the representative of the landed interest.

The tendency of universal suffrage is to jeopard the rights of property and the principles of liberty.

Pound manages to combine the gist of both statements:

Kent said they wd. 'deplore in sackcloth and ashes
if they preserved not a senate
to represent landed interest, and did they
jeopard property rights?'

One alteration – 'preserved not' – shows the liking later expressed in *Guide to Kulchur* for an ancient and strong construction; but what makes the passage perform its message is the switch from indicative to interrogative, together with the line-break which exposes the rather unusual verb 'jeopard'.

In E. M. Shepherd's *Martin Van Buren*, Jackson is said to have told Congress that 'the resources of the nation beyond those acquired for the immediate and necessary purposes of government can nowhere be so well deposited as in the pockets of the people'. In Canto 37, this becomes:

> 'Nowhere so well deposited as in the pants of people,
> Wealth ain't,' said President Jackson.

'Pockets' has been revised to the more demotic 'pants', and the idea of depositing the wealth of the people therein emphasised by removal to the head of the sentence. Jackson's verbose subject-clause, boiled down to 'Wealth ain't', has been held over to another line.

This is history rewritten in the image not of the fetishist but of the dictator, according to a model of performative public utterance (or social gest). Mussolini soon obliged by confirming the model, and Pound's hallelujah followed with equal alacrity in the *Criterion* of January 1935, between the American and English publications of *Eleven New Cantos*. Pound reported that on 6 October 1934,

> Mussolini speaking very clearly four or five words at a time, with a pause, quite a long pause, between phrases, to let it sink in, told 40 million Italians together with auditors in the U.S.A. and the Argentine that the problem of production was solved, and that they could now turn their minds to distribution.

Here, at last, was the ultimate gest, a statement that was immediately and without compunction an act: 'Dead, at 4-14 in the Piazza del Duomo, Milano, anno XII. Scarcity Economics died.' Some utterance.

Pound was understandably intrigued by the art of this magical pronouncement. He thought that Mussolini had found 'the unassailable formula, the exact equation for what had been sketchy and impressionistic and exaggerated in Thos. Jefferson's time and expression'. There could no longer be any nostalgia for the poise and elegance of the idiom so lovingly salvaged from Jefferson's correspondence, because the Duce's new sort of expression had superseded it, achieving a mysterious autonomy and a self-evident truth: 'The more one examines the Milan speech the more one is reminded of Brancusi, the stone blocks from which no error emerges, from whatever angle one looks at them.' These blocks of verity seemed immediately apprehensible from any angle, not framed by political or rhetorical convention; they allowed no indecision, no gap between saying and doing. Here, at last, form-sense had become dictator-sense.

But the pale anticipations of this Brancusi-like utterance which Pound had sown in *Eleven New Cantos* sat uneasily beside other elements of the book, such as Jefferson's 'last moment' composure. For the unity of thought and action acquired by Mussolini's style and by Pound's gestic writing was bound to be disrupted by a rhetoric which fetishised the last moment *before* some decisive event. Our reading of the poems switches us from the convention of dotted lines to the convention of performative utterance, and back again. Should we admire these new sorts of expression for their newness, or for their promise to restore a lost world?

7 Going over

Among English writers the scramble for dictators was less fierce, although not without incident. H. G. Wells buttonholed Stalin in 1934, and the resulting conversation was published in the *New Statesman* of October 27:

> WELLS: . . . Now I have come to you to ask you what you are doing to change the world.

> STALIN: Not so very much.

Hardly a cup-tie atmosphere. As the occasion progresses, its hollowness becomes increasingly apparent. 'It would be a good thing,' Wells quipped, 'to invent a Five Year Plan for the reconstruction of the human brain, which obviously lacks many things needed for a perfect social order. (Laughter.)'

Comment on this interview in subsequent issues of the *New Statesman* ranged from millennial fantasy to disputes about Wells' method of entry into the Kremlin: had he walked, or trotted, or perhaps sidled? A writer had penetrated to the innermost sanctum of history, but he was not allowed to forget, even there, the peculiarities of his gait. The gaze of his audience flinched from Stalin's immense opacity, from Five Year Plans for the reconstruction of the human brain, and came to rest on a more homely detail. This disparity between the scale of the regeneration envisaged and the language available to describe it was to characterise a great deal of English politics and English writing during the thirties.

Since 1928 Western opinion had been fascinated as much by the land as by the dictator. It was in 1928 that Stalin announced the doctrine of 'socialism in one country' and inaugurated the first Five Year Plan. At a stroke the Russian revolution mellowed from world-wide insurgency into a social experiment taking place at a safe distance. 'Immediately,' David Caute observes, 'a tide of pent-up goodwill, optimism and moral idealism flooded from the West into Russia.' The Americanists of the twenties were superseded by the Russianists of the thirties. Caute regards this tide of goodwill as a 'postscript to the Enlightenment', admiration for a rationally planned and governed society. But it seems to me that an interest in social engineering, although important, was often outweighed by a desire to begin again (anyhow) at some furthest limit. The West did not want a model for its own reconstruction so much as the faint glow of liminal experience, a glow which meant that somehow somewhere a society had been reduced to a generic human bond and made anew. All the better that it should be happening a long way away, and thus require a dramatic quest, moral and physical departure. The Soviet Union had become the biggest margin in the world, and to that extent we should regard fellow-travelling as a postscript to Romanticism.

Intourist certainly did its best to enhance this marginality. Its first brochure announced that the tourists who were beginning to visit Russia in the early thirties would 'have access to what is doubtless the most interesting country on earth, where at the present moment the greatest upheaval in the history of the world is taking place'. These lucky travellers would witness nothing short of 'the birth of a new era in the history of mankind' and 'the feverish construction of a new social order'. (The breathless tone is somewhat qualified by five pages of advertisements for such unreconstructed activities as game-hunting.)

Subsequent brochures like *A Pocket Guide to the Soviet Union* (1931) or *Moscow. Past, Present, Future* (1934) retained this emphasis on making-anew. Attention was drawn to the fruits of economic planning, particularly those fruits likely to be of immediate concern to the traveller: 'The streets of Moscow are being completely repaved with amazing speed.' But it was also suggested that the creation of 'new forms of social life' would prove as interesting as signs of economic progress. 'In this beginning of a new collective life a young generation is growing up which neither knows nor remembers the tsarist regime.' So the tourist strolling along streets being repaved at amazing speed in front of him might catch a glimpse of what it was like to begin again. The captain of the ship taking the trade unionist Walter Citrine to Russia in 1935 knew what to say: 'Oh, you will find very great changes! Everything is different now. We are even changing human nature.'

But Citrine's countrymen still did not have the terms to describe this change in human nature or their own relation to it, a failure which became cruelly apparent in the reports of the two Congresses of Peace and Friendship with the USSR held in 1935 and 1937. Here the biggest margin in the world was endlessly acclaimed, usually in language and conception so threadbare that one wonders whether anyone stayed to hear the end of it. At the first Congress, Boothby (a Tory MP) declared that 'in spite of many faults and many cruelties, experiments are to-day being carried out in Russia in the social, economic and political fields, which may well prove to be of infinite value to humanity in the future'. That 'infinite'' warns us that Boothby, like his fellow Russianists, had no way of assessing the 'value' of the Soviet experiment, and thus no way of accounting for its many faults and cruelties.

Other speakers resorted to bonhomie. Bernard Shaw, who had been particularly insistent about Wells's method of entry into the Kremlin, announced that capitalism was sick of itself, while communism had a healthy radiance: 'The Russians are bursting with Communism.' Sidney Webb agreed, observing that in Russia the workers 'go mad in their desire and determination to turn out more stuff, to do more than they have ever done before.' Mrs Cecil Chesterton thought that because of the spiritual independence of Russian women 'there are growing up children who have shed all their inhibitions, and we hear so much of inhibitions these days'. During a debate on Soviet peace policy at the second Congress, Vyvyan Adams rose to follow a peroration by Geoffrey Mander: 'While that speech was going on I have been interjecting such words as "Marvellous", "Splendid", "Red-hot" – this last expletive being customary in my youth, and singularly appropriate this afternoon.'

Whereas the Americanists of the twenties had developed a language (a ferocious banter) which brought home to them the consequences of the technology they coveted, the Russianists of the thirties had to make do with bonhomie and Public School slang.

Of course, Congresses of Peace and Friendship tend to be rather cynical exercises. But the same inadequacy haunted the most famous and intellectually respectable account of the Soviet

Union's cultural achievements, *The Mind in Chains,* published in 1937. According to its editor, Cecil Day Lewis, the book had been inspired by the belief 'that the mind is really in chains to-day, that these chains have been forged by a dying social system, that they can and must be broken – and in the Soviet Union have been broken'. But enthusiasm for this regenerative margin was again marred by the lack of any terms with which to describe what was going on there. 'In 1934,' Alistair Browne reported,

> Dr. Rosenstein, of the Moscow Institute of Mental Hygiene, could not find a case of manic-depressive insanity to show to his students, after three months' search; this would be inconceivable in Europe or America. Prostitution and alcoholism are both being rapidly 'liquidated'.

Liquidation was at that time still a relatively new term in the political vocabulary, and Brown's simultaneous appropriation and disavowal of it reveals a deep moral failure. The same failure had rendered audiences oblivious to the irony of the final lines of Auden's 1933 play *The Dance of Death,* spoken by Karl Marx over the hero's body:

> The instruments of production have been too much for him. He is liquidated.

No wonder the streets of Moscow were free of manic-depressives. Aesthetic judgement fell victim to a similar disparity between the scope of the quest and the resourcefulness of the quester. Anthony Blunt found it hard to like Soviet art, but contented himself with the reflection that it was the 'right kind' for Russia. However, an essay by Edward Upward did at least give some sense of the difficulties inherent in any idealisation of the quest:

> In the classless society of the future the writer will no longer be faced with the necessity of going over to a new way of life: he will be born into a new way of life. Nor will he be compelled to give the best of his time and energy to the political struggle, since that struggle will have died away . . . Such a happy situation for the writer has not yet arrived, though in Russia it is on the way, and in Russia already writers are better off than anywhere else in the world.

There were two ways of entering the new life: by going over to it, or by being born into it. Russia fascinated Western intellectuals because it seemed the only place where rebirth – rather than a painful and deeply compromised switch of loyalties – was possible. Russia promised that the guilt would not be in vain.

Fellow-travelling is still often regarded as an organic process, although usually as a disease rather than a rebirth. 'Recurrent as malaria,' John Lehmann wrote, 'a bout of rentier-guilt laid me low.' A more recent visitor to the sick-bay, Andrew Boyle, has diagnosed a 'distemper' of 'epidemic' proportions. But before rushing to blame the wily mosquito, we should consider the extent to which politics in the thirties depended on the *interplay* between organic metaphors and metaphors of decision.

Boyle mentions a 'farewell letter' written by Julian Bell to Cecil Day Lewis, in which Bell renounced Communism and declared that 'revolution is the opium of the intellectuals'. It was in fact an open letter to Day Lewis, and Bell was not deploring revolution – 'the arguments for socialism, and for civil war, and the resultant barbarism, are irrefutably strong' – but criticising the *type* of revolutionary commitment envisaged by Auden, Spender and Day Lewis. He objected to the submerging of middle-class guilt in organic metaphors for political process and in a sentimental identification with the proletariat. His own alternative strategy represented an attack on the existing social order, but also on certain proposals for putting an end to that order.

Bell argued that intellectuals should cultivate 'cold and soldierly virtues' rather than enthusiasm. Fascism would be defeated by 'tricks, stratagems, manoeuvres and the resources of war as an art, not a paroxysm of emotion'. Meanwhile the principal sufferings of an upper-class English socialist arose from listening to the speeches on his own side (perhaps Bell had been at the first Congress of Peace and Friendship?). However, a military attitude would enable one to cooperate with such irrelevant enthusiasms and at the same time prepare for the real struggle ahead: 'it averts imbecile discussions about goods and concentrates on means and practice'. This last remark comes from an open letter to E. M. Forster, written in January 1937. In his 'Notes for a Reply', Forster demurred from the main thrust of the argument, while accommodating the occasional practicality: 'Julian's tips may come in useful over corpses.'

It was an argument over cultural as well as political strategy. 'Just as intelligence and impartiality seems to me better,' Bell declared, 'more effective in action than enthusiasm, so they seem to me more effective in the arts.' Eight years before, he had joined the Cambridge Apostles, at a time when the society's meetings were dominated by two issues: 'a classic, post-impressionist view of the arts . . . and anarchism (of the most philosophical kind)'. This view of the arts he made his own, polemicising on behalf of clarity and common sense – notably in the pages of *The Venture*, a magazine founded by another Apostle, Anthony Blunt. *The Venture* was against whatever its enthusiastically avant-garde rival, *Experiment*, was for: abstraction, surrealism, Eliotic obscurities. It thus played its small part in the turn against 'Modernism' in the late twenties. Blunt contributed erudite and stylish essays on art or architecture to all six numbers (October 1928–June 1930), writing against the subservience of much modern art to theory or fashion, and defending the few artists who had 'kept painting to its normal course'. The final number included a dispassionate survey of Cubism by Blunt and an attack on poetic obscurity by Bell.

Blunt gave further expression to this 'classic' view of culture during his stint as art critic of the *Spectator*, from 1936 to 1938. In one piece he described Surrealism as the last phase of a development which had started with Impressionism and had led to the abandonment of realism in favour of 'abstraction' or 'emotionalism'. In another, he deplored the contemporary taste for the 'non-rational, emotional and fantastic art of earlier periods':

> So, for instance, it is no matter for surprise that, at any rate recently, in the room of every young upper-class intellectual in Cambridge who belonged to the Communist party there was always to be found a reproduction of a painting by van Gogh. They had the feeling of revolt against society which van Gogh expressed so keenly.

Such scruples were dropped from his contribution to *The Mind in Chains*, where Van Gogh becomes an example of 'proletarian realism'. But he clearly felt considerable distaste for the kind of political or cultural commitment which did not extend beyond emotional identification. Another *Spectator* piece praises the author of a book about Richelieu for having revealed 'the essential greatness of Richelieu's policy: its concentration on purely practical matters and its subordination even of religious questions to reasons of state'.

So there was a neo-classicism of the Left: confidence in the imminent demise of capitalism, accompanied by a revulsion from those who allowed 'emotionalism' to resolve their artistic and political dilemmas. It may have been the revulsion rather than the confidence which produced an unsentimental study of means: Bell's 'militarist daydreams' (a subject on which he addressed the Apostles in 1937, just before travelling to Spain); Blunt's more oblique defection. Contempt for fantasies of rebirth which obscured the harsh process of going-over perhaps led them to regard that process as an end in itself, and to cultivate the art of what Bell termed 'reservation and privacy': tricks, stratagems, manoeuvres. It was an art which had long been practised by the English ruling-class, and so came naturally to both men. But would it have taken the forms it did, the forms of militarist daydream and espionage, except by reaction against all those journeys to the Soviet margin?

*   *   *

The interplay between metaphors of rebirth and metaphors of going-over shaped the writing as well as the politics of the thirties. At its best – and for me that means in Auden – the poetry and prose of the period tested the quests and the marginalising rhetorics of Romanticism against the monstrosity of the dictators on one hand, and the new fluidity of a middle-class readership on the other. Rebirth and going-over criss-crossed incessantly in the minds of poet and audience alike. At the start of his career Auden does not seem to have given much thought to his readers. The success of 'Modernism' had created a small but identifiable audience for elliptic writing, an audience which he could address without having to explain himself. Much of his work up to and including *The Orators* (1932) was more or less impenetrable to his contemporaries. When doubts arose, and he suggested adding an elucidatory preface to *The Orators,* Eliot told him never to apologise for impenetrability. As a result his metaphors for regeneration were keyed to his own obsessions rather than to any chance his readers might have had of changing their lives.

The most important of these metaphors was the Airman whose journal forms Book II of *The Orators,* a prototype redeemer and full-blown Romantic marginal. 'The symbolic position of the airman,' Stephen Spender wrote, 'is, as it were, to be on the margin of civilisation.' Being an airman, 'he is not tied down in any way'; and being homosexual, he has 'broken away from the mould of the past and is compelled to experiment in new forms'. Auden did not mean to endorse the Airman. He was conducting an enquiry into his own fondness for marginality and for what Edward Mendelson calls 'the privileges of the seigneurial mind'. To do so, he drew on a paper by his friend John Layard about the 'flying tricksters' of Malekula. These tricksters fell into epileptic fits during which, Layard argues, they took over such incidental features of epilepsy as the sensation of flight, irresponsibility and homosexuality. They were undoubtedly marginal figures, but their marginality had more relevance to Auden's self-diagnosis than to the essential and generic human bond underlying Western society.

Auden had not bothered to ask what his readers might make of the Airman, and after publication he found that many of them supposed him to be endorsing a fascist outlook (fascist hero-worship). He admitted that Hermann Goering was an example of the kind of figure he had in mind, but flying had long been the supreme symbol of technological progress, a symbol often appropriated by Fascism. In 1909, the year Blériot flew the channel, Marinetti's Futurist manifesto celebrated the sleek flight of planes whose propellers seemed to cheer like an enthusiastic crowd. But who were those propellers cheering *for?* When Brecht wrote a play about Lindbergh's solo flight of 1927, the wretched aviator immediately identified himself with the political Right, and the name of the play's hero had to be altered to 'The Flyer'. Meanwhile Pound was praising the Fascist spokesman d'Annunzio for his prowess in the cockpit rather than on the page. Mussolini loved planes, and so did Oswald Mosley, as the introduction to the first volume in the Fascist Shilling Library made clear:

Through the hesitant decade of the 'twenties, in the presently complacent 'thirties, this ex-airman has symbolised the challenge of his generation to all the accepted values of a senescent civilisation.

Furthermore, the embarrassing shortage of Marxist pilots was compounded by the strange things which happened to those who did get into the air. On 3 October 1931, Lauro de Bosis, an anti-fascist Italian poet, flew from Marseilles to Rome in order to drop political leaflets, and was never seen again. He left behind him a bizarre document, 'The Story of My Death', which described his flight in symbolic terms and was published in *The Times* of 14 October. Auden, who wrote his 'Journal of an Airman' between August and October of that year, revising through November, cannot have been unaware of such a quixotic adventure. But his readers may well have thought first of Goering or Mosley or Lindbergh.

Auden could have expected similar difficulties with a symbol he used in a 1936 collaboration with Christopher Isherwood, *The Ascent of F6*. The hero of this play, Michael Ransom, wants to redeem mankind by climbing the mountain F6 and so achieving international acclaim. As Mendelson points out, mountaineering is 'a romantic enterprise, which achieved its isolated early triumphs at the end of the eighteenth and the start of the nineteenth centuries, before it became institutionalised in the Alpine Club'. Details of Ransom's climb were lifted from Byron's *Manfred*. Auden was trying to exorcise an outdated and damaging redemptive impulse, a delight in the seigneurial mind. The play dealt unambiguously with the packaging of this impulse as legend, propaganda and news-item. It is the cynical and bombastic Lord Stagmantle who offers an encomium of loyalty and adventure.

Yet the symbolism of mountaineering proved as easy to appropriate as that of flying. A pamphlet published by the British Union of Fascists in 1938 announced that Fascism 'is a daily battle against the forces of corruption and complacency, against slothful acceptance of economic evils; it glories in the sublime spirit of mystic comradeship and hates the materialistic sensuality of plutocratic democracy. The Spirit of Everest as opposed to that of the night club.' The front cover shows a snow-capped peak surmounted by the B.U.F. emblem. It would not be impossible for anyone conversant with such symbolism to interpret parts of *The Ascent of F6* as an endorsement of it.

Auden was still dealing with fantasies of rebirth and marginality, a whole Romantic rite of passage. He thought he had demonstrated their fallibility by relating them to the harsh and lonely process of going-over which was all his own experience yielded by way of rite of passage. But he failed to realise that the new political movements, Communism and Fascism, were machines for the appropriation and recirculation of such fantasies *in their pure form*; what came back to him was a polished version of symbols which had interested him because of their shabbiness. He had to find a rhetoric which would elude the machines and make contact not only with his own fallibility, but also with the fallibility of his readers.

* * *

At some point in the early thirties, Auden passed beyond 'Modernism', as Pound did in *Eleven New Cantos*. Both began to give a front-name, a hind-name and an address to the references they made. But whereas Pound tended to give these references a name and address supplied by the Fascist machine, Auden tuned the 'Modernist' rhetoric of unfulfilled specificity until it played wonderfully on the nerves of his middle-class readers.

This had begun to happen in the 'Journal of an Airman', whose dazzling exuberance was not mere virtuosity, in that it quite cannily sorted out from the herd of promiscuous readers those who were doing more than snatch a glance. Auden may have intended his catalogue of the shortcomings of Enemy behaviour to represent the middle-class as seen from the point of view of the distinctly imperfect Airman. But many of his readers were able to bring their own experience and their own guilt to bear on its needling aggression:

Three kinds of enemy walk – the grandiose stunt – the melancholic swagger – the paranoic sidle.

Three kinds of enemy bearing – the condor stoop – the toad stupor – the robin's stance.

Three kinds of enemy face – the fucked hen – the favorite puss – the stone in the rain.

Eliot, with inscrutable aplomb, emended 'fucked hen' to 'June bride' before publication. But neither detail would seem to have any necessary connection with bourgeois physionomies.

In each case the definite article does all the work. It seems to suggest that middle-class faces look like something specific – a fucked hen, a favorite puss – but relies on the reader to complete the identification, to bring to mind a particular face which might be thought to resemble a fucked hen or a favorite puss. That is precisely what Auden's readers did, taking on themselves the responsibility for interpretation which had previously rested unhappily between his inner world and the machines of Communism and Fascism. 'These are excellent descriptions,' Spender wrote, 'of the kind of people whose pictures we see in society newspapers.' They are excellent descriptions not only for the Airman but for those readers who follow the society newspapers and can therefore complete the identifications proffered by the definite article.

Auden had modified the reliance of the early Eliot and the early Pound on demonstrative reference. The definite article – like demonstratives, unlike the indefinite article – is a specifying agent, which serves to identify a particular individual or sub-class within the class designated by the noun it precedes. But the demonstratives differ in that they themselves provide part of the information needed to identify the individual or sub-class; they position it along a scale of proximity, and their associations of intimacy or distance survive even if we cannot identify what they are referring to. The definite article, on the other hand, has no semantic content and does not position the individual or sub-class it refers to. Auden exploited not only its specificity, but also its neutrality: a neutrality which allows the reader more scope for interpretation than a demonstrative would, assuring him that he can identify the item in question from his own experience. If Auden had compared the middle-class walk to 'this' grandiose stunt or 'that' paranoic sidle, the relevance of our own familiarity with grandiose stunts and paranoic sidles would have been severely curtailed. *The* grandiose stunt and *the* paranoic sidle are a different matter: we all know them, if we have been following the society newspapers.

Auden explained the purpose of this rhetoric in his introduction to *The Poet's Tongue* (1935):

> The poet writes of personal or fictitious experiences, but these are not important in themselves until the reader has realised them in his own consciousness.

> Soldier from the war returning
> Spoiler of the taken town.

It is quite unimportant, though it is the kind of question not infrequently asked, who the soldier is, what regiment he belongs to, what war he had been fighting in, etc. The soldier is you or me, or the man next door. Only when it throws light on your own experience, when these lines occur to us as we see, say, the unhappy face of a stockbroker in the surburban train, does poetry convince us of its significance.

The poem itself will identify neither soldier nor war nor town. Instead, it asserts that they are identifiable (*the* war, *the* taken town) and encourages the reader to supply the necessary information from his own experience (of commuter trains, or whatever).

Yet we need something more than a season ticket if we are to feel the force of these lines. For the choice of a stockbroker to represent the spoiler of a taken town was hardly accidental. It suggests that the identifications we make should be based on political attitude, and should therefore serve to identify *us* as socialists. It helps to fulfil Auden's promise, in *The Dance of Death,* to portray 'the decline of a class' ('Our class', the bourgeois chorus adds helpfully). The process of interpretation, of connecting 'Spoiler of the taken town' with the unhappy face of a stockbroker, itself confirms whose side you are on, where you stand. 'The weakness of the Enemy captions,' Spender observed, 'is that they apply to the people whom one doesn't like. One's own little set draws closer together.' Auden's definite articles encouraged his own little set, and the larger 'set' which grew out of it, to supply information which only it could supply, and thus draw closer together. They were making a readership.

They could do so because their audience was politically fluid, ready to put some distance between itself and certain features of a world it knew only too well. That audience wanted change, but knew that it was part of what had to be changed, and so found itself committed to a painful and guilty switch of loyalties. 'I longed to be on the side of the accusers,' Spender has written,

> the setters-up of world socialism. But at this stage, having shifted the centre of the struggle within my self from the

bourgeois camp to the communist one, I failed to find myself
convinced by Communism.

The dream was of rebirth, the reality a shifting of the centre of
the struggle within oneself, a going-over from one camp to
another.

Auden's rhetoric was so perfectly matched to this reality that it
became available to anyone who had something to dissent from,
and served a considerable variety of radical positions. When
Auden complained about the influence of 'the great malignant /
Cambridge ulcer', he expected his reader to recognise and dissent
from Bloomsbury liberalism. When the Marxist poet John
Cornford wrote his 'Keep Culture Out of Cambridge', he
expected the reader to recognise and dissent from such
Audenesque preoccupations as 'the kestrel joy' and 'the change of
heart'. Cornford was attacking certain attitudes, while exploiting
the idiom in which they had been formulated, and even admiring
that idiom in other poets. Thus he contrasted the subjectivism of a
poem by Spender with the revolutionary fervour of some lines by
Louis Aragon which display (in translation at least) the rhetorical
device found so often in the work of the Auden gang:

> I am a witness to the crushing of a world out of date,
> I am a witness to the stamping out of the bourgeoisie.

And although Julian Bell would have despised the romantic
identification with the working-class of both Auden and
Cornford, the *Spectator* review of his *Work for the Winter* rightly
perceived no difference at the level of language: 'Mr. Bell's verse
is a cocktail of the younger "contemporary" poets with a little
Housman plus Omar Khayyam by way of sweetener. It abounds
in easy adjectival *clichés* – "The lost battle, the long defeat".' The
definite articles, rather than the adjectives, gave him away.

All these poets wanted to dissociate themselves from a
moribund culture: their definite articles track down its most
unsavoury features, and invite the reader in for the kill.
Isherwood's Mr. Norris, addressing a group of Berlin
communists, expressed the hope that the cries of starving Chinese
peasants would soon drown 'the futile chatter of diplomatists and
the strains of dance bands in luxurious hotels'. A few days before
leaving for Spain in January 1937, Auden put the same
sentiments into the mouth of the satanic dictator of 'Danse
Macabre':

> It's farewell to the drawing-room's civilised cry,
> The professor's sensible whereto and why,
> The frock-coated diplomat's social aplomb,
> Now matters are settled with gas and bomb.

Although both men took care to dramatise these apocalyptic visions, they did expect their readers to identify the dance bands and the drawing room and the diplomat from whatever experience they could bring to bear. They also expected their readers to feel the chill of 'gas' and 'bomb', terms as refreshingly free of definite articles as they are of inherited privilege, and the chill of inevitable catastrophe: 'It's farewell', not 'We must say farewell'. History speaks, offering total destruction and rebirth, but we must count the cost of losing experiences which only we can identify and which to that extent possess us. 'It is goodbye to the *Tatler* and the *Bystander*,' Orwell said in 1940, 'and farewell to the lady in the Rolls-Royce car'. A Rolls-Royce clearly signifies the privilege about to be destroyed by gas and bomb, but 'the' lady has been put there only for the reader who can consult the pages of a mental *Tatler*: she is the harder to lose.

Auden had pursued such strategies for more than a decade, for example in the first stanza of '1929', where he detailed the terrible lethargy of 'the loud madman' and announced 'the destruction of error'. It is time, the poem says, for regeneration:

> The old gang to be forgotten in the spring,
> The hard bitch and the riding-master,
> Stiff underground; deep in clear lake
> The lolling bridegroom, beautiful, there.

The old gang, which we must identify through our knowledge of hard bitches and riding-masters, will transform itself by shedding its definite articles, 'deep in clear lake'. Auden's friend Rex Warner advised any of his readers who might still belong to the old gang to throw away, before it was too late, 'the eau de Cologne which disguised you', not to mention 'the tennis racquet' and 'the blazer of the First XV'. Day-Lewis was more militant, suggesting that the proud possessors should be junked along with their trophies. His long poem *The Magnetic Mountain* (1933) attacked all those who had nothing to fight for except 'the silver spoon', 'the touched hat', 'the expensive seat'. Silverware seemed to cause particular offence, and even the mild-mannered Louis MacNeice was ready to pour scorn where tea might have been expected. How would the gentry feel, he asked in 'An Eclogue for Christmas',

> Without the bandy chairs and the sugar in the silver tongs
> And the inter-ripple and resonance of years of dinner-gongs?

The eau de Cologne, the blazer, the touched hat, the expensive seat, the silver tongs: it is goodbye to all that.

Finding things to say goodbye to had been a more or less full-time occupation for many writers since the end of the First World War. But Auden and his contemporaries were also looking for things to say hello to. They required their readers to spot both decadence and signs of the birth of a new social order. 'If the poet reproduces within his audience his own sense of disintegration,' wrote Day Lewis, 'he also recreates within them his instinctive movement towards a life which is forming and gathering strength.' Guilt felt at association with the old order might be cancelled by an altruistic embrace of the new one.

Unfortunately, however, the life which was forming and gathering strength during the thirties began to yield prospects of infinite horror, including a sticky end for altruists. E. M. Forster, contemplating the technological marvels on display at the 1937 Paris Exhibition, tried to fathom the cryptic message transmitted by 'the Angel of the Laboratory'. For Auden, in the final poem of his 1936 collection, they only had one nightmarish meaning:

> For the wicked card is dealt, and
> The sinister tall-hatted botanist stoops at the spring
>   With his insignificant phial, and looses
>   The plague on the ignorant town.

The future promises to be even nastier than the decadent present. In 'Postscript to Iceland', MacNeice assured Auden that he just about had time to drink his health before the gun-butt rapped on the door. By 1939 such anxieties had become sufficiently commonplace to trouble the blowsily dyspeptic hero of Orwell's *Coming up for Air*: 'The bombs, the food-queues, the rubber truncheons, the barbed wire, the coloured shirts, the slogans, the enormous faces, the machine-guns squirting out of bedroom windows. It's all going to happen.' Stop around long enough to compare *those* faces with a fucked hen and it might just be your last comparison.

This vision of the future, faithfully shepherded by definite articles, was so daunting that it could not always be held within any objective frame of reference. George Barker allowed public and private anxieties to merge in a long poem whose view of the world was signalled by its title, *Calamiterror* (1937). Where MacNeice had envisaged the gun-butt rapping the door, Barker envisaged the descending hand on the shoulder, a hand as frightful as 'five bananas'. The only hope was that 'the coming struggle', in John Strachey's phrase, might prove surgical or redemptive. David Gascoyne's 'Cavatina' suggests as much in its listing of cruel catharses, each one introduced by a definite article:

> Now we must bear the final real
> Convulsion of the breast, for the sublime
> Relief of the catharsis; and the cruel
> Clear grief; the dear redemption from the crime,
> The sublimation of the evil dream.

Auden, on the other hand, tended to set non-specific instruments of change against a specified corruption, as in 'Sir, no man's enemy':

> Send to us power and light, a sovereign touch
> Curing the intolerable neural itch,
> The exhaustion of weaning, the liar's quinsy,
> And the distortions of ingrown virginity.

Here the metaphors for rebirth – power and light, a sovereign touch – remain discreetly (and honestly) out of focus, while the world to be changed seems much closer to home, because its identity rests in our keeping. We know the intolerable neural itch, and we know that going over from it may well not bring us into the kingdom of power and light.

Some poems also encouraged the reader to identify the means by which present was to be transformed into future. Spender touches on this problem when discussing his attitude to a proletarian friend: 'I imagined, I suppose, that something which I was now beginning to call in my mind "the revolution" would alter his lot, and I felt that as a member of a more fortunate social class I owed him a debt.' But how much of the debt was owed to the friend and how much to that provocative definite article? *The* revolution was a kind of club, a meeting-place for the like-minded, a readership.

Day Lewis found other terms for the transformation: the hour of the knife, the break with the past, the major operation. As so often, the absolute certainty of apocalypse is immediately qualified by phrases whose meaning depends on us and on our willingness to make the adjustments they demand. The precise reference of those slogans is less important than their momentum: the revolution, the break with the past, the hour of the knife, the major operation, and so on indefinitely, for it hardly matters which nouns are introduced into the series. Although the poet announces our imminent demise in ringing tones, we cannot be sure where the blow will fall, and there seems a fair chance of becoming separated from a favourite limb in the ensuing surgical *mêlée*.

But the poem which most coherently imagined the interplay between organic metaphors of rebirth and a going-over provoked by definite articles was Auden's 'Spain 1937'. (In discussing this poem, I shall base my remarks on the longer 1937 text, which represents his immediate and unqualified response to the Spanish Civil War.) Its first six stanzas concern a past whose identity clearly lies in our keeping: 'yesterday the invention / Of cart-wheels and clocks,' and so on. It is a rapid summary, a classroom version of the past whose importance lies less in its truth than in the security it offers us – the sense of a knowledge encapsulated and possessed. Soon, however, a more enigmatic and unresolved present intrudes: 'But to-day the struggle.' Samuel Hynes suggests that this is not simply the class-struggle, but also 'the struggle or moral choice that goes on occurring *every* today, because in the present in which men live they must choose and act'. It is the process of going-over, the shifting of a centre within oneself which would produce a new political alignment and a readership.

In the next eight stanzas, poet and scientist and pauper request the intervention of History. They long for some superior force, some rite of passage, which will elide their struggle and usher them smoothly into a new life:

O descend as a dove or

A furious papa or a mild engineer, but descend.

It is a supremely witty summary of the age's demand for an accelerated and thoroughly modern rebirth. However, History's reply throws the responsibility for decision back on to the human subject: 'I am whatever you do.' There can be no rebirth which is not supported at every point by particular willed acts of going-over.

Or can there be? In 1937, of course, a particular struggle beckoned: 'I am your choice, your decision: yes, I am Spain.' The next five stanzas (two of which were dropped in 1940) describe a journey to the margin, a Romantic quest which promises the new life at a stroke. For those who went to Spain, Bernard Bergonzi points out, 'crossing the frontier from France meant a transition to a new world of faith and hope and meaning'. Suddenly it seems that a particular willed going-over might after all amount to regeneration, as Auden imagines a release from social structure ('the institute-face, the chain store') into liminal comradeship:

> Madrid is the heart. Our moments of tenderness blossom
> > As the ambulance and the sandbag;
> Our hours of friendship into a people's army.

This is Tennyson's 'equal temper of heroic hearts', the rediscovery of an essential and generic human bond. Tenderness *blossoms* into a sense of community, and the organic metaphor concludes (as Mendelson has pointed out) a sequence of naturalising terms: the volunteers 'migrated like gulls or the seeds of a flower,' they 'clung like burrs' to the sides of trains and 'floated over the oceans' like clouds. In no previous poem had Auden so exuberantly thrust such metaphors into the centre of political occasion.

The dream of organic change inspires the vision of the future which unfolds over the next four stanzas. But it is a dramatically curtailed and arbitrary vision, dramatically off-hand in its celebration of such memorable events as 'the enlargement of consciousness by diet and breathing'. The details of the future rest in our keeping, as though Auden had realised that he could not carry his account of the blossoming in Spain through, and that it was already dissolving into what each of us can make it. *We* imagine the future: the rediscovery of romantic love, the photographing of ravens, the winter of perfect communion, the bicycle races. The very arbitrariness of these details, their sponsoring of ostentatiously relative values, drains off the optimism generated by the heroic comradeship of Madrid.

Finally the poet resigns himself to the present, to 'the expending of powers / On the flat ephemeral pamphlet and the boring meeting' (which were what Auden expended *his* powers on during his brief visit to Spain). The concluding stanza registers the exhaustion of organic and natural metaphors, and a new pragmatism:

> The stars are dead, the animals will not look;
> We are left alone with our day, and the time is short and
>   History to the defeated
> May say Alas but cannot help or pardon.

In the hubbub surrounding the politics of this stanza, its virtuosity has been overlooked. The metrical unit of the poem is a five-stress line incorporating a varying number of syllables, shortened to three stresses in the third line of each stanza. Here, though, the first and last lines are regular pentameters with no loose syllables, and it is this freezing exactness which gives such a force to Auden's conclusion. The second line, by contrast, is baggy and shapeless and at the very last moment resignedly gathers way again; it is in perfect accord with its subject, the role of human decision in history. As organic process on one hand and History on the other draw back into their oblivious shells, we are left alone with our day and with the imperfect continuing of utterance.

'Spain 1937' attempts to locate a Romantic rite of passage amid contemporary political circumstances, to describe a journey to the margin. But the organic metaphors sponsored by such a project do not 'take'. They are ornamental, a frivolous sub-plot to the main (and true) story of a guilty and incomplete going-over. *That* story is told by the definite articles, as they tempt us to dismiss a past which only we can identify, or join in a struggle which will be intensified rather than resolved by our participation, or put our names to a blueprint of the future. When Auden left for Spain, he may have thought that he was embarking on a regenerative rite of passage; when he came back, he knew that he had simply gone over and come back. His poem testifies to the reality of that experience, and to its failure to become a metaphor for rebirth.

When he came to revise 'Spain 1937' for publication in *Another Time* (1940), Auden excluded its major commemoration of liminality (the hours of tenderness blossoming into a people's army); by that time the fantasy perhaps seemed too dangerous even to acknowledge. Later, of course, he disowned the poem altogether. But I believe that in its original form it articulated more powerfully than any other contemporary work the interplay between rebirth and going-over which preoccupied so many people during the thirties (and which is not exactly unheard-of today). Orwell's response to it is well-known, and has formed the basis for much subsequent comment. Less well-known is Eliot's oblique rejoinder to its final stanza in the third section of 'Little Gidding'; he had after all seen *Another Time* through the press. Eliot suggested that if History cannot help or pardon the defeated, we can:

> Whatever we inherit from the fortunate
> We have taken from the defeated
> What they had to leave us – a symbol:
> A symbol perfected in death.

He at least tried to meet the force of Auden's argument.

* * *

Eliot is often admired for his principled aloofness from the compromising political raptures of his contemporaries; that is certainly how Auden came to see him. But like Pound he modified the rhetorical strategies of his early writing in order to make an identifiable readership, and like Auden he spread a panoply of definite articles in order to do so. His readership, like theirs, was to identify itself politically, by a militant and self-conscious Christianity.

An occasional passage in *The Waste Land* had employed the definite article as a form of external reference, but his most Audenesque poems were the unsatisfactory 'Choruses from "The Rock"',' which inveighed against the horrors of modern life (including daughters who 'ride away on casual pillions'). These Choruses invoke familiar details – the broken chimney, the peeled hull – but they have none of Auden's vigour, and indeed almost justify Pound's remark that Eliot had achieved his position of eminence among English men of letters by pretending to be a corpse.

Eliot was at this time much preoccupied with the use of private experience in poetry, and with the ways such experience might be made to signify for other people. An author's imagery, he claimed, derives partly from his reading and partly from

> the whole of his sensitive life since early childhood. Why, for all of us, out of all that we have heard, seen, felt, in a lifetime, do certain images recur, charged with emotion, rather than others? The song of one bird, the leap of one fish, at a particular place and time, the scent of one flower, an old woman on a German mountain path, six ruffians seen through an open window playing cards at night at a small French railway junction where there was a water-mill: such memories may have symbolic value, but of what we cannot tell, for they come to represent the depths of feeling into which we cannot peer.

These memories mean something to us, without having any 'symbolic value' or intrinsic significance. They are particular and stirring, but we cannot classify or identify them. To use them in a poem would therefore involve the reader not so much in interpretation as in the recall of similar moments from his or her own life.

In 1935 Eliot was exploring the theme of lost childhood, and 'Burnt Norton' reiterated his belief that some of our most important memories have an unidentifiable content: 'I can only say, *there* we have been: but I cannot say where.' He had said 'there' without adding 'where' before, in *The Waste Land* and 'The Hollow Men'. But in 'Burnt Norton' he began to dispense with the protectiveness of 'here' and 'there', and 'this' and 'that'. Its moments in and out of time were left open for the reader to identify:

> To be conscious is not to be in time
> But only in time can the moment in the rose-garden,
> The moment in the arbour where the rain beat,
> The moment in the draughty church at smokefall

Be remembered; involved with past and future.
Only through time time is conquered.

Rose-garden and draughty church are, thanks to the definite
article, more accessible than red rock and Perilous Chapel had
ever been. Eliot had begun to modify the rhetoric of his early
writing.

Four years separated 'Burnt Norton' from the next of what
were to become *Four Quartets*, 'East Coker'; during that time Eliot
conceived, and gave in 1939, a series of lectures which were then
published as *The Idea of a Christian Society*. These lectures were
written with the events of the previous September – Neville
Chamberlain's appeasement of Hitler – very much in mind.
Many people, he said, had been shaken by those events, 'in a way
from which one does not recover'. 'The feeling which was new
and unexpected,' he went on,

> was a feeling of humiliation, which seemed to demand an act of
> personal contrition, of humility, repentance and amendment;
> what had happened was something in which one was deeply
> implicated and responsible.

He felt responsible for the failure of his adopted country to match
conviction with conviction, and inclined to ask whether English
society was built around anything more permanent than 'a
congeries of banks, insurance companies and industries' and
whether it had any faith more deeply-rooted than 'a belief in
compound interest and the maintenance of dividends'. The third
section of 'East Coker' damns the congeries unequivocally,
perhaps as Eliot's act of contrition. Under the pressure of a
national crisis, a collective failure of will, he began to experiment
with less secretive forms of address. When the poem appeared in
New English Weekly in March 1940, it proved so popular that
Faber immediately published it as a pamphlet. At its conclusion
Eliot records his conviction that, for 'old men' at any rate, life is
not sustained by epiphanies – such, perhaps, as the one which
provoked *The Waste Land* – so much as by less temporary and less
exclusive recognitions: 'Here or there does not matter.'

After all, Eliot had been among those who changed 'around
1926'. He had been received into the Church of England and had

acquired British nationality, and most critics notice a greater emphasis on social and political issues from this point on. Like Pound, he began to imagine his audience differently. In 1930 he drew attention to the power of what he called the 'esthetic sanction', the prospect that some readers may be attracted to a poet's beliefs by the beauty of the art to which those beliefs gave rise. He also suggested that some readers may be attracted to a poet's art by the conformity of his beliefs with their own: 'We aim to come to rest in some poetry which shall realize poetically what we ourselves believe.' Either way, the relation between poetry and belief must be close.

Eliot argued in *The Idea of a Christian Society* that writers address other writers, or 'a hypothetical audience which we do not know'. His problem was the familiar one of identifying that audience, of excluding those who merely snatch a glance and encouraging those who read for the right reasons. Like Pound and Auden, he began to make use of social and political alignments which would do the work of identification.

In the same book he argued that anything like a Christian faith transmitted from generation to generation within the family would soon disappear, and that then 'the small body of Christians will consist entirely of adult recruits'. When that happened, Christians like readers would have to be made rather than brought up. The recent history of the Christian faith had come to bear a striking resemblance to the recent history of the audience for literature; the Common Believer had gone out with the Common Reader. In the modern world, to recruit a congregation was perhaps to recruit a readership. Eliot's last three Quartets were written, I think, for those who aimed to come to rest in a poetry that would realise poetically what they already believed, and so confirm their identity as Christians *and* as readers.

'The Dry Salvages' returned to Eliot's preoccupation with the way in which personal memories acquire value. He seems to have decided that the only way to define that value was by summoning the 'god' who watches and waits in all our epiphanies:

> His rhythm was present in the nursery bedroom,
> In the rank ailanthus of the April dooryard,
> In the smell of grapes on the autumn table,
> And the evening circle in the winter gaslight.

The definite articles acknowledge the specificity of such memories, but leave it to us to identify them in terms of our own experience. The passage which follows is a litany of definite articles, denser even than 'Spain 1937'. Eliot could afford their neutrality (the relative freedom they allowed to the poem's secret complement), because he was now addressing a socially distinct readership: the minority of Christians in a non-Christian society.

But it was the last of the *Four Quartets*, 'Little Gidding', which finally united poetry and belief. The titles of the first three had a purely personal significance, whereas 'Little Gidding', as Helen Gardner says, 'proclaims by its title that its scope goes beyond the personal and involves the history of a nation and its Church'. It refers back to his assumption of British citizenship and of Christian faith in 1927, and it brings to a resolution his part in the changes he had noted as starting 'around 1926'. It is his most concerted attempt to define liminality not only for himself, but for his place and time.

The encounter with the ghost in Section II and the salvage of meaning from history in Section III contribute to this project. But the tone of the poem is set by the opening description of the sacred margin itself, Little Gidding. There are other sacred places, Eliot says, but 'this' is the nearest, the most relevant today. For once he not only specifies but identifies a margin. Or at least he names it. Whether it emerges into its full identity will depend on whether we seek out the religious community at Little Gidding – and not just to visit, but to pay our respects to the tradition it embodies. Those who merely snatch a glance will not be welcome, those who attend for the right reasons will find their faith clarified and strengthened. Eliot is quite aggressive about this, announcing that we are not 'here' to gratify our curiosity, but to kneel in a place where prayer has been valid for centuries. Intimations of pilgrimage and quest dominate the description. But for once we know what 'this' and 'here' refer to. Eliot forestalls any other questions we might have by telling us exactly why we are there. Unless you have come for the right reasons you are neither a 'true' believer nor a 'true' reader of the poem.

Eliot and Auden found their way past 'Modernism' by developing a rhetoric which spoke to an audience already to some extent segregated by religious or political tendency. They did not set out to exploit that segregation, and their poems were and still are read for a variety of reasons. But both men regretted the passing of the age of the Common Reader. Both looked back enviously to the eighteenth century, a time when, as Auden said in his 'Letter to Lord Byron',

> Each poet knew for whom he had to write,
> Because their life was still the same as his.

The thirties offered Eliot and Auden readers whose lives were the same as their own, if only by virtue of a shared opposition to the lives led by everyone else. They knew that they were reaching people who had already identified themselves by their dissatisfaction with contemporary English society. The secret complement articulated by the poems they wrote during the thirties was a process of going-over, a shifting of the centre of the struggle within oneself.

Of course, we should not forget that other poets took a different view. In the preface to her 1938 *Collected Poems*, Laura Riding observed that Auden wrote, and was read, for political rather than poetic reasons. 'And T. S. Eliot, on leaving his university, wandered free without a muse until, his reasonlessness becoming unendurable to him, he made himself a tailor's-dummy muse of Religion.' She insisted that her own work answered only to 'reasons of poetry':

> Truth is the result when reality as a whole is uncovered by those faculties which apprehend in terms of entirety, rather than in terms merely of parts. The person who writes a poem for the right reasons has felt the need of exercising such faculties, has such faculties. The person who reads a poem for the right reasons is asking the poet to help him to accentuate these faculties, and to provide him with an occasion for exercising them.

Wallace Stevens might well have agreed with her. His 1935 volume, *Ideas of Order,* consistently fought shy of social and political reasons, and was consistently attacked for doing so. One critique drew from Stevens the comment that, although the social situation was 'the most absorbing thing in the world today', he would not become a propagandist. Poems like 'Sailing After Lunch' and 'Farewell to Florida' and 'Sad Strains of a Gay Waltz' and 'How to live. What to Do' flaunt their unfulfilled specificity, their use of demonstrative reference. But it was the poets who turned to the definite article who set their mark on the decade.

8 The serious action

Louis MacNeice's 'Carrickfergus' describes the town in County Antrim where he spent much of his childhood. It was a town divided irrevocably into opposing camps: rich and poor, Protestant and Catholic, soldier and civilian. But when MacNeice left for England, the division and the mutual hostility began to recede:

> I went to school in Devon, the world of parents
>   Contracted into a puppet world of sons
> Far from the mill girls, the smell of porter, the salt-mines
>   And the soldiers with their guns.

Although it is the prep school which seems like a puppet world, Ireland also has contracted. Unified by the backward glance and warmed over with nostalgia, Carrickfergus has become a set of stable impressions: the mill girls, the smell of porter, the salt-mines, the soldiers. Whereas in Auden's poems the definite article had presented a world to be acknowledged and disowned (or acknowledged and owned), here they present a world to be admired for its pungent remoteness.

A couple of years later, in Section 16 of *Autumn Journal*, MacNeice returned to his feelings for Ireland, this time in a less forgiving mood:

> The land of scholars and saints:
>   Scholars and saints my eye, the land of ambush,
> Purblind manifestoes, never-ending complaints,
>   The born martyr and the gallant ninny;
> The grocer drunk with the drum,
>   The land-owner shot in his bed, the angry voices
> Piercing the broken fanlight in the slum,
>   The shawled woman weeping at the garish altar.

This time, it seems, division will not recede and no sentimentality about the land of scholars and saints will be allowed to obscure the brutal particulars of sectarianism and civil war: And yet born martyr and gallant ninny and shawled woman are figures as hazily representative as the mill girls and the soldiers of Carrickfergus, while those angry voices might pierce any fanlight in any slum in Europe. Only the grocer and the land-owner have the potential definiteness of one of Auden's Enemy-captions. Again, MacNeice's rhetoric does not invite us to take sides so much as to review a distant and contracted world, a land held ruefully up to the backward glance. Educated and living in England, he feels well out of it. Yet Ireland tugs at the imagination, because of its remoteness from more commercialised cultures,

> And because one feels that here at least one can
> Do local work which is not at the world's mercy
> And that on this tiny stage with luck a man
> Might see the end of one particular action.

By its resistance to commercial and technological progress, Ireland contracts itself, holds itself up to the backward glance. On this 'tiny stage' local work and family feeling are still the appropriate frames of reference.

However bloody the differences played out on that stage, they matter less to the expatriate than the difference between everything that happens there and everything that happens in the industrialised countries. Seen against the international background, Ireland dwindles to a unified miniature tableau which must either be cherished or abandoned. Better close the horizon, MacNeice concludes, send her no more fantasy.

His desire to close the Irish horizon was itself perhaps a fantasy of the industrialised world, a longing even more powerful and elusive now than it was then. But it did show the definite article in a new light. Whereas Auden's readers had been provoked to identify and act upon differences within their own society, MacNeice's readers were able to imagine a remote society unified despite appearances by its exclusion from historical process.

In this respect MacNeice had been anticipated by Graham Greene, whose 1935 novel *England Made Me* suggested that the birthplace of industrial revolution had itself become a tiny insignificant stage; it is worth pausing over, because it rewrote Dickens's 'condition of England' novel *Hard Times* in Audenesque terms. The relationships between Greene's characters – Kate Farrant, her brother Anthony and the Swedish industrialist Krogh – duplicate those between Louisa Gradgrind, Tom Gradgrind and Josiah Bounderby. Neither brother returns his sister's love with equal intensity; despite this, their fecklessness makes them more attractive than the suitors, Krogh and Bounderby, who are self-made men better able to handle figures than human beings. Both sisters turn out to be sterile and their sterility reinforces the general sense of a thwarted and moribund culture.

But there is an important difference. Whereas Bounderby represents a moral danger, Krogh threatens the political and economic identity of the English middle class:

> 'We're national. We're national,' Kate said, 'from the soles of our feet. But nationality's finished. Krogh doesn't think in frontiers. He's beaten unless he has the world.'

Dickens's England had been threatened from within by the spirit of egotism and calculation. Greene's England is threatened from without by the power of international capital, by an enterprise and ruthlessness it cannot match. Like MacNeice's Ireland it has been reduced to a tiny stage where local work and family feeling still count. So although Anthony Farrant travels widely, he never 'has the world'. At each frontier and in each foreign city he performs on the tiny stage of his own Englishness (part of the novel turns on his false claim to be an Old Harrovian).

Throughout the novel definite articles create an England as remote and contracted as MacNeice's Carrickfergus. Kate tries to make Anthony settle in Sweden, but 'she couldn't build up his London inside the glass walls of Krogh's as a seaside landlady can construct Birmingham with the beads, the mantel ornaments, the brass-work in the fender'. England has made him, and made him nostalgic:

> Autumn was the few leaves drifted from God knows where upon the pavement by Warren Street tube, the lamplight on

the wet asphalt, the gleam of cheap port in the glasses held by old women in the Ladies' Bar. 'London', he said, 'there's nothing like it.'

The bleak indefiniteness of Sweden – 'It was windy on the terrace: a few trees with yellowing leaves, an attempt at topiary, outside a door in one of the wings a bottle of milk' – contrasts with these fervent memories of an identifiable past: 'He dug his nails into his palm with a spasm of longing for the tea urn, the slattern with the clean towels, the stacks of English cigarettes.' Anthony's past is an object of nostalgia or disgust rather than decision, a world as immutable as it is redundant. If we can identify it, then we too have been made by England, and made nostalgic.

Of course, Swedish industrialists did not represent the only threat posed in the late thirties to the integrity of that world. Roy Fuller's 'Soliloquy in an Air-Raid' was soon to find an equivalent use for the Audenesque, at a time when gas and bomb really were obliterating the drawing-room's civilised cry:

> It is goodbye
> To the social life which permitted melancholy
> And madness in the isolation of its writers,
> To a struggle as inconclusive as the Hundred
> Years' War.

The gestures are perfectly grooved: specification and farewell wave. But they have been produced by a general cataclysm rather than by any personal going-over. It is high explosive which has broken with the past. As a result issues which once provoked division and commitment – the role of the writer, the 'struggle' – now contract to a tiny stage, a 'world that never was'. Not surprisingly, Fuller found it hard to discern an audience: 'But who shall I speak to with this poem?'

MacNeice and Greene and Fuller were not using external reference to identify a readership, but to announce the end of the world which had made such identification possible. Other bombs and other developments were soon to reduce its frontiers and its aching miniature attachments still further. The post-war political order did not seem to allow much scope for the margins on whose magical apartness the poets had marshalled their readers. However, we should not be too quick to declare an End of

Ideology or a Beginning of Tourism or whatever. At the very moment when MacNeice's Carrickfergus was contracting to an object of nostalgia or revulsion, the 1937 Irish Constitution acknowledged that frontiers and the bitter loyalties they provoked would continue to dominate the political life of its citizens.

Even so, although the Second World War did not abolish politics, it may have contributed to the demise of rhetorics which co-existed – blithely, knowingly, critically – with politics. That particular method of identifying a readership lost its appeal. When Auden left for America in 1939, he abandoned a major subject of his poetry – Europe under the threat of fascism and war – and an audience which could be expected to register the nuances of that subject. The proportion of definite articles in his poems dropped steadily from this point onwards. He also rewrote much of the work he had produced during the thirties, erasing wherever possible the definite articles. In the 'Foreword' to *Collected Shorter Poems 1927–1957* he described his earlier preference for those items as a 'disease'. He was in effect dismantling a particular rhetoric, sealing off the places in a poem where the reader had been invited to step forward and become known by distancing himself from what he alone could identify. It was an important disavowal from an important writer.

Other rhetorics faltered at the same time. *Four Quartets,* its identification of an ideal English community sharpened by wartime crisis, was Eliot's last major poem. Ezra Pound reverted to a lyrical accounting for his predicament, to the intimate aura of demonstratives. In the *Pisan Cantos* his attachment was to 'this grass or whatever here under the tentflaps' (Canto 74), 'this air as of Kuanon' (Canto 74), 'this wind out of Carrara' (Canto 76), Mercury's emblem on 'this packing case' (Canto 77). He greeted mythic presences who 'suddenly stand in my room here' (Canto 76), lamented 'this calvario' (Canto 80), entered a bibulous plea (Canto 79):

> Guard close my mountain still
> Till the god come into this whisky

(Here 'still' acquires a sense which neither Keats nor Stevens had anticipated.) The only difference from the early Cantos is that the aura of intimacy surrounding these glimpses of truth is now movingly provisional: 'this grass *or whatever* here', 'this air *as of* Kuanon'. With the *Pisan Cantos* the poem settles into the pattern it will sustain until the end: an alternation between lyricism and documentary, between an utterance which represents the speaker and one which excludes him. While Pound was reverting to lyricism Wallace Stevens, who had never made any appeal to a politically-grounded readership, entered the period of his greatest achievements. When Faber published his *Selected Poems* in 1953, he even found an audience in England, which had hitherto resisted him.

* * *

I have tried to show in this chapter how one particular rhetorical strategy (the Audenesque) was adapted to new political circumstances and expectations, and finally superseded. I want now to draw out one implication of this development, rather than to chronicle it and its historical context more fully. When Auden removed the definite articles from his early work he was removing more than a nuisance, an embarrassing mannerism. He was renouncing a rhetoric tied very closely to particular circumstances and expectations, and therefore very efficient in its making of readers. Once the circumstances had changed, the rhetoric perhaps came to seem otiose. But in any case it seems to me that nobody, including Auden himself, has since achieved as memorable and as effective a use of external reference. I may be wrong in this, and I certainly would not claim omniscience where modern poetry is concerned. But I know that my reading of more recent work has not been helped by the kind of analysis which has enabled me to say something about Yeats and Eliot and Auden. New factors have been entered into the relation between poem and reader, new circumstances and alignments. This does not mean that it is now impossible to deploy demonstratives in the way Eliot did, or to identify a politicised readership in the way Auden did. But it does surely suggest that we should try to find other terms for the relation between poem and reader.

In the 'Age of Criticism' (to borrow Randall Jarrell's phrase), literature has become more firmly established on school and university curricula, and the reading of it more firmly directed by discourses produced within those institutions. Anxiety about the diffuseness of the audience for literature has persisted, but the grounds upon which that audience (or a part of it) might be reassembled have perhaps changed. In 1959 Donald Davie, today our leading poet-critic, wrote an essay called 'Remembering the

Movement'. Looking back at what the Movement had achieved, he declined to regret its academicism. 'Academic is no bad thing to be,' he wrote, 'and in any case becomes inescapable, as the philistinism of Anglo-American society forces all artists – not just writers – back into the campus as the last stronghold.' In Davie's view the sin committed by the Movement poets (and by most of their English and American contemporaries) was not to address an academic audience, but to address whatever audience they had too humbly, forever anticipating its objections and appeasing its prejudices. There was too much flattery of temporary and accidental readers, and not enough selection, not enough making. Davie claimed that he himself *had* on occasion tried to select, by addressing himself 'not to the academic profession but to a group within the profession, very consciously at odds with the rest and more or less committed, appropriately enough, to the idea of a "minority culture".' Whereas Auden had addressed a group within a social class, Davie addressed a group within a profession. Those who taught and studied in the universities had to formulate, 'very consciously', their literary preferences and their position with regard to the current orthodoxy; they thus fell into identifiable readerships. Unlike the outside world, the academy provided a setting in which the poet might once again know for whom he was writing and in which his readers would become apparent through their choice of professional discourse.

Davie was no happier about the elusiveness of the Common Reader than Eliot or Auden. His *Purity of Diction in English Verse* (1952) lamented the collapse between Goldsmith and Wordsworth of a 'homogeneous society'; while a Movement colleague, John Wain, argued that from about 1800 onwards 'the English poet found himself with the chance of addressing a public so large that its outlines were blurred . . . The trouble was that this larger audience could not be known, could not be physically felt as a presence.' In this respect the poets of the fifties held the same view as the poets of the thirties. Cecil Day Lewis, for example, had claimed in *A Hope for Poetry* that poetic achievement depends on the existence of 'small, compact, homogeneous communities such as the Greek city state or Elizabethan England.' However, modern communities are neither small nor compact nor homogeneous, and the poet therefore has to create for himself

a world of manageable proportions . . . a point from which he may begin to work outward again; and in the process he is bound to be obscure, for he is talking to himself and to his friends – to that tiny, temporarily isolated unit with which communication is possible, with whom he can take a certain number of things for granted.

By the time of the second edition of the book, in 1936, Day Lewis had decided that there was a hope: 'The revival of interest in poetry, accepted in the foregoing pages with some hesitation, must now be taken as an accomplished fact.' Auden and his colleagues had managed to work outwards, and they had done so by identifying a more or less political readership. Where the Movement differed was that it worked outwards by identifying an institutional readership, a readership separated off along professional rather than political lines.

Anxiety about the diffuseness of the audience for poetry remained constant, but the models on which plans for reconstituting an audience might be based did change. We can see this in more general terms if we examine the preoccupation of many twentieth-century writers with getting organised. It is a preoccupation which derives from and modifies a nineteenth century view of the role of the intellectual in society.

As Ben Knights has shown, that view came increasingly to centre around the idea of a 'clerisy', an influential élite whose disinterestedness would be guaranteed by their relative exclusion from power and privilege. It was an idea stated most concisely by John Stuart Mill in a series of articles written for Leigh Hunt's *Examiner* in 1831, and later published as *The Spirit of the Age*. Mill claimed that society is in a natural state when governed by the 'fittest persons' available, and in a transitional state when it contains 'other persons fitter for worldly power and moral influence than those who have hitherto enjoyed them'. Since no government ever seems conspicuous for its display of probity and talent, those 'other persons' have been given plenty of scope to dream of organising themselves in such a way that their superior fitness might produce effect.

This has been particularly true of times when the shortcomings of parliamentary democracy have become, for whatever reason, apparent; as they did, for example, in Ireland after the fall of Parnell in 1891. Maud Gonne chose that moment to deliver a series of uplifting lectures in Paris. 'Looking backward now,' Yeats was to write,

I see that a mastery over popular feeling, abandoned by
members of Parliament through a quarrel that was to last for
nine years, was about to pass into her hands. At the moment I
was jealous of all those unknown helpers who arranged her
lectures . . . and I had begun to dream of a co-ordination of
intellectual and political forces.

Maud Gonne was not the only person to bid for mastery. 'The
modern literature of Ireland,' Yeats said, 'and indeed all that stir
of thought which prepared for the Anglo-Irish war, began when
Parnell fell from power in 1891. A disillusioned and embittered
Ireland turned from Parliamentary politics . . .' His own part in
this co-ordination of intellectual and political forces was to help
found Literary Societies in London and Dublin. A modest
contribution, perhaps, but one which reveals how important it
has seemed at such times to *organise*: to produce a set-up and an
exchange of ideas more cohesive than the system whose failure
has made the opportunity. In 1901 Yeats said that he had 'spent
much of my time and more of my thought these last ten years on
Irish organisation'.

During the next ten years new models for that organisation
appeared, as new political movements began to assert themselves.
One thinks of James Joyce's interest in the Congress of the Italian
Socialist Party held at Rome in 1906. Joyce sympathised with the
syndicalist faction led by Arturo Labriola, which was contending
against the reformist wing of the Party:

They assert that they are the true socialists because they wish
the future social order to proceed equally from the overthrow of
the entire present social organisation and from the automatic
emergence of the proletariat in trades-unions and guilds and
the like. Their objection to parliamentarianism seems to me
well-founded . . .

But Joyce's socialism was (as he himself said) 'thin', and he was
certainly no organiser, no joiner of trades-unions and guilds. In
any case, it was only when the New Model political parties
(Communist, Fascist, National Socialist) triumphed, during and
after the First World War, that they became a force whose
emphatic cohesion the clerisies might emulate. These Parties
assumed that society was in a transitional state and that they
themselves were 'fitter for worldly power and moral influence'

than the present ruling class; fitter, very often, because more resolute and better organised. The consequences of their success were registered most clearly by H. G. Wells.

Wells found himself at the turn of the century 'a complete outsider in public affairs', a man 'debarred from any such conformity as would have given me a career within the established political and educational machinery'. But rather than fight his way into the machinery he decided to create and organise a group of like-minded outsiders, a 'voluntary nobility', whom he wished to be known as Samurai. His decision was reinforced by a belief that 'life regarded as a system of consequences' was at that very time giving way to 'life regarded as a system of constructive effort'. A ruling class would henceforth have to be *made*: 'The problem of world revolution and world civilization becomes the problem of crystallizing, as soon as possible, as many as possible of the right sort of individuals from the social magma, and getting them into effective, conscious co-operation.'

At which point history intervened. For while Wells was trying without much success to persuade Bernard Shaw and Beatrice Webb to behave like Samurai, Lenin and Mussolini triumphed. His emphasis on the crystallisation of an élite was superseded by the example of political parties which had begun as tiny minorities outside the established system of government and fought their way to power. In his autobiography Wells said that the achievement of these 'successful organizations' had greatly strengthened his belief in 'the essential soundness of this conception of the governing order of the future'. Even if he found little to admire in the doctrines of either Party, he could still recognise them as examples of conscious and effective co-operation. In 1924 Yeats suggested that the tendency towards 'authoritative government', in Ireland and throughout Europe, was 'part of a reaction that will last one hundred and fifty years. Not always of the same intensity, it is, still, a steady movement towards the creation of a nation controlled by highly trained intellects.'

The Parties themselves, of course, did all they could to confirm this impression. 'In the close community life of both sexes,' declared the organisers of a 1920 festival of Working Youth in Weimar, 'we shall crystallize aristocracy within ourselves.' The Hitler Youth aimed to crystallise the right sort of leaders from the social magma by rigid discipline:

This cult of individualism of past generations, this caressing of one's own peculiarity down to the most insignificant matters, we deplore. Therefore we also despise those circles of the present bourgeoisie which are incapable of organising themselves into forceful movements because they cannot and will not subordinate themselves, in the perpetual fear of losing a minute quantity of their own individuality.

Hence the uniforms, the military command-structure, the parades: ways of imprinting organisation into the individual mind. In Britain, anyone joining the British Union of Fascists had to sign a form containing this declaration:

I recognise the necessity for the voluntary discipline of the British Union of Fascists and I, therefore, pledge myself to accept its discipline and at all times to be loyal to its leadership.

The leader himself, Oswald Mosley, laid great stress on the cohesion which such loyalty made possible. While admitting that Fascism was as much of a universal creed as Socialism or Liberalism, Mosley claimed that unlike 'those creeds of the past, it has found an organised form in Britain within a few years of its birth. That organisation is necessary because the old civilisation crumbles to collapse, and we can lose no time in the building of the new.'

This emphasis on triumphs of organisation rather than doctrine does seem to have had some effect on people who were neither Fascists nor politicians. In his book *Beyond Politics*, published in 1939, Christopher Dawson argued that consensus, which had once been 'an unconscious fact arising out of the natural structure of society', could no longer be taken for granted: 'And it is on this ground, rather than in the field of politics in the strict sense, that it is necessary to plan and organise, if any fundamental reform is to be made in the life of the nation.' What in an earlier age had been given would now have to be made; made, furthermore, according to the most successful models available: 'the form of organization appropriate to our society in the field of culture as well as in that of politics is the party – that is to say a voluntary organisation for common ends based on a common "ideology".' And the most successful political Parties were those which had seized power in Russia and Germany and Italy: 'we must organise as completely as the totalitarian States have done, but in a different way'. Thus the cohesiveness of the new Parties appealed even when their doctrines did not. Dawson's book was one of the few whose influence Eliot acknowledged in his own contribution to the debate, *The Idea of a Christian Society*.

By 1926 Wyndham Lewis was suggesting that the banding together of people into 'an ever more and more rigid system of clans, societies, clubs, syndics, and classes' had left no room for the play of an independent mind. Examples of the organisational imperative pressed in from all sides, and Lewis thought that even the most independently-minded would not be able to resist for much longer:

> All these *odd men out* stand at present glaring at each other as usual, remarking perhaps to themselves that adversity brings them strange bedfellows. But the time must arrive when *they*, too, in spite of themselves, form a sort of syndic. That will be the moment of the renascence of our race, or will be the signal for a new biological transformation.

That the prospects for biological transformation should be taken so seriously is perhaps a tribute to the growing power of another 'syndic', the scientific élite. J. D. Bernal, declared that in order to close the gap between technological advance and natural evolution, 'man himself must actively interfere in his own making – and interfere in a highly unnatural manner'.

Bernal was not joking. He planned to 'interfere' by extracting from the human body those functions rendered useless by technology and grafting new functions on to whatever was left. The result would be a cylinder – 'rather a short cylinder' – containing a brain immersed in fluid, with an array of microscopes and telescopes hooked on to the casing. Bernal supposed that a fanatical élite of scientists would transform themselves into cylinders and then use their newly acquired powers to gain control over the non-cylindrical majority. At this point people might realise what was going on, but by then it would be too late for them to 'do anything about it'.

One cannot imagine Lewis's odd men out turning themselves into cylinders without a great deal of protest, but the example of the successful syndics was hard to ignore. 'Much more research needed,' Auden's Airman was to note, 'into the crucial problem – group organisation (the real parts).' As early as 1914, Pound had praised Allen Upward's 'propaganda . . . for a syndicat of intelligence; of thinkers and authors and artists'. He himself moved to Italy at a time when the Fascist Party was trying to establish syndicates of similar kind (although with a primarily technical emphasis). The Futurist Marinetti had advised the creation of a body made up of young men under thirty, to be called *L'Eccitatorio,* which would act as a stimulus and corrective to the bureaucracy. During the early years of Fascism, from 1919 until 1924, its leaders showed considerable interest in this project, and bodies known as Competence Groups were in fact set up in 1921. According to Michael Ledeen, these represented 'an attempt, of the sort advocated by Marinetti, to create structures parallel to those of the bureaucracy in order to stimulate the creation of new programs and rational attempts to solve problems'. Pound, a lifelong opponent of bureaucracy, no doubt approved.

His own ideas, however, were more broadly cultural. In 1928 he suggested to James Vogel that if 'the 243 Americans who ever heard of civilisation wd. quit crabbing each other and organize, it wd. be a start'. 'An intelligentzia,' he told the readers of the Mosleyite *British Union Quarterly,* 'cannot exist unless there be some open square, or some roofed space or aggregation of printed pages where these sincerities can come together and compare notes on tomorrow.' (The B.U.F. did in fact make vague gestures at some such roofed space: one pamphlet proposed replacing the House of Lords by 'a Chamber which will enquire into the cultural needs of the nation'; another talked about a corporation of artists.) A year later, in 1938, Pound returned to the theme:

> To ORGANISE in our barbarism, in our utter and rabbity inconsequence, an hierarchy and order is not an affair of decades. We can not, or at any rate we have not organised one clean book club, we have not organised even committees of communication, we have not one publication that serves as postal system for ideas between the few hundred top-notch (however low the top be) intelligentsia. And until a selection of the intelligentsia can organise something, until they can set up at least a model they can not expect the 120 or whatever million to copy it.

Book club and committee and journal were ways of organising what might in a previous age have possessed a self-evident coherence, ways of forcibly crystallising a syndicate out of the social magma.

However, these methods of organisation have proved less durable than, and have often been incorporated into, the universities. 'Watch the beaneries,' Pound said mistrustfully; yet the beaneries are now the only roofed spaces where an intelligentsia gathers to read him. Even as he fulminated, the universities were organising a readership by means of the kind of programme set out in his 1931 essay *How to Read, or Why*. This essay shows Pound in a rummaging mood, plunging into remote corners of the literary attic after a gleam from some forgotten (or maliciously suppressed) heirloom, deciding what can usefully be dispensed with. All kinds of things come flying out of the window (Pindar, Vergil, the 'Rhoosuns'), not because they are worthless, but because they do not form part of the 'serious action': the literature which teaches you how to read, and why. Pound was offering a method and a programme, not a survey. He was trying to get the reader organised. 'I am not talking about the books that have poured something into the general consciousness, but of books that show *how* the pouring in is done or display the implements, newly discovered, by which one can pour.' Readership does not require encyclopaedic knowledge, but skill in the use of certain 'implements'. As Pound said two years later, in 1933, 'you cannot get the whole cargo of a sinking paideuma on to the lifeboat'.

In the same year F. R. Leavis sent up an answering flare from *his* lifeboat, *How to Teach Reading: A Primer for Ezra Pound*. Although he wished to retrieve some of the lumber Pound had hurled out of the attic window, Leavis concurred in proposing to equip people with 'a technique of reading, a trained sense for the significant'. He too thought that 'if literary culture is to be saved it must be by conscious effort; by education carefully designed to meet the exigencies of the time – the lapse of tradition, the cultural chaos and the hostility of the environment.' So both men agreed about the necessity for 'conscious effort': the audience for literature (like the syndicate of intelligence) would now have to be made and organised, where once it might just have appeared.

The shift of emphasis from Pound's title to Leavis's title, from *How to Read, or Why* to *How to Teach Reading*, indicates both the continuities and the differences between their respective positions. Leavis dropped the 'Why' and baulked at Pound's version of the serious action. But he persevered, as did the universities as a whole, with Pound's belief that in an age of 'utter and rabbity inconsequence' readers would have to be *made*. Ivor Richards, for one, had a vivid sense of cultural chaos; the modern mind, he remarked in a moment of particular gloom, is like a bed of dahlias whose sticks have been removed. His criticism emphasised the responses of the 'fit' or 'adequate' or 'right' reader, and set about training students up to that standard. Empson's *Seven Types of Ambiguity* claimed to show 'how a properly-qualified mind works when it reads'. Such minds would now have to qualify for readership through 'conscious effort', where they might once have done so simply by living, Leavis said, in a 'homogeneous culture'.

Since the Second World War, the literary syndicates have been almost wholly absorbed into higher education. As a result, it is now not so much the development of academic criticism as developments within academic criticism which create readerships. One such development within academic criticism has been the attempt, recently renewed with great vigour, to guarantee its autonomy as a discipline. Thus while Northrop Frye's *Anatomy of Criticism* (1957) assumed that the allusions of a Yeats or an Eliot would still signify for 'the properly instructed reader', it also suggested that the grounds for such instruction should be made more secure: 'just as there is nothing which the philosopher cannot consider philosophically, and nothing which the historian cannot consider historically, so the critic should be able to construct and dwell in a conceptual universe of his own'. As matters stand, Frye argued, 'the absence of systematic criticism has created a power vacuum, and all the neighbouring disciplines have moved in'. Readers were being trained, but they were being trained to read historically or philosophically – that is, for the wrong reasons. These are Yeats's temporary and accidental readers, now found within the academy rather than outside it. Frye's insistence on the autonomy of literary criticism was a way of counteracting them, a way of ensuring that some people at least would be able to read for the right reasons. 'I suggest that it is time for criticism to leap to a new ground from which it can discover what the organizing or containing forms of its conceptual framework are.'

Many critics have since leapt, and their athleticism has often involved the tacit recognition that they were making readers. For example, conceptual frameworks such as that recently elaborated by a group of critics at Yale tend to be organised around certain canonical texts, and in their turn organise a readership for those texts. They are erected against what is felt to be the 'utter and rabbity inconsequence' of literary studies as a whole, and so fight Pound's battle all over again inside rather than outside the academy. Thus Geoffrey Hartman's *Criticism in the Wilderness*, a defence of literary theory and assault on Leavis's 'anti-theoretical bias', nevertheless incorporates some distinctly Leavisite assumptions:

> Books are already like gardens, a small cultivated area that miniaturizes what is lost. But what is lost is not books themselves or print-capability, but the wish, need, or motive to read what is being written in a world where publication has utterly changed its character.

Unless criticism can restore that wish, need, or motive, the audience for literature will disappear: 'our problem today is that as the quality of writing increases, the quality of reading should also increase to preserve the great or exceptional work as something still possible.' Leaving aside the question of how the quality of writing might be said to 'increase', we have here a familiar anxiety about people not reading for the right reasons, and a familiar defensive nurture of small cultivated areas and miniature nostalgias. Hartman and Leavis agree about the situation of literature, even if they disagree (instructively) about how it should be remedied.

For Hartman, the remedy lies with a declaration of independence. Literary criticism should free itself from the imperial grasp of neighbouring disciplines and from intimidation by political bandits. 'The reader-critic,' he says, 'is deeply involved in not allowing art to be shunted aside or co-opted by the newest ideology.' Deep involvement to the exclusion of the newest ideology is now what distinguishes the properly instructed and authoritative reader-critic from the temporary and accidental one. So Walter Benjamin is praised for the literary and religious analogies his work fosters, rather than for his 'ideologically induced social interpretation'; while the context provided for the deconstructive enquiries of Jacques Derrida is noticeably less plural than those provided in the early seventies by Anthony Wilden's *System and Structure* or by the Anglo-French collection

Signs of the Times. Behind Hartman's concern for the 'quality of reading' and behind Harold Bloom's, one senses a deep distrust of the sixties: of 'countercultural students' and their intellectually promiscuous mentors.

Hartman does not offer us a conceptual universe so much as a room of our own, an ideal seminary where the properly-instructed may gather. He is always referring to 'famous' texts. Eliot and Ransom have 'famous' essays, Kafka has a 'famous' parable, Thoreau a 'famous' chapter, Emerson a 'famous' statement, Heidegger a 'famous' formula, Milton a 'famous' axiom, while Benjamin even manages a 'famous' phrase. Conversation in the seminary obviously covers a wide variety of literary and critical texts. All the texts are familiar (almost wearisomely familiar) to the seminarists, and it is only good manners that they should recognise this by introducing each quotation with an apologetic 'famous'. Here, surely, is Pound's roofed space, where each bit of the serious action has its certifying tag.

* * *

Models for the identification and organisation of a readership have varied according to historical circumstances. Where Pound looked to the political party or the syndicate, Davie looks to a party or syndicate within the educational system. Although other models have sometimes supervened, there can be little poetry published today on which the shadow of an institutional readership does not fall.

'Academics,' Christopher Logue said recently, 'have the power to influence and form taste at a time when there isn't the excitement we had in the Fifties and early Sixties – and because there isn't that same excitement and energy released elsewhere, that academic taste seems almost as though it is the only possible one.' In this view a university audience has replaced an audience created, in part at least, by poetry readings. 'Like a sermon,' Seamus Heaney points out, 'a reading is a conventional mode of behaviour.' It serves to identify a particular readership. Those who attend (perhaps on a cold January night) are the 'party activists', the permanent and essential among readers; by attending regularly they commit themselves to the idea that poetry is above all a spoken medium. Such readings may indeed have become, as Logue suggests, a convention less powerful than academic fiat, an assembly harder to identify than the group which occupies seminar room 35b on alternate Tuesdays.

If so, there is an important consequence. Pound tried desperately to bring an organisation into existence, to make a certain group of people identify themselves as a group by falling in with his schemes and his poems. The group Davie was addressing, on the other hand, already existed. It had already acquired a distinct identity by enrolling or teaching at a university, and then by attending a particular seminar or writing a particular article. The logical consequence of this change would be a shift in the balance of power between poem and reader. A readership which many modern poems sought to create by particular rhetorical strategies would now be created independently of any single poem by institutional practices and discourses.

To put it like this is perhaps to exaggerate the difference. One could argue that Eliot's Christian readership and Auden's left-wing readership existed long before they were licked into shape by the caress of definite articles. Yet religious and political groupings are not necessarily predisposed towards poetry, and a further and more distinct identity must have been drawn out of them by the rhetoric of *Four Quartets* or 'Spain 1937'. After all, 'Little Gidding' does not simply propose faith, but a particular and rather chastening kind of faith (there is some evidence that Eliot meant to rebuke outbreaks of evangelical fervour, as he does in *The Idea of a Christian Society*). An audience made available by common religious or political interests, and then brought to a greater awareness of its identity by the rhetorical strategies of particular poems, surely differs from an audience identified once and for all by its commitment to the academic study of literature (or at least to the study of literature as taught at a particular institution). It seems to me an important difference, although I would only want to explain what can happen in different circumstances rather than what invariably does.

Attempts to define the prosody of contemporary verse have provided some corroborating evidence. Like the use of external reference, prosody is a semantic convention, a set of rules which enables the reader to make sense of what the poet has written. 'A wholly new ("hidden") meter,' Charles Hartman observes, 'is not a prosody as far as the reader is concerned, because he does not share the secret.' An effect of language must be recognised by both reader and writer if it is to serve as a semantic convention. As long as poets continue to obey generally accepted conventions such as the use of iambic pentameter we will recognise that they are writing poems rather than letters to a newspaper, and interpret what they have to say accordingly.

But many modern poets have been notoriously reluctant to use the iambic pentameter, or indeed any equivalent prosody; they have written free verse instead. It is now conventional to abandon convention. Of course, their poems are read and understood, which presumably means that their new and hidden metres have somehow acquired the status of prosodies. This has happened in two ways. On one hand, the 'threshold' of what constitutes a metre has been lowered dramatically; some of us now think that poems are simply texts which never make it all the way across to the right-hand margin. On the other hand, certain poets (notably Charles Olson) have been able to publicise their eccentric prosodies so successfully that we now know more or less how to read their poems. So far so good.

But what about poets who have no gift for propaganda and yet feel that their writing is characterised by something more specific than its failure to get all the way across the page? Who will read them for the right reasons? Only, I would guess, those readers who have access to academic research into the prosodies they have invented. For example, Louis Zukofsky developed a metre which arranges the distribution of 'n' and 'r' sounds according to the formula for a conic section. But unless we have read the book in which Hugh Kenner describes this system we will not be able to identify it. Similarly, William Carlos Williams intended each line in his three-line stanzas to occupy the same time-span. But his attempts to explain this system only left the matter in total darkness, and the reader seeking guidance will have to follow up Hartman's reference to an unpublished dissertation by Emma Kafalenos. Neither Zukofsky nor Williams is exactly unknown. Yet the most basic convention on which their work relies has only been revealed by meticulous academic study.

The consequence of this shift in the balance of power between poem and reader is serendipity. The rhetoric of a poem by Eliot or Yeats or Auden had sought out a readership among a diffuse potential audience. The rhetoric had caused a readership to exist by identifying it (by identifying those among the diffuse potential audience who did not merely snatch a glance). But the audience for poetry today is no longer diffuse, having been to a larger extent preselected and trained by academic study. Whether or not a contemporary poet is read for the right reasons may well depend less on his rhetorical exertions than on the way that audience has been taught. In principle an English Department could (over a number of years) create a readership for any poet it chose, and the popularity of 'reader-response criticism' has shown that the academy does relish this kind of power.

If the relation between poem and reader has been substantially modified by the growth of institutional audiences of various kinds, then we must surely pay some attention to the protocols which organise and identify them. My final chapter will try to initiate an enquiry along these lines. At the same time, of course, poems still address a reader (how could any utterance not do so?), even if they conceive that reader differently. Since this is a book about the language of modern poetry, I want also to account for some of the rhetorical effects produced by the address of more recent work.

In my next three chapters I shall argue that the major rhetorical axis of much contemporary verse is based on pronomial rather than on demonstrative reference, and on the status of the speaker rather than on that of any marginal figure. The sense of a place being marked out for a reader – a place in discourse, a place in society – seems less acute. Instead there is a continuous testing of the extent to which a speaker can occupy his or her words, can fill them to capacity; and a contrary urge to let the words dictate and to incorporate types of utterance which appear to exclude subjectivity. I believe but cannot prove that this change of rhetorical emphasis is in some cases related to a change in the balance of power between poem and reader. It is not that these poems are any more assured of who their reader might be, but that the means of assurance no longer lies in their keeping.

9 *Les blancs débarquent*

If Geoffrey Hartman's seminary were to acquire a poet in residence, it could well be John Ashbery, whose famous obliquities are already beginning to compete with Kafka's famous parable and Emerson's famous statement. Ashbery's career has been transformed by the growth of a particular institutional audience, an audience not of his own making. When *Self-Portrait in a Convex Mirror* won all three of America's most prestigious literary awards in 1976, he attained, in the words of David Lehman, 'a degree of fame that few would have thought possible a mere half-dozen years earlier'. Introducing a collection of essays about Ashbery, Lehman claims that the poet has survived the neglect which usually attends literary innovation and now finds himself on 'everybody's reading list'.

Ashbery's advance on to Everybody's Reading List – that is to say, his capture of a ready-made institutional audience – was foreshadowed in a lecture he gave at the Yale Art School in 1968, when his work was still relatively unknown. In this lecture he contrasted the current visibility of avant-garde art with its virtual invisibility twenty years before, and illustrated the point by referring to a performance of Schoenberg's *Trio for Strings* given at Harvard in 1949:

> My friend the poet Frank O'Hara who was majoring in music at Harvard went to hear it and was violently attacked for doing so by one of the young instructors in the music department, who maintained that Schoenberg was literally insane. Today the same instructor would no doubt attack him for going to hear anything so academic. To paraphrase Bernard Shaw, it is the fate of some artists, and perhaps the best ones, to pass from unacceptability to acceptance without an intervening period of appreciation.

It was during such intervening periods of appreciation that the selective rhetorics of Yeats and Eliot and Auden had come into play, sorting out from among a diffuse potential audience those readers who could be 'physically felt as a presence'. But the institutional audiences which ensure for avant-garde art an immediate passage from unacceptability to acceptance are identified not so much by their response to a particular rhetoric as by their enrolment at the academy and by the degree of their loyalty to one or another of the critical discourses available there. An artist or a musician or a writer who has made no effort to identify an audience may find himself suddenly transported to that nirvana where all utterances are always already famous: Everybody's Reading List. Among contemporary poets none has passed more rapidly from unacceptability to acceptance than Ashbery himself.

Even he, however, has not yet arrived on *everybody's* reading list, because institutional readerships tend to make themselves known by dissenting from academic orthodoxy rather than by proclaiming it. It is not so much that an institutional readership has replaced the more general one addresssed by Yeats and Eliot and Auden, as that the institutions are now the general ground on which selections can be made. Thus for the contemporary poet there is always the chance of somebody's reading list, but rarely the chance of everybody's reading list. Even Ashbery's more recent books have not always found favour with English publishers or English critics. Reviewing five miscellaneous volumes in December 1979, John Carey lavished the good news on some unexceptional performances by English poets, and saved the bad news for a concluding sentence on *Houseboat Days*: 'It's a collection of obscure, pretentious, self-indulgent meanderings, exemplifying with remarkable comprehensiveness the features which have alienated the general reader from modern poetry'. Even Ashbery's enemies might feel that such hostility exemplifies with remarkable comprehensiveness the features which have alienated the modern poet from the general reader. But it does at least suggest that the writer passing from unacceptability to acceptance will have to chose his moment carefully, or be carefully chosen by his moment.

A sector of the institutional audience – 'a group within the profession,' to use Davie's terms, 'very consciously at odds with the rest' – has been alerted to something in Ashbery's work (or something 'about' Ashbery's work) by its own heterodox ambitions. David Lehman, for example, claims that critics hostile to Ashbery are 'simultaneously resisting Pollock and de Kooning, or Webern and Cage, or "literary America", or semiology, or any of the proliferating ripples of cultural implication'. He lines Ashbery up not only with avant-garde artists and composers, but with that energetically proliferated ripple, Harold Bloom. We are not asked to agree with Bloom, but to respond with the same kind of aggressively specialised attention (Lehman and his contributors aim at 'a level of critical discourse as advanced in its way as the poetry that occasions it'). Do these advanced critical discourses form the secret complement of the poems they address or of the institutions within which they are asserted?

It is a question one might ask of David Shapiro, who characterises Ashbery's work as 'a precursor of Derrida's critique of a metaphysics of presence':

> The poet does not speak, but constantly is involved in that mute science of Derrida's grammatology. Ashbery deflates our expectations of sense, of presence, by giving us again and again the playful zone of *deferred sense*. There is an icy autocratic humiliation of the reader, who expects again and again a center, only to be decentered.

Shapiro does not offer a Derrida-like critique of the poems (which might have been interesting). His book is an introduction, and his allusion to grammatology is meant to let us know where we are on the map of academic discourses. If 'deferred sense' is our callsign, then we are ready: only those with a copy of *Positions* and a taste for Siberian torments need apply.

Ashbery seems to have decided very early on that there was not going to be any intervening period of appreciation for him, and that he would just have to hang around until history exchanged unacceptability for acceptance. Or so he told Gerrit Henry, immediately after *Self-Portrait* had picked up the third of its awards:

> When my first book was published and it bombed, I realised that no one was going to be very interested in my poetry – ever, it seemed to me – so I thought I'd just forget about the reader and write for myself. Not that I *wanted* to forget about the reader, but he left me no alternative.

Even now, I don't feel that these three awards mean a sudden wave of acceptance of my work. I feel pretty much the same way about my work as I did when I started writing – now that I've received public approval, I can still write as I choose.

Forgetting about the reader means that the poems no longer make the same kind of provision for their secret complement by the use of external reference; the provision they do make is both more welcoming and more fugitive, opened instead by the play between subjectivity and its constant fading or eclipse. To put it another way, pronominal reference is a more important device in Ashbery's writing than demonstrative reference.

Indeed, conventions such as metre and demonstrative reference often become mere curiosities, bits and pieces awash in the flow, part now of the poem's content rather than of the way it should be read. *The Double Dream of Spring* (1970) includes a short poem called 'Parergon' which exemplifies this process. Like the 'Prologue' to Auden's *Orators,* it records the passage from centre to margin of a prophet: his separation out, his speech against the world, a journey on which he is rebuffed or misunderstood. Here is part of its concluding section:

> As one who moves forward from a dream
> The stranger left that house on hastening feet
> Leaving behind the woman with the face shaped
>   like an arrowhead,
> And all who gazed upon him wondered at
> The strange activity around him.
> How fast the faces kindled as he passed!
> It was a marvel that no one spoke
> To stem the river of his passing . . .

Some of these lines proclaim that they are iambic pentameters: the fourth, whose length has clearly been measured by metrical rather than semantic requirement; the sixth, whose stressed words are given unmistakable prominence by alliteration and internal rhyme. But it does not seem to me that Ashbery is writing with oblique reference to a regular metre, as Eliot had done, challenging us to listen for departures from and returns to a norm. The pentameter is not really a convention at all in this instance, because it does not serve to identify a particular mode of address or a particular meaning. It is rather itself an object to be interpreted in the light of whatever convention the poem as a whole proposes. Metre has, so to speak, passed from the level of form to the level of content, as have the uses of external reference: 'that house', 'some court'. These are no longer the places where the poem's secret complement can be brought into play. Indeed, they barely signify at all. Nothing hangs on the invitations they proffer, and they can scarcely serve to sort out the accidental and temporary among readers since they are themselves accidental and temporary. Whatever it is that marks them as such must be said to constitute the poem's system of organisation.

The passage might recall another tradition. For the figure assimilated to a universal category by 'one' is perhaps a distant descendent of Wordsworth's silent monitors. The people who gaze upon him still wonder at his apartness, as they had in 'Animal Tranquillity and Decay'. But this silent monitor does not live up to his billing; the apt admonishment he offers has no effect, and his lesson eddies far into the night. In Wordsworth's poem, the reference item 'one' had sealed the pronomial chain, so that the traveller had already entered into his ritual function before being named as 'the Old Man'. Here, the ritual function cannot be sustained, and dissolves back at the end of the poem into a pronomial chain whose reference becomes increasingly uncertain. There is for example a 'he' who may be the stranger, or each onlooker in turn. Ashbery cannot hold to the community of perception evoked by 'one', or even to the far more fragile community evoked by the demonstrative and the definite articles of the 'Prologue' to *The Orators*. 'Parergon' reduces demonstrative reference from the level of form to the level of content, from code to message. A parergon, after all, is an ornamental accessory.

This does not mean that Ashbery's poems are unintelligible. They can be read, and by a process short of the 'icy autocratic humiliation' recommended by David Shapiro. For they are governed, as Donald Davie had said, by 'the necessity – once the poetic engine has been started – to keep it ticking over, not picking and choosing among the moments that present themselves, but consuming them one and all, burning them as fuel for the enterprise that, once started, must at all costs be kept going'. The convention, in other words, by which these poems are to be interpreted is their own remorseless spate: the belief that poetry is 'something coterminous with lived actuality, not rescued

or salvaged from it'. An Ashbery poem is coded by the knowledge
that there are many like it in the books he has already written and
that there will be even more like it in the many books to come. I
myself think that this makes for dull reading, and that the act of
rescue or salvage – of moral and political thinking – can be more
strictly 'coterminous' with 'lived actuality' than the flow it
impedes. But I would not deny, as John Carey does, that the
writing has its own principle, its own poetics of spate. That a poet
as uncompromising as Ashbery should pass so nimbly from
unacceptability to acceptance seems small cause for Jeremiads.

* * *

It is sometimes maintained that during the sixties many American
poets turned away from the guarded complexity associated with
Eliot and the later Auden towards another, equally resilient
literary ideal: direct and intimate utterance. These poets are said
to have been consumed by the pathos of straight talking about
lived actuality. Yet the straight talking was often quite
remarkably oblique. John Berryman's *Dream Songs* make copious
reference to actual friends and actual circumstances, but their
protagonist is 'not the poet, not me'. Other poets struck off
personae whose circumstances were very different from their
own, but whose opinions and feelings seemed quite similar.
'These two disclaimers,' Robert Pinsky argues, 'are explicit or
implicit in much modern writing: that the statement by or about
oneself is only seemingly a personal statement in words; and,
conversely, that the seemingly objective ''character'' in fact
presents a statement about oneself.' The new authenticity soon
broached its own antidotes.

Pinsky himself provides an excellent account of the way the
resulting literary convention – 'that the poet can at once say, yet
somehow not-say' – operates in Lowell and Berryman. John
Bayley has written well about a poetry which 'reveals but does not
confide': about the 'aesthetic cautery' applied by Lowell, and
about the way Berryman makes intimacy impossible while
appearing to invite it. But I want here to take up the case of two
writers, Frank O'Hara and Ed Dorn, who instead of reducing the
opposition between saying and not-saying to a taut ambiguity
have taken it to extremes. Their concern has been with saying

in the fullest sense (a shameless intimacy, a declaration of allegiance) and not-saying in the fullest sense (an utterance or an awareness which erases subjectivity). Saying may pass into, and perhaps even depend on, not-saying; but it is impossible to locate any midpoint, any equilibrium.

Frank O'Hara knew just how invisible avant-gardes can be, and how easy it is to assimilate them. He remained relatively unknown at a time when the avant-garde New York painters who were his close friends had achieved celebrity; he himself contributed to that celebrity through his art criticism and his work at the Museum of Modern Art, where he was employed by the foreign exhibitions department. The techniques of Abstract Expressionism are sometimes said to have had consequences for his writing (and for Ashbery's), but perhaps mattered less than its celebrity, which demonstrated that an unacceptable art could become accepted. If O'Hara was (in the title of Marjorie Perloff's study) a 'Poet among Painters', he was also a 'Poet among Museums', a poet who knew at first hand the importance of institutional audiences. He saw that a deliberately experimental art was now finding a ready-made audience, an audience made ready by the proliferation of museums and galleries. In 1965 he remarked to Edward Lucie-Smith that museum-going had only recently become 'an event' for Americans: 'only recently have Americans even bothered, for instance, to trot off to Philadelphia to see the museum on a Saturday. It's perfectly available.' People trot off to Philadelphia, he added, because of 'what their forbears told them about these marvelous things,' or because 'it's something they just love because it's an event'. Avant-garde art was now a large part of that event, with its own institutions (Museum of Modern Art, Tate Gallery). O'Hara pointed out that there was a whole Cinematheque on Lafayette Street devoted to 'underground' movies – a privilege few commercial directors could claim.

Knowing of the existence of ready-made audiences for avant-garde art and film and music, if not yet poetry, O'Hara did not compromise the intimacy or the adventurousness of his writing. He avoided the discriminatory and identifying rhetorics found in his 'modernist' predecessors, choosing instead a continuous apostrophe to the people and places and events which imposed on his everyday life. Whereas Stephen Spender had seen in parts of *The Orators* a device for making readers, Ashbery and O'Hara saw a wonderful verve and flippancy, a dense accumulation of idioms.

This reading of the book 'washed back', as O'Hara said, on to the original and gave it 'a marvelous tone'. Like Ashbery he subscribed to a poetics of spate; and yet there are acts of rescue and salvage which check the flow. In O'Hara's work the speaker is the poet, a poet fully committed to the pathos of authenticity and the pathos of love; yet his Songs of Myself provoke their opposite, an anti-pathos which founds them and which they in their turn support. By recognising that this opposition between pathos and anti-pathos could neither be avoided nor accommodated, O'Hara was able to articulate new and powerful versions of subjectivity.

Even the aspect of the poems which might be thought to guarantee their intimate manner – the constant reference to a small circle of friends – in fact denies it. For O'Hara does not simply refer to his friends, or talk about them; he gossips. Gossip becomes a way of ensuring a certain fluidity in his relationships with other people, and then a specific practice of writing. To gossip about someone is, after all, to distance oneself from them and from one's feeling for them, to view them temporarily as the objects of an impersonal curiosity. We do it to our closest friends as well as to our enemies, and so recognise that we always have at least the capacity to erase our feelings for other people. My closest friend becomes, for a moment, an object for the subject my curiosity represents. Yet of course I don't break with that friend, and I do not think any the worse of him or her for supposedly doing what my curiosity demands that they should have done. I know that I in my turn will become an object for the subject his or her curiosity represents; I too will be gossiped about. For the function of gossip may be to guarantee the circulation of subjectivities. We all gossip and are gossiped about; we swap roles continually – now subject, now object – and so the group is sustained without ever separating into permanent alignments. This may well have been important for O'Hara, whose life was shaped, according to Ashbery, by 'the many passionate friendships he kept going simultaneously (to the point where it was almost impossible for anyone to see him alone – there were so many people whose love demanded attention, and there was so little time and so many other things to do, like work and, when there was a free moment, poetry)'. For these relationships to be kept going, it was essential that there should be no hierarchy, no pair of subjects for whom everyone else was always an object, no permanent alignments. Gossip ensured a continuous redistribution of roles, whereby the object of one curiosity was always becoming the subject of another.

These are the opening lines of a poem – 'Adieu to Norman, Bon Jour to Joan and Jean-Paul' – whose title announces its gossipy intentions:

> It is 12:10 in New York and I am wondering
> if I will finish this in time to meet Norman for lunch
> ah lunch! I think I am going crazy
> what with my terrible hangover and the weekend
>   coming up
> at excitement-prone Kenneth Koch's
> I wish I were staying in town and working on my poems
> at Joan's studio for a new book by Grove Press
> which they will probably not print
> but it is good to be several floors up in the dead of night
> wondering whether you are any good or not
> and the only decision you can make is that you did it.

Later it transpires that Allen has just got back from somewhere and is talking about God a lot, that Peter is also back but not talking about anything, and that Joe has a cold and so won't be going to Kenneth's although he is having lunch with Norman . . . The star of this marvellously off-hand yet cunning piece, Kenneth Koch, was a close friend of O'Hara. Helen Vendler imagines him as a member of a cosy writers' circle: 'O'Hara has a line in one poem about writing poetry to cheer people up, and there is an air of determined social duty about a lot of these poems, as though the balloon of group cheerfulness had to be batted back to the next player – over to you, Kenneth – and Kenneth Koch, himself equally noble in his obligations, serves a jaunty poem back, and so on through the clan . . .' Yet Koch does not appear in 'Adieu to Norman' as a friend and collaborator, but as the object of a really quite dispassionate curiosity. He is there to be gossiped about rather than to be liked or congratulated or cheered up. Such, indeed, would appear to be his function throughout the *Collected Poems*. An entire play *(Kenneth Koch, a Tragedy)* considers his attitude to homosexuality, while another poem ('The fluorescent tubing burns') accords him a precise role in the social life alluded to by Ashbery. O'Hara knew that the desire to be everything to everybody everywhere involved a certain adaptability; and that meant no exclusive alignments. By gossiping about Koch, he put some distance between himself and one of his closest friends, and so ensured a perpetual redistribution of roles.

'Adieu to Norman' is as decisively organised around its pronouns as any poem by Ashbery. It opens with a pronominal reference item – 'It is 12:10 . . .' – whose empty generality suggests that the poem will not have much use for demonstratives. Generalised reference – '*it* is good to be several floors up' – is an important and consistent feature of O'Hara's rhetoric, focusing attention on the mind which perceives rather than on its objects: 'the only decision you can make is that you did it'. The decision has more bearing on 'you' than on what 'it' was that 'you' did. For the objects and the people in O'Hara's poems (unlike those in poems by Eliot and Auden) are named, self-evident; what counts is, to adapt one of his own phrases, the speaker's thinking towards them.

Even more crucial, perhaps, is the distinction between the 'I' and 'you' implied by a conversational tone and the nouns and pronouns which designate the gossiped-about. Within the system of pronominal reference we can distinguish between pronouns like 'I' and 'you' which refer to speech-roles (to participants in the act of communication itself) and those which refer to everyone and everything else. Gossip underlines that distinction, because it makes a temporary clan of the two or more people engaged in a particular conversation and sets them off from whoever they are talking about. 'I' and 'you' meet to discuss Allen and Peter. But when Allen and Peter meet one of 'us' may become the topic of their conversation, and thus slip back to a 'he' or a 'she' again. Knowing this, the poem can happily distribute roles and make its distinctions.

Gossip was not O'Hara's only means of approach to the relation between pathos and anti-pathos, as anyone who has read 'In Memory of My Feelings' will know. The title of this great and unaccommodating poem conveys pathos, indeed a double pathos: not just the poet's feelings but his pious feelings about those feelings (there won't be a dry eye in the house). The poem is dedicated to a close friend, Grace Hartigan, and refers frequently to the details of O'Hara's own life. Its opening lines establish the self as a kind of pathos-machine constantly turning out impulses which have to be rescued from their own generosity and vulnerability. The impulses never learn. They launch themselves repeatedly into improbable and irretrievable escapades. Far from being able to do anything about this, the poet can only invite commiseration ('I'm too blue') as the rueful possessor of weapons which will not defend him adequately. Yet he does not disown these impulses, or subject their alternating torpor and hysteria to ironic revision as a Lowell or a Berryman might have done. Instead, he allows the frenzy of his 'naked selves' to produce its own opposite: .

> So many of my transparencies could not resist the race!
> Terror in earth, dried mushrooms, pink feathers, tickets,
> a flaking moon drifting across the muddied teeth,
> the imperceptible moan of covered breathing,
>   love of the serpent!
> I am underneath its leaves as the hunter crackles and pants
> and bursts, as the barrage balloon drifts behind a cloud
> and animal death whips out its flashlight,
>   whistling
>
> and slipping the glove off the trigger hand. The serpent's eyes
> redden at the sight of those thorny fingernails, he is so smooth!
>   My transparent selves
> flail about like vipers in a pail, writhing and hissing
> without panic, with a certain justice of response
> and presently the aquiline serpent comes to resemble the Medusa.

The transparent selves love this aquiline serpent because it stills their panic. Yet it is not only their culmination but their strange and implacable opposite: a Medusa-head which turns all who look at it to stone, an anti-pathos. Is subjectivity itself founded on and forever returning to a state of no-feeling?

The next three sections of the poem ask this question in different contexts: family life, history, autobiography. Section 2 deals with family romance, that nominally airtight bonding which so often discloses pockets of hostility and guilty indifference.

O'Hara's 'coolness' towards his father, his uncles and his aunts is a kind of minimal anti-pathos, a 'lucidity' which cuts the nerve of family romance. Its Medusa-head is comparable to the gaze which reduces a barge full of terrified Marines to an image, a flippancy ('A hit? *ergo* swim'). We can all recognise such small but terrifyingly abrupt reductions in our feelings towards even those whom we love and respect.

Section 3 is more general in emphasis, coping with the panic induced by time:

> And the mountainous-minded Greeks could speak
> of time as a river and step across it into Persia, leaving the pain
> at home to be converted into statuary. I adore the Roman copies.

But can the pain ever be converted into statuary? Its reflux tends to be immediate and potent. Immense longing for a glamorous past – including, now, the death of an uncle, a death grown fond in the recollection – sweeps over the poet. His transparencies reassert themselves as a nostalgia for the *ancien régime* which will not allow itself to be converted into statuary. One remembers Stevens's 'Sad Strains of a Gay Waltz', where the memory of gay waltzes and the solitude of 'mountain-minded Hoon' are threatened by an 'epic of disbelief' (another advance into a new land). The epic of disbelief is an anti-pathos, like the Greek statuary in 'Examination of the Hero in a Time of War':

> The hero is not a person, The marbles
> Of Xenophon, his epitaphs, would
> Exhibit Xenophon, what he was, since
> Neither his head nor horse nor knife nor
> Legend were part of what he was, forms
> Of a still-life, symbols, brown things to think of
> In brown books. The marbles of what he was stand
> Like a white abstraction only, a feeling
> In a feeling mass, a blank emotion,
> An anti-pathos, until we call it
> Xenophon, its implement and actor.

The white abstraction has abolished rather than memorialised

Xenophon, reducing him to a blank emotion, a still-life. Yet
Stevens knew that we will continue to recreate Xenophon as a
person, from the reflux of a fierce nostalgia: 'Unless we believe in
the hero, what is there / To believe?' O'Hara would have agreed
that no anti-pathetic epitaph can rid us of the vulgar
sentimentality ('I adore the Roman copies') which sustains
heroism. We cannot purge the hero of his transparencies, because
without them none of us would join any race at all. And the
section concludes by springing some wonderfully nimble and
vulgar transparencies from a 'meek subaltern' and his mistress:
'How many selves are there is a war hero asleep in names?'

Section 4 switches back to more personal concerns:

> Beneath these lives
> the arden lover of history hides,
>   tongue out
> leaving a globe of spit on a taut spear of grass
> and leaves off rattling his tail a moment
> to admire this flag.

We are recalled from history to consider the project announced by
the opening lines of Whitman's 'Song of Myself':

> I celebrate myself, and sing myself,
> And what I assume you shall assume,
> For every atom belonging to me as good belongs to you.
>
> I loafe and invite my soul,
> I lean and loafe at my ease observing a spear of summer
>   grass.

The confidence to lean and loafe – to become a pathos-machine –
challenges O'Hara, as it has challenged so many other American
poets. A bit later in 'Song of Myself', a child asks Whitman what
the grass is:

> How could I answer the child? I do not know what it is
>   any more than he.
>
> I guess it must be the flag of my disposition, out of
>   hopeful green stuff woven.

O'Hara tries to locate the flag of a similar disposition in his own experience, starting with the memory of a trip to Chicago five years before. But the challenge presented by Whitman's subjectivity was its careless spawning of transparencies, its claim to contain multitudes, its 'profound lesson of reception' ('Song of the Open Road'). While recognising this – 'Grace / to be born and live as variously as possible' – O'Hara seems driven to exceed rather than to extend himself; to break rather than to celebrate that leaning and loafing subjectivity. He embarks on a catalogue of 'sordid identifications', which concludes as follows:

> I am a child smelling his father's underwear I am an Indian
> sleeping on a scalp
>   and my pony is stamping in the birches,
> and I've just caught sight of the *Nina*, the *Pinta* and the *Santa*
> *Maria*.
>   What land is this, so free?
>   I watch
>
> the sea at the back of my eyes, near the spot where I think
> in solitude as pine trees groan and support the enormous
>   winds,
> they are humming *L'Oiseau de feu!*
>   They look like gods, these whitemen,
> and they are bringing me the horse I fell in love with on the
>   frieze.

As Marjorie Perloff points out, this echoes *Saison en enfer,* where Rimbaud suddenly appears as a noble savage in the deserts of Arabia, awaiting the whitemen: 'Les blancs débarquent'. O'Hara does not aim, like Whitman, to contain a society; but rather, like Rimbaud, to evade one, to enter a world which does not recognise his vulnerability. Yet he cannot get rid of his paleface mannerisms, the transparent selves with their relentless production of pathos. For his Indian self covets something which has already been represented to him in the terms of the colonisers, the horse on the frieze.

The first two sections of the poem had noted the persistence in human behaviour of a lucidity which on occasion (and without our having willed it) suspends our feelings for other people and our anxious memorialising of those feelings. The next two sections had attempted to will some such suspension, some lucid

estrangement; but each advance into a new land had immediately
triggered a reflux of sentimental longing, whether for ball gowns
or horses on a frieze. So O'Hara begins the fifth and last section
on a more sober note:

> And now it is the serpent's turn.
> I am not quite you, but almost, the opposite of visionary.
> You are coiled around the central figure,
> > the heart
> that bubbles with red ghosts, since to move is to love . . .

The heart remains a pathos-machine, bubbling with red ghosts,
committing itself to other people or to memory each time it
moves. The poem concludes – obscurely but justly, I think – that
the heart's ease will only be assured by a full and ruthless
acknowledgement of its opposite, the implacable Medusa-head:

> . . . and I have lost what is always and everywhere
> present, the scene of my selves, the occasion of these ruses,
> which I myself and singly must now kill,
> > and save the serpent in their midst.

It hardly seems a triumphant conclusion, as it is sometimes said to
be, because the killing has yet to be done. Indeed, the presence of
a rather gaunt pentameter – 'which I myself and singly must now
kill' – gives it an air of grim resolution. But then a poet celebrated
for his feeling cannot have found it easy to acknowledge the
necessity of no-feeling. Dismantling his ruses in order to save
their occasion, he was working against the grain of his talent in
order to make a truthful poem.

The nonchalance and exuberance of O'Hara's poetry recalls
the spirit of anti-pathos abroad in the twenties. His most
outrageous play, *The General Returns from One Place to Another*, was
inspired by 'a wonderful production of Brecht's wonderful *In the
Jungle of the Cities*'. 'Personism: a Manifesto' takes very seriously
the business of refusing to take anything seriously. Yet O'Hara
was beginning to explore the implications of anti-pathos in a way
no twenties writer did, and his poems reveal more than a soldier
of humour. He tried to say that love has pitched its mansion not
in the place of excrement but in the place of no-feeling.

*   *   *

Like O'Hara, Ed Dorn featured in Donald Allen's seminal anthology, *The New American Poetry,* although he found himself among Black Mountaineers rather than New Yorkers. Both men have been concerned with the play between subjectivity and its eclipse. But their concern has, as Allen's classification would suggest, found different levels and different terminologies.

If O'Hara was a poet among museums, then Dorn has been a poet among academies (although they have sometimes been rogue academies, such as Black Mountain, and he has usually stayed among rather than inside them). Dorn's poems speak more openly about political and cultural identity than O'Hara's, sometimes in terms first assembled by Charles Olson, and so perhaps does his readership. 'My readers,' he told an interviewer,

> are the people who have read me. I know almost exactly how many they are, and I even know a large percentage of them personally. And by statistical extension I know them all.

Auden might have said the same during the mid-thirties, although the extension from some to all of his readers was registered by the language of his poems rather than by statistics. Olson might have said it during the sixties, and his rhetoric too identified an audience and made it known to him. Dorn can say it in the eighties and mean an audience identified by its acquaintance not only with his poems, but also with idioms already formulated in an academic context ('which when it's the best I admire completely'). Allusions to Heidegger and astrophysics serve the same purpose as Auden's definite articles and Olson's jagged syntax, without demarcating or characterising a particular mode of address.

What I mean by this is that Dorn's allusions are not – as Eliot's literary allusions and Pound's historical allusions sometimes threaten to become – the sole criterion by which our reading of his poetry is to be judged. They assume the kind of acquaintance with certain subjects that would be provided by up-market newspapers, and they are in the poetry now because they were once in the newspapers. At the same time, the academic community has provided Dorn with a powerful image of what the relation between a poet and his readers might be, and so freed him to pursue the line of his thought: 'From the beginning I have known my work to be theoretical in nature and poetic by virtue of its inherent tone.' Or perhaps one should again speak of groups within the academic community. Douglas Oliver remarks that of contemporary poets Dorn and J. H. Prynne 'have most interestingly concentrated upon the following consequence: if scientists trying to plumb the birth processes of nature are, for greatest accuracy and insight, driven to investigate the largest possible birth processes in macro-space-time (black holes, etc.) and the smallest possible in micro-space-time (sub-microscopic growth, internal cell events, particle physics, etc.), then the birth processes of ''mind'' itself and of its acts will most accurately find its reflection in such events'. I believe that this indicates not simply an investment in scientific idioms, but an investment in the image of the communities which produce and are confirmed by those idioms. Dorn does not write for Heideggerians or astrophysicists, but he does write in the knowledge that such groups exist, and sometimes even flourish.

The play between subjectivity ('the birth processes of ''mind''') and its opposite articulates Dorn's writing at a different level from O'Hara's reckoning with pathos and anti-pathos. Subjectivity turns out to mean finding an argument or a decision or a loyalty which will represent you to other people as you are during those moments when you believe that you really have got it right – words spoken, in the fullest sense, with respect to yourself. Argument, decision, loyalty: these acts involve or imply a *thesis* (from the Greek word for 'putting' or 'placing'). In prosody the term 'thesis' originally meant the stressed syllable in a foot or the stressed note in music. Your thesis is what positions you and holds you to a determinate identity; it bears your stress. Dorn's prompting of subjectivity might be described as an exploration of thesis.

However, it is not all that often that we get things right and we do not spend our lives proposing theses: 'When people speak, other than arguing (but even there to a certain extent), they're often saying what they think other people might like to hear. And I think that's a definitely honest act.' Such non-thetic speech is produced in common, with respect to other people rather than to oneself. It is colloquial in the sense that it involves a talking together, and it tends to merge the subjectivity of the speaker into shared values and idioms. These idioms help to constitute and define our societies, for they represent the fading of one subjectivity into the desire or the control of another. Dorn has always been open to this colloquy: 'I hear an awful lot of what I repeat just on the air. That would be: radio, conversation on the corner, in a cafe, things my children tell me, reports of all kinds coming in from many sources.' His work operates between the extremes of thesis and colloquy, among the public idioms where our moral and political decisions must find their place.

In an essay published in 1960, Dorn tried to define the thetic aspect of Olson's voice, its self-assertiveness, by referring to a scene in Melville's *Redburn*. Redburn, an American sailor on his first voyage to England, is exploring the town of Liverpool when he comes across a starving woman and her two children in a filthy cellar. He is so moved by their plight that he decides to intervene:

> Leaving Launcelott's-Hey, I turned into a more frequented street; and soon meeting a policeman, told him of the condition of the woman and the girls.
> 'It's none of my business, Jack,' said he. 'I don't belong to that street.'
> 'Who does then?'
> 'I don't know. But what business is it of yours? Are you not a Yankee?'
> 'Yes,' said I, 'but come, I will help you remove that woman, if you say so.'
> 'There, now, Jack, go on board your ship, and stick to it; and leave these matters to the town.'

This interference in other people's business establishes Redburn's identity, his sense of himself (in Dorn's words) 'as a placement on this earth, as an environment in which things are pronounced'. Moral strength must be seen to depend on placement, on becoming an environment in which a thesis can take shape. Thesis of this kind has been a major concern not only in Olson's *Maximus* but also in Dorn's work from *Hands Up!* (1964) to *Hello, La Jolla* (1978) – not least in the titles of those books, since greetings can be propositions.

Some of the poems in *Hands Up!* seem fiercely determined to represent their author, to claim authorisation and placement. For example, 'The Land Below':

> They simply get
> what they want –

> an economy is *never*
> more intricate
> than that

An italicised word bears the stress of the poet's identity, his presence in what he says, his thesis. As others do elsewhere in the poem:

> The chipping off of invert reality
> *is* alright . . .
>
> It is a *real* mystique, not a
> mystique.

We are meant to feel that these pronouncements are one man's purchase on existence, his grasp and his only: he in turn is pinioned by the determinacy of his investment in a particular thesis. Such ferocity can of course become a problem, as it does in *The North Atlantic Turbine* (1967), a book whose opening poem is entitled 'Thesis' and which is almost wholly engrossed by the thetic:

> I want to say something
>   I want to talk
> turn myself into a tongue

The book is humourless and shrilly self-assertive; indeed, it comes close to undermining Dorn's perception of the social basis of speech. *Gunslinger,* foreshadowed by 'An Idle Visitation' in *The North Atlantic Turbine,* subsequently led him away from the thetic, although *Hello, La Jolla* returns to the business of placement from a different angle. Dorn has said that in writing the latter he was 'trying for a tone to see how actually flat and rigorously final you could make a line.' He describes one poem in the book as 'exhortatory and pontifactory', and remarks that the tone he was aiming at had been 'left over from a certain bounciness of *Gunslinger* motion.' His emphasis on finality is important, because thesis depends on closure as well as on authorisation for its validity. *Hello, La Jolla* evinces a freewheeling dogmatism, sealing exhortation into each utterance without worrying too much where it came from. But the most challenging of the books directly concerned with placement and thesis is *Geography* (1965), which asks whether the announcing and situating of a subjectivity by acts of perception will authenticate it. Does observation 'earth' the observer morally and politically? Dorn touches on the science of geography, which offers the poet concerned with thesis tempting terms of definition. Olson's *Bibliography on America for Ed Dorn* praised the geographer Carl Sauer's 'space of time and precision on roots', while Sauer's essay on 'The Morphology of Landscape' provides the epigraph for the longest poem in Dorn's book, 'Idaho Out': 'The thing to be known is the natural landscape. It becomes known through the totality of its forms.' According to Sauer, a knowledge of natural landscape will make possible a knowledge of the cultural landscape. 'Under this definition,' he wrote, 'we are not concerned in geography with the energy, customs, or beliefs of man but with man's record upon the landscape.' So on one hand geography does seem to concern itself with a kind of thesis or placement, 'the impress of the works of man upon the area'. The cultural landscape is 'man expressing his place in nature as a distinct agent of modification'; in so far as it studies that landscape, geography offers clues to anyone proposing a thesis and thereby expressing his place in discourse as a distinct agent of modification. On the other hand, geography cannot elucidate the energy, customs or beliefs of man – surely the major preoccupation of Olson and Dorn. It remains a parallel vocabulary, a mocking echo of the desired placement; no study of man's impress upon the landscape will, in the end, locate him.

'Idaho Out' entertains that mocking echo with beautiful tenacity. It is the statement of someone at variance with the energy, customs and beliefs of his society:

> But I am ashamed of my country
> that, not as areal reality, but as act
> it shames me to be a citizen in
> the land where I grew up

The question is whether exploration of that 'areal reality', with its attendant lightness of tone –

> But not to go too much into
> that ethnic shit, because
> this is geographic business

– will yield a more authentic placement, alternative beliefs. It will not, finally, Idaho, the place Dorn speaks from, remains 'unannealed / by a real placement'; recognising this, the poem shifts back inexorably from geographic business to the harsh reality of ethnic shit.

However, Dorn's writing has never been exclusively preoccupied with versions of thesis. In 1972, looking back at *Hands Up!*, he remarked that he found the feeling of the book 'very dogmatic and insistent, adamant, concerned': 'That kind of responsibility to say how you feel about things which I hope has gone entirely from my writing.' But even there he had begun to explore the possibilities of undogmatic statement, in poems such as 'On the Debt of Mother Owed to Sears Roebuck'. Although the title implies proposition, the first two stanzas seem lazily unconcerned to take a line; they pause over intransitive actions (grinning, brooding) and each is brought to a close by events rather than by any necessity of argument. At this point the poem could turn to polemical use the credit it has already won by its fidelity to a particular situation, or it could with stoic fatalism decline to rise above mere description. Instead, Dorn produces a rhetorical effect which has some consequence for his work as a whole:

> On the debt my mother owed to sears roebuck?
> I have nothing to say, it gave me clothes to wear to school,
> and my mother brooded . . .

The poem's title spins interrogatively on its author, inviting him to take a line. But he refuses and in doing so refuses the thetic; his 'I have nothing to say' is the opposite of that obsessive propositioning found in *The North Atlantic Turbine* ('I want to say something'). It makes possible an altogether different form of statement. The mother broods on her debt; she cannot do more than brood because she has not the terms which would enable her to comprehend it and so at least know herself as a 'distinct agent', of protest if not of modification. She does not have entry to the thetic. But what she cannot say, and what her son refuses to say, has been said for them. The stanza continues:

> In the rooms of the house, the kitchen, waiting
> for the men she knew, her husband, her son

from work, from school, from the air of locusts
and dust masking the hedges of fields she knew
in her eye as a vague land where she lived,
boundaries, whose tractors chugged pulling harrows
pulling discs, pulling great yields from the earth
pulse for the armies in two hemispheres, 1943
and she was part of that *stay at home army* to
keep things going, owing that debt.

The debt cannot be comprehended from the point of view of
individual or family; it has been produced by the exigencies of an
immeasurably larger moral and economic system. Since no poetic
thesis could ever size up that system, or establish the place of a
single debt among its million transfers of wealth and loyalty,
Dorn withholds judgement. A phrase written 'on the air' in 1943,
a phrase eclipsing the mother's subjectivity, moves into the space
left by his retraction: 'she was part of that *stay at home army* . . .'

Yet this is no sullen capitulation, for the phrase has been
admitted only that it may be stripped of its authority. A swell of
compassion for the mother has built up through the poem, and
now wrenches the phrase which has wrenched her. *Stay at home
army*, has been doubly spoken, doubly figured: once by the
propagandist's trope, which makes a soldier of a farm-labourer,
and once by a disbelieving voice which can tell the two apart.
That disbelief is no routine sophistication, but the voice of a
community Dorn knew as a child:

> The social basis of the central Illinois farmer is extemely thin
> and it's also characterized by a kind of skepticism – a social
> skepticism. You know farmers tend to be skeptical about both
> weather and people.

It is that thinness which the poem speaks for, by its brooding
accommodation of fat lies. Ironic or sidelong utterance delivers a
scepticism which does not lend itself to thesis, and which will not
be heard at all unless the poet refuses to say what he thinks. The
tenacity and poise of Dorn's scepticism reasserted itself
magnificently in the late sixties, when he began to publish his
masterpiece in the sidelong mode, the comic epic *Gunslinger*.

If the social basis of the central Illinois farmer counts as thin,
then that of the characters portrayed in *Gunslinger* must seem

positively membranous. Reading an account of the Kansas cow towns which Dorn mentions as an 'influence' on the poem, one is struck above all by a sense of manic impermanence: cities which boom and slump overnight; men who keep the peace for months with great resolution and then are casually murdered; the sheer insistence of stray bullets. The characters in Dorn's poem who enact the 'cultural phenomenology' of the late sixties and early seventies in frontier dress are equally impermanent, distinguished by mannerism and turn of phrase rather than any more inward design; distinguished, in short, by the kind of self-presentation appropriate to that eminently colloquial event, a long journey. (One remembers Johnson's hilarious account of the gradual transformation of pained camaraderie into outrageous posturing on a long journey by stage-coach.) Early in Book I the narrator and the Slinger meet up with Lil, the Madam of the local brothel:

> *Shit, Slinger! you still got that*
> *marvelous creature, and* who *is this*
> *funny talker, you pick him up*
> *in some sludgy seat of higher*
> *learnin, Creeps! you always did*
> *hang out with some curious refugees.*
> *Anyway come up and see me*
> *and bring your friend, anytime*
> *if you're gonna be in town we*
> *got an awful lot to talk about* . . .

Lil merges with Mae West, because the word is already out and the characters do not so much express themselves as occupy temporarily the place marked for them in some already charismatic utterance. They rise to the occasion of a style rather than a subjectivity, and the emphases in their speech denote a sidelong glance at these utterances whose charisma has been produced elsewhere. (Dorn admits that when reciting the poem he sometimes gives an ironic or sarcastic twist to certain words.) The 'social basis' of the characters is so thin that they have no other thesis or placement than this sly punctuation of the idioms which envelop them.

The narrator, indeed, proves more temporary than most. He passes away in Book II and is then resurrected by a massive dose of LSD. Instead of providing a unifying and authoritative view of events, he becomes an event himself, a peripatetic pronoun, a suave derangement of grammar:

I is now an organ Ization
a pure containment

He has become a Five, Gallon, Can
I is now a living Batch

Dorn elicits a good deal of knockabout comedy from this transformation, but it also demonstrates that he is not proposing a thesis. In this respect, we might compare *Gunslinger* with James McMichael's 'Itinerary', published in *The Lover's Familiar* (1977), another narrative poem which incorporates idioms and locations from the American past. 'Itinerary' opens in the twentieth century on the Western plains, and moves eastward across the continent and backwards in time until it reaches Puritan New England. A single narrative voice unites the various episodes, sinking back through layers of idiom until it begins to sound like Cotton Mather. It is this impressively managed continuity of voice which sustains the poem's thesis or assertion of national and individual identity. By emphasising *dis*continuity – 'I is now an organization' – Dorn has denied any such metaphysical status to the narrative act of *Gunslinger*.

McMichael, of course, is by no means the only modern American poet to attempt a steadfast fix on origins. The sprawling epic poems of Dorn's immediate predecessors – Pound, Williams, Olson – had involved an enquiry into the birth processes of nationhood, a nostalgia for the moment when things were relatively uncomplicated and therefore easier to get right. They seem to have believed that imaginary kinship with the men and women of that moment would stabilise and justify poetic utterance. Dorn, however, revises Olson's revision of Pound. His neglect of thesis serves to prevent any fix on origins.

Olson had seen and criticised in Pound's writing 'the moan for the lost republican purity, the wish to return America to its condition of a small nation of farmers and city-state patricians, all Boston brahmin, and Philadelphia brick'. Whereas Pound sought the birth processes of nationhood in Jeffersonian republicanism, Olson wanted to look further back, in search of the fundamental dynamism which might be said to characterise American life from the time of the original settlers until the present. He found this dynamism in an aspect of 'lost republican purity' which had escaped, or been ignored by, Pound.

Canto 31 had Jefferson writing to Thomas Paine in March 1801 with an offer of sanctuary. But other correspondence from the same year, not included by Pound, shows Jefferson in a less favourable light. For example, a proposal that slaves should be allowed to colonise the empty spaces of the American continent met with this less than enthusiastic response:

> However our present interests may restrain us within our limits, it is impossible not to look forward to distant times, when our rapid multiplication will expand itself beyond those limits, and cover the whole northern, if not the southern, continent, with a people speaking the same language, governed in similar forms, and by similar laws; nor can we contemplate with satisfaction either blot or mixture on that surface.

The man who welcomed Paine was not willing to see any negro blots on his shiny new empire, and seems at times rather less indifferent to dreams of domination and rather more indifferent to the rights of slaves than Pound cared to admit. Jefferson's policies were unashamedly expansionist. In his first Annual Message to Congress, in December 1801, he argued for a rapid increase in population, with a view to 'the settlement of the extensive country still remaining vacant within our limits'. Successive Annual Messages reported a steady purchase of land from the Indians. It was this expansionist impulse which Olson traced back to its origins in the enterprise and tenacity of the New England settlers.

At the leading edge of each expansion stood the frontier, which thus had to be defined as the perpetual birth process of national identity, the place where everything was always done for the first time. 'It is not a line to stop at,' Walter Prescott Webb noted in 1953, 'but an *area* inviting entrance . . . In Europe the frontier is stationary and presumably permanent; in America it *was* transient and temporal.' The remark about the permanency of European frontiers sounds strange coming from a man who had just lived through the Second World War. Still, it enabled Webb to establish the American frontier as something completely different, as a rite of passage which 'acted as an abrasive on the metropolitan institutions, wearing them down until man stepped forth with old human restraints stripped off, old institutions of aid or hindrance dissolved, leaving him relatively free from man-made masters'. The frontiersman moves forward out of a world made rigid by social structure, divesting himself of his old metropolitan identity until 'little remains but the individual standing alone in the presence of novel condition'. Arrived at the frontier-margin, he begins his life again, rediscovering the value of an essential and generic human bond.

According to Webb, the philosopher of the frontier-margin was Frederick Jackson Turner, who could 'tell what was its meaning'. Turner's well-known paper on 'The Significance of the Frontier in American History', published in 1893, provided a definitive account of the frontier as a regenerative space:

> American development has exhibited not merely advance along a single line, but a return to primitive conditions on a continually advancing frontier line, and a new development for that area. American social development has been continually beginning over again on the frontier. This perennial rebirth, this fluidity of American life, this expansion westward with its new opportunities, its continuous touch with the simplicity of primitive society, furnish the forces dominating American character.

Thus the expansionist impulse was reclassified as a Romantic rite of passage, its aggressive makeshift ambitions glossed as a desire to begin again at the margin. Many thought that even after its closure in 1890 the frontier would continue to shape the American character; among them Webb's contemporary, Charles Olson. In *Call me Ishmael*, Olson insisted that the next frontier was the Pacific ocean. Beyond the ocean lay the markets of Asia. 'With the closing of our own frontier,' Nelson Rockefeller told the Committee on Foreign Affairs in 1951, 'there is hope that other frontiers still exist in the world'. This time the pioneers would be wearing smart suits and broad grins. Olson did not merely acknowledge the durability of the myth of 'perennial rebirth'. He sought to return it to its original purity and so renew it, by a meticulous recording and honouring of the acts of the first settlers.

Gunslinger also returns to a frontier, but not with any idea of celebrating perennial rebirth. The margin it locates is one painfully aware of its own belatedness and instability. During the period from 1840 to 1885 the agricultural frontier first jumped across the Great Plains to the Pacific slope and then began to work backward into them. Webb explains that the 'last stage of frontiering consisted, therefore, of a movement from both the east and the west into the Great Plains'. During this last stage, as the Industrial Revolution closed in from both sides, 'there arose in the Plains country the cattle kingdom,' a 'world within itself, with a culture all its own'. By occupying that precarious and increasingly redundant margin, *Gunslinger* announces its revision of American foundation-myths. Its social scepticism and its discontinuous spread of idioms demonstrate that the last frontier offers neither placement nor rite of passage.

* * *

I cannot claim that Frank O'Hara and Ed Dorn are representative figures. But I hope that my discussion of their work will provide terms – pathos and anti-pathos, thesis and sidelong utterance – of some use to our understanding of the opposition between saying and not-saying which characterises much contemporary literature.

10 Declarative voices

The opposition between saying and not-saying which I have described in the work of some American poets seems to me an equally prominent feature of the recent history of English and Irish poetry. The pathos of subjectivity, the 'responsibility to say what one feels about things': these imperatives have come and gone on this side of the Atlantic as well as on the other. My next chapter will deal with their coming at a particular moment in the careers of Philip Larkin and Seamus Heaney, the one after that with their going at a particular moment in the careers of Ted Hughes, Geoffrey Hill and J. H. Prynne.

I shall approach Larkin's work through a type of poem which he has returned to so consistently and so successfully that it might be regarded as a genre in its own right. This type of poem tries to define the relation between the actions and perceptions of a narrator, and the social and cultural significance of the events he witnesses; the relation, in short, between individual experience and shared meaning. I am thinking of 'Church Going' and 'I Remember, I Remember' in *The Less Deceived* (1955); of 'Here' and the title poem in *The Whitsun Weddings* (1974). Like the dramatic monologues of Browning and Tennyson, the genre seems to spring fully-formed from the poet's head, so perfectly is it adapted to his basic preoccupations.

'Church Going' pursues Eliot's thought that ritual observances which were once dominant in English life are now ancillary, but with a jauntiness Eliot would have shrunk from. Its opening lines show the narrator bobbing around in the entrance to the church, trying to claw off his bicycle-clips. Further indignities ensue, boosting among other things the circulation of Irish sixpences, but there is such a determined air about them that an outbreak of piety seems imminent. And the poem does eventually work through from jauntiness to an appraisal of the enduring significance of holy ground. In the concluding stanzas, the narrator wonders who will be the last person to seek 'this place' for what it once was. It could even be, against all the odds, his own 'representative',.

> Bored, uninformed, knowing the ghostly silt
> Dispersed, yet tending to this cross of ground
> Through suburb scrub because it held unspilt
> So long and equably what since is found
> Only in separation – marriage, and birth,
> And death, and thoughts of these – for which
>   was built
> This special shell? For, though I've no idea
> What this accoutred frowsty barn is worth,
> It pleases me to stand in silence here;
>
> A serious house on serious earth it is,
> In whose blent air all our compulsions meet,
> Are recognised, and robed as destinies.
> And that much never can be obsolete,
> Since someone will forever be surprising
> A hunger in himself to be more serious,
> And gravitating with it to this ground,
> Which, he once heard, was proper to grow wise in,
> If only that so many dead lie round.

The demonstrative 'this' refers back, on each occasion it is used here, to the description of the church given in earlier stanzas. Yet because these items bunch so in one stanza – 'this cross of ground', 'this special shell', 'this . . . barn' – they signify as much by their usual association of closeness and intimacy as by their reference to a particular building. The sacredness of Larkin's church, like that of the Perilous Chapel, is given to the reader to imagine. But we do not altogether lose sight of the reference back to a particular building. For Larkin's pilgrim, unlike Eliot's, does not sink into holy ground, leaving us to be harried by thunderous voices. He remains distinctly sceptical about his own motives and about the redemptive aura of a barn which is, after all, frowsty. If he were to return to it, he would surely still have trouble with his bicycle-clips and still resort to Irish sixpences. There is a gap between experience and meaning, between what he feels and what he feels he might feel if pushed.

Roughly the same thing happens in 'I Remember,' except that

the intention there is to *deny* meaning to the place ('I was born here') whose ritual function in our lives we usually take for granted. The meaning of this place is that it has no meaning. For in the stanzas which follow the speaker is as surely characterised by the absence from his childhood of prize-winning poems and tumultuous initiations as he would have been by their presence. Nothing, like something, does happen; although as in 'Church Going' we do not quite know how or why. Both poems complete their descriptions of a particular event before paying attention to the feelings it has aroused: the narrator has signed the book in the church, donated his Irish sixpence and reflected that the place was not worth stopping for; the train has pulled out of Coventry and the two travellers sit back, staring at their shoes. Only then, in the ebbing of event, does the significance of either occasion become apparent. Meaning occurs after the event, as a release from tension (a sprawl) which nevertheless does not quite take account of what occasioned it. Larkin relates individual experience to shared significance by organising them into a temporal succession: first event, then meaning. It is a relation which emphasises difference as much as identity.

He returned to the problem in his next volume, *The Whitsun Weddings*, published in 1964. The first poem, 'Here', describes another journey, but anyone anticipating the clipped impatient tone of 'Church Going' or 'I Remember, I Remember' might well have been taken aback by its enormous opening sentence, which buffets across three intricate stanzas before beaching on a fourth. The length of the sentence announces Larkin's determination that this time the event described (a swerving night-journey into the north-east of England) should last until the poem ends, and that it should produce *by some logic of its own* the necessary shared meaning. If the length of the sentence startles, then so should another feature: the absence of a grammatical subject. Who is the agent of this journey? Who or what is it that, in the long-delayed main clause, 'gathers' to the surprise of a large town? A traveller in a train, presumably. But the traveller does not draw attention to himself, and so insist on the eccentricity of his points of view; he does not remove his bicycle-clips, or decline a British Rail sandwich. He is a spectral presence, a hole in the syntax.

As a result, the narrative itself is able to produce a social symbolism, by making the transition from one landscape to another (from town to countryside to coastline) a movement across different categories of experience and across fractionally different idioms. The town which surprises us first of all is a caricature of materialism, a consumer paradise where all the verbs have become nouns in a dream of pure instrumentality: mixers, toasters, washers, driers. Participial adjectives dominate the description, as though a weight of commercial activity had sunk into people and objects. Beyond the town lies a countryside which clearly belongs to a different category of experience, in that it allows natural process to thrive: leaves thicken, weeds flower, waters quicken, air ascends. Beyond this vegetal abundance of clauses, the land ends: 'Here is unfenced existence.' The coastline is as much a regenerative margin as the frowsty barn in 'Church Going'. But no pilgrim descends to feed his Irish sixpences into the beach-telescope and train it on passing oil-tankers. This time there is no gap between event and meaning, because the journey across different landscapes and different states of mind has itself produced the recognition that somewhere, right out at the edge, purity exists.

As it does in 'The Whitsun Weddings', a more complex and more beautiful statement of the theme. Whitsun is still a holiday, if not any more a Christian one, and the weddings which take place on this particular Whitsun will constitute a rite of passage of some kind, a half-carnival and half-spiritual threshold. But what brings this symbolism home to the sceptical observer who has been caught up by chance in its unfolding? Not so much his saintly benevolence, it would appear, as the sense of an ending (at once physical sensation and moral qualm) produced for all passengers alike by the train's entry into the station:

> I thought of London spread out in the sun,
> Its postal districts packed like squares of wheat:
>
> There we were aimed. And as we raced across
>   Bright knots of rail
> Past standing Pullmans, walls of blackened moss
> Came close, and it was nearly done, this frail
> Travelling coincidence; and what it held
> Stood ready to be loosed with all the power
> That being changed can give. We slowed again
> And as the tightened brakes took hold, there swelled
> A sense of falling, like an arrow-shower
> Sent out of sight, somewhere becoming rain.

Again, the shared meaning is labile: something loosed, something which swells, release into a not unfamiliar image for the relation between lives in a big city. (In Chapter 38 of *Martin Chuzzlewit,* Tom Pinch brushes past Mr. Nadgett, whom he has never met but whose thoughts at that moment are identical to his own. Dickens remarks that in any city the size of London 'there are a multitude who shooting arrows over houses as their daily business, never know on whom they fall'.) But this time meaning does not occur in the aftermath of event. It is produced by the final act of the journey, the moment when the tightened brakes take hold.

For although the narrative does have a grammatical subject, 'I' or 'we', its presence is more spectral than that of 'Church Going', and to some extent offset by the dummy subjects which control two sentences in the final stanza. (A dummy subject is an item of language which fills in for the subject at its usual place before the verb, and which seems empty because it has a syntactic but not a semantic function. In a sentence from the penultimate stanza of 'Church Going' – 'It pleases me to stand in silence here' – the subject clause 'to stand in silence here' has been moved to a position after the verb and replaced by a dummy, 'it'.) On two occasions in the final stanza of 'The Whitsun Weddings' –

> . . . and it was nearly done, this frail
> Travelling coincidence . . .

> . . . there swelled
> A sense of falling . . .

– a dummy replaces the subject phrase. The effect, I think, is to diminish or attenuate the sense of transitive process. 'There swelled a sense of falling': who, exactly, is doing what to whom? Event and meaning, so distinct in 'Church Going' and 'I Remember, I Remember', have begun to merge.

The metaphoric equivalent of this syntactic masking is the trajectory of the journeys undertaken: one a 'swerving' movement east, the other a 'slow and stopping curve southwards'. We are carried across rather than with the grain of the landscape, and so take in by a lateral movement its graduated textures. At the same time, it is important to recognise that these are agnostic journeys, journeys which celebrate the connection between individual experience and shared meaning if and when it occurs, but do little to seek it out or defend it as a moral and political principle.

But by the time Larkin came to publish his next volume, *High Windows,* his work had taken on a different tone, and now showed an unmistakable anxiety about social and political developments during the sixties. This anxiety took comic form in 'Annus Mirabilis', and rather more serious form in 'Going, Going' or 'Homage to a Government', a poem protesting about the withdrawal of British troops from East of Suez. Larkin objects to the decision because it was motivated by expediency rather than by principle. 'I don't mind troops being brought home,' he told an interviewer, 'if we'd decided this was the best thing all round, but to bring them home simply because we couldn't afford to keep them there seemed a dreadful humiliation.' His poem claims that such decisions have made Britain 'a different country', a nation governed according to economic rather than moral or political criteria. Larkin sustained this line of attack throughout *High Windows.*

What gave offence was the pragmatism usually associated with the Labour governments of 1964–6 and 1966–70. Harold Wilson had famously inaugurated a 'white-hot technological revolution' at the 1963 Labour Party Conference. 'In cabinet and boardroom alike,' he declared, 'those with responsibility must be able to speak with the language of the technical age.' The new mood was well, if rather skittishly, caught by Anthony Sampson's *Anatomy of Britain Today.* The first edition of the book had been written in 1962; now, three years later, a second edition registered a 'quite spectacular' change. In the intervening period rationalisation had become a national slogan: 'Even Buckingham Palace has called in efficiency experts.' Wilson had become Prime Minister, the first civil servant and the first Englishman outside the middle or upper class to do so. He may never have got past page 2 of *Das Kapital,* but he had 'acquired, as early as the General Strike (when he was ten), an ability to see individual emotional problems in rational economic terms, which gave him his intense personal interest in (for instance) the dry subject of economic organisation.' It was the translation of those problems into those terms which was to cause Larkin such dismay. As for Harold Wilson, he could be summed up as 'a technocrat of phenomenal efficiency, but with no strong political line'.

The bravado of this utilitarian prodigy combined with Britain's decline as a world power to sanction expediency. Britain, as Dean Acheson remarked, had lost an empire and not yet found a role; or, as others suggested, it had lost its sense of responsibility and found Carnaby Street. 'The old nonconformist ethos,' Sampson reported, 'the sense of work being itself virtuous and self-improving, is being undermined by the new prosperity.' And he cited a government advertisement aimed at the carbuncular young men of the sixties:

> There was a clerk with a worried frown
>   Who got his fellow workers down
> Until one happy day he found
>   He'd won a prize – £1,000.

Teenagers were spending £850 000 000 a year on themselves and admen were being hailed as 'consumption engineers'. 'The crowd / Is young in the M1 café'; Larkin observed in 'Going, Going', 'Their kids are screaming for more . . .' Certainly things had changed between 'the end of the Chatterley ban / And the Beatles' first LP'.

A different but related pragmatism shaped the programme of social reform which was to characterise the decade more effectively than any political or economic developments. The new Labour MPs of 1964 and 1966 were young, middle-class, well-educated and sceptical; to them, social reform was as urgent an issue as, say, nationalisation. And they had a considerable measure of success in this field. In July 1967 homosexual acts between consenting adults over 21 ceased to be an offence. In October 1967 the Abortion Act enabled a woman to have an abortion if she could satisfy two doctors that it was justifiable on medical, social and psychological grounds. In October 1969 the divorce law was amended: divorce could now be granted after two years if it could be shown that the marriage had broken down irretrievably. In 1968 the Theatres Bill ended the reign of the Lord Chamberlain over the London stage. The death penalty, suspended for five years in 1964, was abolished in 1969.

These reforms were of course important in themselves, but they also embodied a fundamental change of attitude towards social issues. The criteria of public morality were now subjected increasingly to scrutiny on utilitarian grounds, both by the supporters and by the opponents of reform. Take the 1967 Divorce Act. Previously, divorce had been allowed if either husband or wife could be shown to have committed a 'matrimonial offence'; it was thus a kind of moral prize awarded to the innocent party, a punishment imposed on the guilty party. The new procedures, on the other hand, were designed to show whether a marriage had broken down irretrievably rather than to determine guilt and innocence. The old 'offences' (adultery, cruelty, desertion) remained, but only as evidence of breakdown. So the new criteria for divorce were pragmatic rather than moral.

Of equal interest were the terms used in the debates about the Act: the concentration on such issues as the welfare of children and dependents, rather than on moral and religious criteria. Even opponents of the Act did not 'take up the moralistic point of view implicit in the old law. They sought rather to justify the old arrangements in terms of the new criteria being used by the reformers.' It was this underlying pragmatism, whether manifested in the divorce courts or in the Foreign Office, that one or two English poets seem to have reacted against. In doing so, they echoed the occasional dissenting voice among politicians. 'I believe,' said Ian Percival, a Conservative lawyer, during the debates about the Divorce Act, 'that there are in this life some things which we cannot understand or put into words although we believe just as sincerely that they matter.'

The increasing dominance of pragmatic criteria in all walks of life may have helped to persuade Larkin that the glancing agnosticism of poems like 'Here' and 'The Whitsun Weddings' was no longer sufficient. For the validity of those things which we believe in even though we cannot understand them was coming under relentless attack; or so it might easily have appeared. And Larkin responded, I believe, by shifting to a far more militant and assertive stance than he had ever adopted before.

Thus the first poem in *High Windows,* 'To the Sea', covers the same ground as 'Here' while marking an important change of emphasis. This time we are already at the coast, and cannot rely on the momentum of a journey to disclose its regenerative purity. Indeed, it is not pure at all, but crammed with activities as ambiguously ceremonial as the Whitsun weddings: 'half an annual pleasure, half a rite'. Whereas the value of the frowsty barn had been implied by a weary after-the-event concession, and the value of the Whitsun weddings had been demonstrated by a

journey's end, the value of these activities on the beach is asserted
by explicit moralising:

> If the worst
> Of flawless weather is our falling short,
> It may be that through habit these do best,
> Coming to water clumsily undressed
> Yearly; teaching their children by a sort
> Of clowning: helping the old, too, as they ought.

'Here' had carried us across teeming townscape and lonely
countryside to the pleasures of 'flawless weather'; 'To the Sea'
stops short of that purity, but it does so decisively and in order to
commit itself to less absolute values. The rhyming of 'sort' with
'ought' hints at reservations, but there can be no doubt that the
connection between individual experience and shared meaning
has been deeply and firmly willed. The speaker has made himself
responsible for it.

Fixed locations replace the swerving trajectories of *The Whitsun
Weddings*, locations such as the beach of 'To the Sea' or the
hemmed-in site of 'Show Saturday'. There is no getting out of it,
the place or the moral response it demands. While the
participants stream away from their half-sacred rite and the Show
'dies back into the area of work,' the narrator stays behind to
utter his valediction: 'Let it always be there.' A superb poem,
'The Building', describes another place whose implications are
not easy to get out of: a hospital waiting-room. Here the narrative
tone is positively imperious, far removed from the prickly
concessions of *The Less Deceived* or the agnosticism of *The Whitsun
Weddings*. Look at the time, the narrator urges, see the people
climbing the stairs, look down into the yard. The sceptical or
remote presences of earlier poems have given way to someone
who refuses on any account to lose sight of those matters which we
believe in even though we cannot understand them. He reappears
in another memorable poem, 'The Old Fools', whose final stanza
turns brutally on a reader lulled into complacency:

> . . . For the rooms grow farther, leaving
> Incompetent cold, the constant wear and tear
>
> Of taken breath, and them crouching below
> Extinction's alp, the old fools, never perceiving

How near it is. This must be what keeps them quiet:
The peak that stays in view wherever we go
For them is rising ground. Can they never tell
What is dragging them back, and how it will end? Not
    at night?
Not when the strangers come? Never, throughout
The whole hideous inverted childhood? Well,
    We shall find out.

Right up until its last line the poem offers us two ways of
appearing to acknowledge the truth of old age while shielding
ourselves from it: an incredulity which shades into contempt and
thus absolves us from the whole pitiful spectacle, and the
Shakespearean grandeur of metaphors like 'extinction's alp' (I
am thinking of Sonnet 63 and 'age's steepy night'). But these
strategies have no power to avert the matter-of-fact conclusion,
where the poet suddenly speaks to us rather than for us. We shall
indeed find out, and all the quicker if we remember earlier poems
by Larkin in which 'well' was a sign of indifference, a shrug of the
shoulders; now it is properly vicious, full of menace.

It seems to me that between *The Whitsun Weddings* and *High
Windows* Larkin began to affirm a connection between individual
experience and shared meaning which he might once have left to
chance. The shaming pragmatism of the sixties drove him to
speak his mind, to give his poems the authority of conscious and
unequivocal dissent.

If I had to find a metaphor for that authority, it would be the
eerie assurance of television correspondents reporting from some
foreign capital. There they stand, babbling about food shortages
and summit meetings, while various citizens peer intently up their
left nostril or aim supermarket trolleys at them from off-camera.
Their sublime indifference to what is going on around them seems
remarkable, until you realise that it is in fact the enveloping
mayhem which gives their reports such buoyancy. After all, to be
the one person reporting back to millions about the state of any
nation must involve a strange accession of authority, and perhaps
makes more sense when the authority is made to rest on the
strangeness. Sit in a studio, and you are assumed to possess a
weight of abstract 'expertise'; stand in the middle of a crowd of
demented foreigners and whatever you say will have been
authorised by your persistence in getting there and your success

in ignoring such frenzied provocations. By the same token, a poet whose 'expertise' concerning public matters may be limited needs some kind of singularity: a voice which will identify not just the speaker, but his or her exhilarating apartness. It is the surrounding Wilsonian mayhem which gives the poems in *High Windows* much of their buoyancy.

* * *

The phrase 'declarative voice' has been used by Seamus Heaney to describe his own attempts, from the early seventies on, to write a more public poetry. Heaney is now as central a figure as Larkin. Reviewing *Field Work* (1979), Christopher Ricks proclaimed him 'the most trusted poet of our islands. (Larkin is now trusted not to produce bad poems, but not necessarily to produce poems.)' Blake Morrison reports that when *North* appeared in 1975, 'it met with the kind of acclaim which, in Britain at least, we had ceased to believe poetry could receive.' Heaney has earned the trust and the acclaim very largely by his response to the Troubles initiated in Belfast in the summer of 1969. 'From that moment,' he has written, 'the problems of poetry moved from being simply a matter of achieving the satisfactory verbal icon to being a search for images and symbols adequate to our predicament . . . I felt it imperative to discover a field of force in which . . . it would be possible to encompass the perspectives of a humane reason and at the same time to grant the religious intensity of the violence its deplorable authenticity and complexity.' This change of emphasis, unlike the one between *The Whitsun Weddings* and *High Windows*, is now a matter of record, and what remains is to consider how far Heaney has been able to take his 'declarative voice'.

The strength of that voice has usually been measured by its provision of 'images and symbols adequate to our predicament', the most famous of which are drawn from descriptions of the Bog People, sacrificial victims of a Danish Iron Age culture. One poem in *North*, 'Punishment', describes an Iron Age adultress who was hung and then drowned in a bog, and compares her fate to that of her 'betraying sisters' in contemporary Ulster – girls who have been tarred and feathered by the IRA for informing or for going out with British soldiers. The image certainly seems 'adequate' to one particular aspect of 'our predicament': the tribal ferocity with which a sectarian group turns on those who have transgressed its laws. But the demand for adequacy of this kind, for the kind of understanding which images alone can bring, is such that it rapidly sponsors extravagant claims. 'It would be going too far,' Blake Morrison argues, 'to suggest that "Punishment" in particular and the Bog poems generally offer a defence of Republicanism; but they are a form of "explanation". Indeed the whole procedure of *North* is such as to give sectarian killing in Ulster a historical respectability which it is not usually given in day-to-day journalism.' But a poem about the way an enclosed society deals with its own can hardly be said to 'explain' more than a limited, if spectacular, part of Irish Republicanism; the analogy should not be taken further than the precise grounds on which it has been made. And if the 'whole procedure' of *North* gives 'historical respectability' to sectarian killing, then it has served only to obscure what has always been a fiercely disputed issue even within the Republican movement: scarcely a reason for preferring it to the accounts given in 'day-to-day journalism'.

Another set of analogies used by Heaney concerns what Morrison calls his 'characteristic compacting of word, territory and sex'. Alarming conflicts within the realm of culture (language, literature, politics) can be explained in terms of a self-evident and immutable distinction within the realm of nature (gender). So Heaney explains the process of composition by comparing it to a 'kind of somnambulist encounter between masculine will and intelligence and feminine clusters of image and emotion'. In this way puzzling and contentious issues can be referred to, and resolved by, a distinction which is supposedly biological and therefore beyond dispute. In poems like 'Ocean's Love to Ireland' and 'Act of Union', and elsewhere, Heaney has cast Britain as an imperialist bruiser and Ireland as a ruined maid. But however vivid such analogies may be, they explain nothing because they are tautologous. For the supposedly natural distinction between masculine will and intelligence and feminine emotion is itself the product of specific cultural forces – including, in Heaney's case, the Roman Catholic faith. It simply reproduces what it is meant to explain, and so prevents any political understanding either of sexual or of national differences.

All these analogies are adequate not so much to the Irish predicament as to the survival of Heaney's poetic gift, and to our expectations about the resilience of poetry. During the Troubles he has perhaps revised and protected an old aptitude, rather than forged a new one. He has not abandoned the 'satisfactory verbal icon', but raised it to a more ambitious vantage. If we receive these new icons gratefully, even where they merge what ought to remain separate, it is because they demonstrate that the imagination can draw coherence and consolation from utter chaos. But I would not want to argue, as Blake Morrison does, that they constitute a public poetry, a form of 'explanation' comparable to those provided by day-to-day journalism.

For public poetry, as Karl Miller pointed out in an essay deploring the failure of writers to confront – in 1971 – the Irish predicament, 'requires a knowledge of and an appetite for public matters'. An appetite for public matters means an appetite for matters which will never yield to coherence or consolation. It means learning the language in which such matters are incoherently and unconsolingly discussed. Whole flotillas of satisfactory verbal icons will not amount to a single public poem if they refuse to say anything at all which (in Miller's words) 'could conceivably be checked or applied or acted on or learnt from'. Heaney himself has recognised this. Miller prints a polemical ballad, 'Craig's Dragoons', written at the time of the Civil Rights marches and circulated anonymously. He also refers to a sequence of poems 'in journalistic vein, with long, loose, conversational lines,' some of which became the second half of *North*. These represent Heaney's most concerted attempt to break with his private idiom and to evolve not simply a public poetry but a 'declarative voice': a voice which declares the speaker as well as his opinions.

However, Heaney's appetite for public matters has never seemed ravenous. The poems in the second half of *North* do speak out, but sometimes only in order to explain that they would really rather not be speaking out at all. They lack the buoyancy and finality of declarative utterance, the sense that a statement has identified the speaker in his singularity and that there can be no going back. Heaney does not find it easy to summon, let alone to emulate, the 'forward youth' of Marvell's 'Horatian Ode'. 'I hate a *moi* situation,' he has said, 'an egotism, a presumption, a *hubris,* and I'm using the bowing down to the mother as a way of saying that.' By this reckoning the poems in the second half of *North* must be said to offer a glance upwards from about the level of the mother's bootstraps.

But there is a gain, because a poem like 'Whatever You Say Say Nothing' does go public. It moves beyond his earlier, more imagistic work in order to take up idioms which a whole range of people might use to articulate their perception of the Troubles.

These idioms have been produced by a dissension which cannot be smoothed over into coherent image or self-evident polarity. Heaney may want to chide their presumption or marvel at their poignancy, but he knows that any poem adequate to the Irish predicament will have to compete with their stern finality: whatever they say, they say something.

Even so, he was clearly not going to make the transition to declarative utterance as smoothly or as emphatically as Larkin had. One has to take into account the organic, inward-looking and rather costive view he holds of his art. He has often spoken of the poet's 'incubating mind', and his discussions of poetry drift relentlessly into talk about motherhood and humility. Lie down, a voice admonishes in 'North',

> Lie down
> in the word-hoard, burrow
> the coil and gleam
> of your furrowed brain.
>
> Compose in darkness.

A poet that conscious of the need to compose in darkness could not have hoped to enter straight away into a fully-fledged declarative voice, a voice in competition with graffiti. He must have expected no more than tiny chemical changes, displacements and resolutions within the word-hoard. I want to follow one such change here, arguing that it eventually served to open rather than seal off the incubating mind.

The piece of the word-hoard in question is a relatively humble one: the modal auxiliary 'would', which often designates a past habit, with the particular sense of characteristic or predictable behaviour. This it does on many occasions in *Death of a Naturalist,* with reference either to habits of the young Heaney or to seasonal occurrences of the world he knew:

> Here, every spring
> I would fill jampotfuls of the jellied
> Specks to range on window-sills at home . . .
> > 'Death of a Naturalist'

> Late August, given heavy rain and sun
> For a full week, the blackberries would ripen.
> > 'Blackberry-picking'

There are other examples of this use of 'would' in 'Churning Day' and 'Follower'. Heaney had of course long since been separated from his rural origins and so, as John Foster remarks, 'his rehearsal of the customs he witnessed or participated in as a child assumes the quality of incantation and commemoration.' What the modal auxiliary does is to relate one custom to another, and thus become for the reader a sign of custom-in-general. The traces of custom and labour cut into it awaken with each subsequent use, for example in several poems from *Wintering Out* ('Fodder', 'The Other Side', 'Fireside', 'Gifts of Rain').

But this sign for custom-in-general was clearly not adequate to Heaney's predicament after 1969. From about that time his poetry began to incorporate, alongside the familiar sense of 'would', a new sense, a fiercer optative mood in which it substitutes for 'would like to'. 'Freedman', a poem from the second half of *North*, marks the change. At first the speaker recalls only his unthinking subservience to habit:

> I would kneel to be impressed by ashes,
> A silk friction, a light stipple of dust –
> I was under that thumb too like all my caste.

But he goes on record how this subservience was broken by a new mood:

> Then poetry arrived in that city –
> I would abjure all cant and self-pity –
> And poetry wiped my brow and sped me.
> Now they will say I bite the hand that fed me.

The second line of this stanza could belong to the past tense of the first and third lines, or to the present tense of the fourth; it could refer to a past habit of abjuring or to a pledge renewed in the present. But the optative sense of 'would' seems much the stronger, linking powerfully with the present moment of the fourth line, and contrasting openly with the habitual subservience described in the earlier stanza. It marks a shift from an identity defined by social and seasonal pattern to an identity defined by pledging declarative utterance. A little too pledging, perhaps, in this case.

For the necessary ritual now has to be fetched from afar, by an act of will which identifies the speaker, rather than simply commemorated. Heaney makes his pledge in 'Funeral Rites':

> Now as news comes in
> of each neighbourly murder
> we pine for ceremony,
> customary rhythms:
>
> the temperate footsteps
> of a cortège, winding past
> each blinded home.
> I would restore
>
> the great chamber of Boyne,
> prepare a sepulchre
> under the cupmarked stones.

Even the stanza-break draws attention to the pining and the pledge rather than the ceremony; that, I think, indicates a considerable difference from the early poems. Heaney has allowed the declarative sense of 'would' to thrust in alongside the commemorative sense which had provided the keynote for much of his previous work. Of course, one subsidence among the word-hoard does not make a public poetry. But it might be regarded as a preparation, like the idioms of 'Whatever you Say Say Nothing'. In his next volume, *Field Work,* Heaney was to extend the optative sense of 'would' to encompass other pledging desires: his own in the fifth of the 'Glanmore Sonnets', that of the poet's wife in 'Afterwards', that of the damned in 'Ugolino'.

Another poem in *Field Work,* 'Casualty', gives some idea of how this change in the word-hoard might open the way towards political statement. 'Casualty' uses the same verse-form as Yeats's 'Easter 1916', and seems to me Heaney's finest attempt at a public poem. Again, though, it has as much to do with the poet's resolve to confront public matters as with public matters themselves; the draft versions, provided for a reading at University College London in 1977, show how much of a struggle he had even to get that far. Indeed, the poem in its final version opens with a straightforward commemoration of characteristic and predictable behaviour:

> He would drink by himself
> And raise a weathered thumb
> Towards the high shelf,
> Calling another rum
> And blackcurrant, without

Having to raise his voice,
Or order a quick stout
By a lifting of the eyes
And a discreet dumb-show
Of pulling off the top;
At closing time would go
In waders and peaked cap
Into the showery dark . . .

The second 'would' picks up swiftly from the first, eliding the
grammatical subject in order to bring into focus the habits which
made up an identity. For this is a proudly commemorative art,
sensitive to the last ungainly detail: that rum and blackcurrant,
for example, tucked into the turn of a line.

But Heaney's attempt to evoke the fisherman's habits is met by
something which never troubled the early poems; it is met by the
fisherman's attempt to evoke *his* habits, to prise out some emblem
of the poetic life. Any curiosity around was mutual, and must be
allowed to touch the nature of elegiac reflection as well as the
nature of the habits commemorated:

But my tentative art
His turned back watches too:
He was blown to bits
Out drinking in a curfew
Others obeyed, three nights
After they shot dead
The thirteen men in Derry.
PARAS THIRTEEN, the walls said,
BOGSIDE NIL. That Wednesday
Everybody held
His breath and trembled.

An earlier version had spoken of a 'kept, wilting art' rather than a
'tentative art'. 'Kept' and 'wilting' recall the self-chastisement of
the poems in the second half of *North*; 'tentative' properly
characterises the poet's uncertainty, without making a song and
dance of it. The final version recognises that Heaney cannot
afford simply to commemorate and then to chastise himself for
being able to do no more that commemorate. He must also
explain, turn his art outwards to the events and the idioms which
produced this death; he owes it to the fisherman's curiosity about
him. So the passage now incorporates what the walls have said as

well as what the poet has said.

The second section of 'Casualty' begins to take account of
political circumstances. A description of the common funeral
accorded to the thirteen men killed in Derry establishes the
strength of Republican solidarity on this occasion, a solidarity
which the fisherman ignored by drinking in the wrong pub at the
wrong time:

> But he would not be held
> At home by his own crowd
> Whatever threats were phoned,
> Whatever black flags waved.

This refusal was both an act of will and an instinctive obedience to
rhythm and routine ('he *would* not be held . . .'). The binding of
individuality to habit makes it impossible to dismiss the
fisherman's behaviour as contrary. His death implies the death of
a social art as well as a pledge, and so becomes a political question
too intractable for commemoration or the fanatic's cursorily
rueful shrug:

> How culpable was he
> That last night when he broke
> Our tribe's complicity?
> 'Now you're supposed to be
> An educated man,'
> I hear him say. 'Puzzle me
> The right answer to that one.'

The earlier version I have already quoted from added seven
further lines at this point, which then formed the poem's
conclusion and gave it an altogether different slant:

> Culpable as the eel
> Obedient to its own
> Rhythms? And as neutral?
>
> Sometimes men obtain
> A power when they betray
> And swim out from the shoal,
> Daring to make free.

These lines resolve the man's stubbornness into its component
parts: on one hand, an addiction to habit as unthinking and as
'neutral' as the eel's obedience to its own rhythms; and on the

other, a wilful and defiant resolve to go his own way. But the stubbornness has political meaning only if it is both at the same time: a tribal loyalty in conflict with other tribal loyalties sponsored by a particular society, and yet also a conscious choice. Then the commemorator cannot avert to the stabilising and cohesive power of ritual, while the fanatic cannot go on about this being no time for romantic individualism. Then we are faced by a real question, and Heaney was right to cut the extra lines and rely on the fisherman's own words to pose it.

The question cannot be answered by any image or analogy which would reduce the conflicting loyalties to coherence, or to coherent polarity. Yeats argued in 'Easter 1916' that Republicanism had transformed haphazard and noncommittal lives into a 'terrible beauty'. Heaney measures the impact of 'terrible beauty' on already purposeful and committed lives: an issue which both the partisan and the indifferent would be unwise to neglect. He has no answer to the question except a voice as declarative in its way as the fisherman's stubbornness, and so his 'tentative art' rises in the third and final section of the poem to a natural eloquence the equal of anything he has written:

> . . . that morning
> I was taken in his boat,
> The screw purling, turning
> Indolent fathoms white,
> I tasted freedom with him.
> To get out early, haul
> Steadily off the bottom,
> Dispraise the catch, and smile
> As you find a rhythm
> Working you, slow mile by mile,
> Into your proper haunt
> Somewhere, well out, beyond . . .
>
> Dawn-sniffing revenant,
> Plodder through midnight rain,
> Question me again.

11 Playing havoc

At the same time as Philip Larkin and Seamus Heaney were evolving declarative voices, other English poets began to modify the pathos and the singularity of their own earlier poems. The dialectic of saying and not-saying stretched at one extreme into forthright thesis and at the other into new kinds of sidelong utterance. The poets I have in mind are Ted Hughes, Geoffrey Hill and J. H. Prynne. Each of them published a book – *Crow* (1970), *Mercian Hymns* (1971), *Brass* (1971) – which marks a significant, although perhaps temporary, change of emphasis. These books vary enormously in style and subject-matter. Indeed, they seem worlds apart: Faber must by now have sold well over 40 000 copies of *Crow*, whereas *Brass* was originally printed by the Ferry Press in an edition of 250 (it can be found in *Poems*, published by Agneau 2 in 1982). I shall none the less argue that they have each played a comparable part in the careers of their respective authors, and that taken together they represent an opportunity for English poetry which is now in some danger of fading.

The terms I shall use to clarify the change of emphasis wrought by each book derive from my discussion of Frank O'Hara. All three English poets have at times attempted to give their work a mythic or historical or political scope which over-reaches what O'Hara took to be his province. But each of them tended in his earlier poems to memorialise feelings (not necessarily his own feelings), and to dote on the pathos of subjectivity. Each of them then wrote a book which reverses this tendency. They have all glimpsed an aquiline serpent coming to resemble the Medusa.

In a recent essay on Hughes and Hill and Larkin, Seamus Heaney has tried to define their differently founded and cadenced memorial acts. 'All of them,' Heaney writes, 'return to an origin and bring something back, all three live off the hump of the English poetic achievement, all three, here and now, in England, imply a continuity with another England, there and then.' He believes that all three have sought a lost origin, the birth processes of mind and language and nationhood. It is not that the other England can be recreated in the present. But the search for another England, the return and bringing back, confers an authentic singularity; put crudely, it gives the poet something to say and a way of saying it. What is at stake is the *pathos* of origins, the rhetorical effect to be derived from an exploration of that fictional moment when things happened for the first time, and when the response to events was not distorted or impeded by the memory of previous encounters. In that moment, perhaps, it might have been possible to act truly and spontaneously. Even though we cannot experience such moments, we must and do cherish their possibility, their pastness and tantalising imminence. The fascination with them runs deep in our literature, as deep as Troilus's first sight of Criseyde in the temple, or Eve's hymn to Adam in paradise. It is a fascination which inflects many a poem by Hughes and Hill and Prynne. But it does not characterise their work as a whole. Each of them turns away from the pathos of origins to meet anti-pathos, a force in human behaviour which will have nothing to do with origins.

* * *

The pathos of a lost spontaneity (a lost unity of thought and action) has long since become the convention according to which the poems of Ted Hughes are read. Hence, I think, the fact that so many critics look to find in them something as direct as a punch on the nose. Geoffrey Thurley speaks of Hughes's 'enormous masculine energy'. 'The language sweats and strains under the load,' he says of 'October Dawn'. Keith Sagar maintains that the words of *Hawk in the Rain* 'leap off the page to strike or grapple with the reader'. John Carey reports 'language as physical as a bruise' in *Moortown*. Reading 'The Jaguar', Robert Stuart is assaulted by a 'solid phalanx of buffeting verbs and steel-heeled nouns'. It all sounds like a bad afternoon down at White Hart Lane.

Such expectations code the poems as direct and spontaneous utterances, utterances so distinct from commonplace speech that they might be held to recreate the flash of thought striking home in the purity of an original moment. Fallen creatures that we are, expelled from any original moment, we can only glimpse the flash in a weapon striking home, a boot going in. By wishing violence and masculine energy on Hughes's poetry, we seek to absolve it from the serpentine indirections of language and the uncertainty they induce. Restored to innocence – to an art without memory or misgiving – the poetry will then cast its aura forward over the violence and masculine energy we want to enjoy. We can thrill to sweat and steel heels. An interest in violence of feeling and action – in anti-pathos – is legitimate, indeed scarcely avoidable. But should we remove it from history, as Hughes's critics have done by denying the discursiveness of his poetry?

In doing so, they are following the poet, who has tended to concern himself with *pristine* anti-pathos; most notably, perhaps, in 'Hawk Roosting'. The hawk sits on a treetop, or hovers expectantly, searching the ground for prey. No falsifying consciousness intrudes between his hooked head and his hooked feet, or troubles his perpetually smooth transition from purpose to deed. His ruthlessness is not commonplace, but *original*, possible only in a mind with no history where things always happen as though for the first time. It is the ruthlessness, Hughes has said, not of a Hitler, but of a primal creator and lawgiver: Nature, Jehovah, Isis.

However, although the anti-pathos Hughes celebrates may not have a history, the image he proposes for it most certainly does. Indeed, the image has a rather pathetic history. His hawk roosts more or less where Satan sits, in Book 4 of *Paradise Lost,* enjoying a prospect of the earth's face and like a cormorant 'devising death / To them who lived.' Satan even makes an affecting speech on the occasion. Keats provided a more homely context for this devising of death. 'The greater part of Men,' he wrote,

> make their way with the same instinctiveness, the same unwandering eye from their purposes, the same animal eagerness as the Hawk – The Hawk wants a Mate, so does the Man – look at them both they set about it and procure one in the same manner – They want both a nest and they both set about one in the same manner – they get their food in the same manner – The noble animal Man for his amusement smokes his pipe – the Hawk balances about the Clouds – that is the only difference of their leisures.

In Keats's eyes the ruthlessness of the hawk was unoriginal and comparable to everyday human behaviour. Bird and man are equally liable to the pathos and the absurdity of instinctiveness.

Hawks balance about the clouds in several of Auden's early poems, including one ('The strings' excitement, the applauding drums') where they represent a very human and unoriginal nostalgia:

> Yet there's no peace in this assaulted city
> But speeches at the corners, hope for news,
> Outside the watchfires of a stronger army.
>
> And all emotions to expression come,
> Recovering the archaic imagery:
> This longing for assurance takes the form
>
> Of a hawk's vertical stooping from the sky . . .

Here the hawk's prey is that which will repair an emotional lack. It is again as recognisable and as fallible as Keats's pipe-smoker.

Hughes's engaging bird cannot altogether escape these associations. It too balances about the clouds for amusement, affably expounding the advantages of its situation. It too is faintly pathetic and faintly absurd, like its pipe-smoking opposite in Keats's fantasy. Hughes's return to an original creator and law-giver, to Nature, has taken a form long since assimilated to our cultural repertoire, long since adapted to express the pathos of lost origins. What speaks in 'Hawk Roosting' is neither Nature nor Adolf Hitler, but Romantic tradition.

What also speaks in the poem is its literary mode, dramatic monologue. Dramatic monologue is a mode designed to convey pathos rather than anti-pathos. The subjectivity of the speaker in Browning's 'My Last Duchess' engages us, however much we might deplore his murder of a first wife and intention to marry a second for her money. 'We suspend moral judgment,' Robert Langbaum says, 'because we prefer to participate in the duke's power and freedom, in his hard core of character fiercely loyal to itself.' Hughes's hawk does not attract us by a display of primal ruthlessness, but by a hard core of character fiercely loyal to itself, by vivid subjectivity. He prides himself on his ruthlessness, and by that tiny flicker of selfhood is displaced from purity of mind.

Two other notable representations of the birth processes of mind, Gog and Wodwo, are similarly displaced by dramatic monologue from utter spontaneity. We warm to them as we do to Browning's Caliban.

I do not want to labour the point. But it seems to me that Hughes's attempt to describe anti-pathos only generates pathos. In the first place, he insists on describing an *original* ruthlessness, and thus invites the pathos attached to any lost paradise, the pathos of exile and distance. In the second place, his image for ruthlessness has long since been assimilated and coloured by Romantic tradition. In the third place, he employs a poetic mode devised to express the pathos of antipathetic characters. Falsifying consciousness may not intrude between the hooked head and the hooked feet of the hawk, but it certainly does intrude between the hooked feet of the poem and the hooked head of the reader. The same could be said of much of the work in *Selected Poems 1957–1967.*

It may be that Hughes has always meant to generate pathos; and it may be the pathos generated by his poems which has ensured their popularity. But his readers will surely have discerned, as well, an interest in anti-pathos, an interest imperfectly articulated by the bulk of his writing but scarcely negligible. I think that *Crow* does articulate this interest, and that it does so by revising the procedures of the earlier poems. Crow's universe has two creators, and is thus un-original from the start. He himself is a constant affront to any idea of animal nobility. And he has great trouble delivering himself of a curse, never mind a dramatic monologue.

The book is incomplete, a fragment of a much longer tale. But one may doubt whether Hughes will complete it, and whether completion would resolve it. It seems unfinishable, rather than unfinished – a quest for origins perpetually and necessarily sidetracked. Ekbert Faas worries that just as *The Waste Land* sent critics in pursuit of the story of the Holy Grail, a story whose coherence would resolve the fragmentariness of the poem before them, so Hughes's sequence will send them on 'a wild goose chase after crows' (or a wild crow chase after geese?). But far from being resolved by the coherence of other narratives, *Crow* manages to render *them* incoherent by multiplying vulgar and horribly garbled versions of them. It might almost be part of the 'Bible of Hell' announced by Blake in *The Marriage of Heaven and Hell*: a counter-myth, Creation and Fall seen from a different point of view. Crow is to the hawk roosting what Blake's Satan is to Milton's Satan, a creature justified but also emptied of pathos.

The Genesis of Blake's Bible of Hell was the *First Book of Urizen*. Urizen is expelled from Eternity for despotism rather than for disobedience, and his expulsion results in the creation of a universe which must be considered a punishment rather than a gift. In the eighth chapter, he surveys his domain:

> 1. Urizen explored his dens –
> Mountain, moor and wilderness,
> With a globe of fire lighting his journey,
> A fearful journey, annoyed
> By cruel enormities, forms
> Of life on his forsaken mountains.
>
> 2. And his world teemed vast enormities
> Frightening, faithless, fawning
> Portions of life, similitudes
> Of a foot, or a hand, or a head,
> Or a heart, or an eye, they swam – mischievous
> Dread terrors, delighting in blood.

Since Urizen's crime was selfishness and unimaginative law-making, the world he creates after his expulsion can only contain nightmare repetitions. It is not unlike the world revealed by 'Crow Alights', a world of 'herded mountains' and fuming stars:

> In the hallucination of the horror
> He saw this shoe, with no sole, rain-sodden,
> Lying on a moor.
> And there was this garbage can, bottom rusted away,
> A playing place for the wind, in a waste of puddles.
>
> There was this coat, in the dark cupboard, in the
>   silent room, in the silent house.
> There was this face, smoking its cigarette
>   between the dusk window and the fire's embers.
>
> Near the face, this hand, motionless.
>
> Near the hand, this cup.
>
> Crow blinked. He blinked. Nothing faded.

Here too Creation looks more like a crime than a gift. The demonstratives – this coat, this face, this hand, this cup – offer an unwanted and redundant intimacy, which we might contrast with the warm particularity of Auden's 'Consider this and in our time':

> The clouds rift suddenly – look there
> At cigarette-end smouldering on a border
> At the first garden party of the year.

The detail takes root in our imagination. But Crow's narrowing inquisitiveness only blights an already blighted landscape.

We are of course seeing things from a point of view other than that provided by the Book of Genesis, whose characters start acting out of character the moment they enter Crow's world (see, for example, 'Apple Tragedy'). The aim is to put about as many stories as possible, or as many versions of one story, rather than to describe a first-coming creator and so nurture the pathos of origins. In Lévi-Strauss's terms, the versions of Crow's world constitute a myth testifying to the transformative power of the imagination, rather than a ritual replete with nostalgia for immediacy.

Crow does not have much time for dramatic monologues. Indeed, he does not have much time for subjectivity, let alone for any desire to express it. He is a sequence of events, of initiatives and sharp rebuffs. David Lodge has quite rightly compared him to the kind of cartoon-character who is propelled through a wall with such force that he leaves a hole corresponding to his own shape, or flattened by a steamroller and then peeled off the ground, but who always survives. Crow, in short, demanded a rhetoric flatter than dramatic monologue, more appropriate to the complete absence of subjectivity.

What Hughes found for him was, I believe, roughly comparable to the gestic idioms evolved by Brecht and Pound during the thirties. Although where Brecht and Pound would have agreed that those idioms were designed to present in one case the contradictions and in the other case the authoritative unity of a particular historical moment, Hughes might claim a more universal frame of reference. But if their versions of gest seem only roughly comparable, they are comparably rough, related by a disregard of delicate harmonies and by the importance they give to the clause as a unit of expression. Brecht had seen each clause as a gest enacting some movement of mind and body; Pound arranged his documentary sources with a similar idea in view, picking out and redistributing their major emphases. In *Crow* the boundary between clauses becomes the boundary between characters or between characters and the world.

In 'Crow's Song of Himself', Crow establishes his identity by capturing the main clause of God's sentence:

> When God buried Crow in the earth
> He made man
> When God tried to chop Crow in two
> He made woman
> When God said: 'You win, Crow,'
> He made the Redeemer.
>
> When God went off in despair
> Crow stopped his beak and started in on the two thieves.

God's departure gives Crow the chance to construct and occupy a gest of his own, to become a subject rather than an object. These when-clauses are a favourite device, because they express so perfectly the cause-and-effect relation which obtains between people and things in Crow's world. Sometimes they are arranged in couplets, as here or in 'Crow and Mama'; sometimes they structure a whole poem ('That Moment', 'Crow and the Birds', 'A Horrible Religious Error'). No trace of subjectivity escapes from these impregnable airtight clauses, nor do they ever become part of a continuous narrative.

The idiom of *Crow*, in short, is not conducive to pathos. It works back over the ground covered by Hughes's earlier poems, revising their tolerance of subjectivity. Whereas *Wodwo's* encounter with the natural world had led him to interrogate his own stirrings of consciousness, Crow's arrival at the sea in 'Crow on the Beach' prompts a question which reveals his armoured separateness:

> He knew he was the wrong listener unwanted
> To understand or help –
>
> His utmost gaping of brain in his tiny skull
> Was just enough to wonder, about the sea,
>
> What could be hurting so much?

The utmost gaping of Wodwo's brain had yielded a first tentative push into subjectivity. Crow's brain just gapes, at a world it can feel nothing towards. 'Wodwo' more or less abandons punctuation in its attempt to follow the mercurial shifts of a particular consciousness. 'Crow on the Beach' sharpens the distinction between lines and between clauses.

'Thrushes', a poem from *Lupercal,* had contrasted the self-admiring stoicism of most human beings with the 'automatic purpose' of genius (Mozart) and with the start and bounce and stab of birds hunting for worms. But Hughes cannot bring himself to admit that such behaviour extends beyond a few glamorously alien beings (Mozart, sharks), those last representatives of a unity of thought and action disrupted by our pusillanimous civilisation. Layers of biblical and sub-Blakean cadence smother the precise image of bounce and stab. 'Crow Tyrannosaurus', on the other hand, finds an idiom flat enough to carry its menace into the heart of commonplace behaviour:

> Crow thought 'Alas
> Alas ought I
> To stop eating
> And try to become the light?'
>
> But his eye was a grub. And his head,
>   trapsprung, stabbed.
> And he listened
> And he heard
> Weeping
>
> Grubs   grubs   the stabbed   he stabbed
> Weeping
> Weeping
>
> Weeping he walked and stabbed
>
> Thus came the eye's
>   roundness
>   the ear's deafness.

Such single-mindedness has been a feature of Crow's world from the beginning, but it does not persist only in those exceptional creatures whose automatic purpose has never been distracted by

any falsifying dream. It also masters those who have been
troubled into consciousness by questions like 'ought I to stop
eating and try to become the light?' In Crow's world, as in ours,
pathos (weeping) and anti-pathos (the eye's roundness, the ear's
deafness) coexist: neither seems all that original any more. Thus
Tolstoy, whose cruelty had been the subject of 'Kreutzer Sonata'
in *Wodwo,* reappears in 'Revenge Fable' as a parenthetic example
of mother-hatred: this time his genius does not so much excuse
him as connect him to the rest of us.

Crow, of course, spends less time drying his eyes than
cultivating their 'roundness'. What separates him from other
beings is the degree to which he is characterised by the spirit of
anti-pathos. If he comes to any conclusion, it is that he owes
allegiance not to the God of pathos but to a more distant and
perhaps equally powerful God of anti-pathos. In 'Crow's
Theology', he works out that the God of pathos loves him, but
also that there are things in the world which the God of pathos
would find it hard to love as much as him:

> And he realized what God spoke Crow –
> Just existing was His revelation.
>
> But what
> Loved the stones and spoke stone?
> They seemed to exist too.
> And what spoke that strange silence
> After his clamour of caws faded?
>
> And what loved the shot-pellets
> That dribbled from those strung-up mummifying crows?
> What spoke the silence of lead?

An earlier poem, 'November', would have found a quick answer
to the last question. There, a gamekeeper's gibbet –

> owls and hawks
> By the neck, weasels, a gang of cats, crows:
> Some, stiff, weightless, twirled like dry bark bits
>
> In the drilling rain

– was a test of the poet's ability to feel with others, to be moved. Those corpses, and the pellets dribbling from them, were the creatures of a God of Pathos. But Crow sees it differently:

> Crow realised there were two Gods –
>
> One of them much bigger than the other
> Loving his enemies
> And having all the weapons.

Hughes's Bible of Hell brings into play a second God, a God who speaks the silence after the clamour of caws has faded. For the moment the God of pathos has the upper hand, but Crow's resilience may yet confound His authority.

Hughes has established the ordinariness of anti-pathos, the sheer frequency of those moments when an 'automatic purpose' overrides our capacity to recognise the feelings of others. He has even tried to give it a seat in the body, a zone equivalent to the consciousness inhabited by the spirit of pathos. 'In the beginning was Scream,' announces Crow's 'Lineage', and like a scream his anti-pathos has no easily identifiable source. Breathtakingly irresponsible, produced neither by mind nor body, it destroys all self-possession. Various other poems, such as 'A Grin', try to define this impulse without origin, domicile or design. What distinguishes *Crow* from the earlier work is a fascination with the way anti-pathos inheres in quite recognisable human experiences. Hughes has been neither the inventor nor the advocate of such behaviour. But it seems plain to me that what he is talking about deserves to be talked about, and that he has found a witty and emphatic language for his thoughts on the subject.

It also seems plain that he would want to put things differently. A recent defence of *Crow* attempts to reinstate the poem as a quest for lost origins, and so manages to sentimentalise it quite balefully. Crow himself, it turns out, represents the 'optimism of the sperm', still chugging along in 'biological glee' after all those millions of years, plucky little fellow. We learn that the morality of the sperm

> is undeniably selfish, from all points of view but its own and the future's ('A standing cock knows no conscience' – Scots proverb) and innate in it is a certain hardness of ego, over-purposeful, nickel-nosed, defensively plated, all attention

rigidly outward and forward: the ego of the sign for Mars. But the paradox is, this spirit has at the same time no definable ego at all – only an obscure bundle of inheritance, a sackful of impulses jostling to explore their scope. And from beginning to end, the dynamo of this little mob of selves is a single need to search – for marriage with its creator, a marriage that will be a self-immolation in new, greater and other life.

My enthusiasm for *Crow* is not exactly heightened by the thought that it might all have something to do with the way Scotsmen defer to their pricks. I can accept Hughes's description of Crow as a sackful of impulses, but I am not convinced by his further assertion that what motivates the sackful is a 'single need' to return to its creator. If we do accept that second assertion, we lose the whole enquiry into an unoriginal and unregenerate aspect of human behaviour, and we gain an eighteenth-century novel: a sentimental picaresque tale about a young fellow who gets laid frequently and beaten up even more frequently but does not forsake the mother he has never known. In their present state the poems provide little evidence to support such an interpretation; they tell us a great deal about the jostling impulses, but precious little about marriage and transcendence. Indeed, it may be the interpretation itself which is the quest for origins: a memory of the moment when *Crow* was conceived and might perhaps have turned out other than it has.

Crow *is* the ego of the sign for Mars. But why should we have to look for a metaphysical frame of reference which might ennoble and sentimentalise his war-lust, rather than for a historical frame of reference which makes it actual? After all, the book was written at a time when the Vietnam war had achieved a murderous and widely-reported stalemate. 'We are dreaming,' Hughes said in 1970, 'a perpetual massacre.' He described people watching their dream unfold on TV 'in attitudes of total disengagement, a sort of anaesthetized unconcern'. I think one might argue that such total disengagement was an attitude bred by the special conditions of the Vietnam war, a war with much technology and much publicity but little reason and less pathos.

There was the anaesthetic of a sense of racial superiority. Michael Herr remembers hearing a colonel explain the whole business in terms of protein: 'We were a nation of high-protein, meat-eating hunters, while the other guy just ate rice and a few grungy fish heads. We were going to club him to death with our meat . . .' The purposes of such an assumption is of course to make it possible (indeed honourable) to feel nothing at all about one's enemy or rival. Then there was the anaesthetic of technological superiority: ' "Air sports", one gunship pilot called it, and then went on to describe it with fervour, "Nothing finer, you're up there at two thousand, you're God, just open up the flexies and watch it pee, nail those slime to the paddy wall, nothing finer, double back and get the caribou." '

Yet this total disengagement from moral and emotional criteria could itself become addictive, a kind of passion, as Michael Herr explains:

> Life-as-movie, war-as-movie, war-as-life; a complete process if you got to complete it, a distinct path to travel, but dark and hard, not any easier if you knew that you'd put your own foot on it yourself, deliberately and – most roughly speaking– consciously. Some people took a few steps along it and turned back, wised up, with and without regrets. Many walked on and just got blown off it.

Whatever this passion is, it does not seem to be all that remote from 'Crow's Battle Fury':

> A hair's breadth out of the world
>
>> (With his flared off face glued back into position
>> A dead man's eyes plugged back into his sockets
>> A dead man's heart screwed in under his ribs
>> His tattered guts stitched back into position
>> His shattered brains covered with a steel cowl)
>
>> He comes forward a step,
>>> and a step,
>>>> and a step –

Battle fury is only one of the many impulses which skid across Crow's ego, but it surely owes something to Hughes's perception of a war which had emptied those who fought it and those who saw it on their TV screens of any concern except unconcern. 'Crow's Account of the Battle' demonstrates how quickly a sense of the overwhelming pathos of war –

Then everybody wept,
Or sat, too exhausted to weep,
Or lay, too hurt to weep

– can turn into a sense of its overwhelming anti-pathos:

. . . shooting somebody through the midriff
Was too like striking a match
Too like potting a snooker ball
Too like tearing up a bill
Blasting the whole world to bits
Was too like slamming a door
Too like dropping in a chair
Exhausted with rage
Too like being blown to bits yourself
Which happened too easily
With too like no consequences.

Striking a match, potting a snooker ball, tearing up a bill, slamming a door: these are gestures of anti-pathos, mechanically efficient releases of energy which may express violence or emptiness but never sympathy. In warfare and in Crow's world they become endemic, and quite possibly terminal. Hughes's poem uncovers the fatal connection between temporary lapses into anti-pathos and our talent for blowing the world to bits.

I believe that *Crow* was produced by an abrupt swerve away from Hughes's obsession with the pathos of origins, and I want to defend its recalcitrance of theme and idiom, and its relevance to a particular time and place. But I would have to concede that his own defence of the poem and his more recent work – particularly the saccharine *Gaudete* (1977) – have fully restored the obsession.

* * *

In the final pages of his book *The Art of the Real,* Eric Homberger speaks of a 'contention' between Geoffrey Hill and Ted Hughes, a 'starkly presented choice between history and transcendence or myth'. There clearly is a choice, but it seems to me a choice between equally vivid obsessions with the pathos of origins. While Hughes returns to a lost unity of thought and action, Hill returns to what he has described, adapting a remark by Christopher Devlin, as 'the lost kingdom of innocence and original justice':

I would want to avail myself of Devlin's phrase, because I think there's a real sense in which every fine and moving poem bears witness to this lost kingdom of innocence and original justice. In handling the English language the poet makes an act of recognition that etymology is history. The history of the creation and debasement of words is a paradigm of the loss of the kingdom of innocence and original justice.

Hill does not believe that his lost kingdom can be restored; but his return to it in imagination identifies and stabilises his poetic voice. For him, the function of poetry is to embody the pathos of our allegiance to and betrayal of a kingdom which can never be restored.

As far as I know nobody has ever admired the physique or the punch-on-the-nose vivacity of Hill's verse, although one critic has ventured the rather more tricky thought that there are moments when 'Hill's power-pack becomes a log-jam'. Yet the poems in his first book, *For the Unfallen* (1959), certainly bulge or choke with something. One mannerism, which could be illustrated from almost any of them, is the use of participial adjectives. 'Drake's Drum' speaks of 'Tide-padded thick shallows' and 'The Death of Shelley' of 'frothed shallows'; we do not see these shallows as they are but as the residue of a process (padding, frothing) which has made them what they are. Again and again a verb those tense refers to the past is used to modify a noun which refers to an object assumed to exist in the present. 'The Lowlands of Europe' describes the 'much-scarred, much-scoured terrain' of Europe, its 'attested liberties' and its produce 'stuffed with artistry and substantial gain'. 'Requiem for the Plantagenet Kings' meditates on 'well-dressed alabaster and proved spurs', on spirits 'secure in the decay / Of blood, blood-marks, crowns hacked and coveted,' and imagines the judgment day when 'sleeked groin, gored head, / Budge through the clay . . .' These participial adjectives carry the pathos of history, the memory of the scarring and attesting and proving and coveting and goring which have expelled us from the kingdom of innocence and original justice. Occasionally they part to allow a glimpse of those who, through virtue or ignorance, still inhabit the kingdom: the 'unfallen' of the book's title. The child-king in 'Picture of a Nativity' rests 'undisturbed' among beasts with 'flesh-buttered' claws. The temptress in 'The Re-birth of Venus' is 'sea-scoured', but nevertheless lies 'unflurried' in an estuary. In other poems a 'bidden guest' cannot leave his heart's 'unbroken room' and Thomas watches 'unsearched, unscratched' as Christ shoulders the cross. Their pathos is not to have entered history.

Hill's next volume, *King Log* (1968), began to experiment with dramatic monologue as a further way of establishing the pathos of certain moments in and out of history. An example would be 'Ovid in the Third Reich', which in the opinion of Christopher Ricks 'says what can be said for those Germans who remained silent' and 'at the same time says what must be said against them'. Hill, in other words, does not go for broke, and any sympathy we may feel for his protagonists is finely balanced against judgment. In his work, the pathos of the subjectivity revealed by dramatic monologue 'bears witness' to the lost kingdom, but is not allowed to become a kingdom in its own right.

This tension characterises the centrepiece of the volume, 'Funeral Music', 'a commination and an alleluia for the period popularly but inexactly known as the Wars of the Roses'. The noblemen it commemorates do speak, but sometimes only to criticise their own relentless clamour for attention:

> 'Prowess, vanity, mutual regard,
> It seemed I stared at them, they at me.
> That was the gorgon's true and mortal gaze:
> Averted conscience turned against itself.'
> A hawk and a hawk-shadow. 'At noon,
> As the armies met, each mirrored the other;
> Neither was outshone. So they flashed and vanished
> And all that survived them was the stark ground
> Of this pain. I made no sound, but once
> I stiffened as though a remote cry
> Had heralded my name. It was nothing . . .'

As in O'Hara's poem, the pathos-machine (the heart bubbling with red ghosts) produces its own antidote: a Medusa-head. But even this irreconcilable opposition seems rather pitiful when seen against the mirrored antagonism of armies on the battlefield. The voice fades out. For the pathos of these fragments of subjectivity must not be allowed an easy victory over the process which has quelled them – the kind of victory, say, that Eliot allowed Richard

III or Yeats allowed Robert Emmet. In a commentary on 'Funeral Music', Hill wrote that he had intended an 'ornate and heartless music punctuated by mutterings, blasphemies and cries for help'. Yet the conclusion of the sequence announces that pathos has, after all, triumphed:

> If it is without
> Consequence when we vaunt and suffer, or
> If it is not, all echoes are the same
> In such eternity. Then tell me, love,
> How that should comfort us – or anyone
> Dragged half-unnerved out of this worldly place,
> Crying to the end 'I have not finished'.

As Andrew Waterman says, the 'grave abstractness' of these lines is offset 'by that personalizing "love", that final cry'. The intimate address to another cuts across the drift of the passage, resurrecting by sheer lyric verve a shape out of the lost kingdom. Poetry has been called in to salvage some comfort from the endlessly discomforting process of history.

King Log left Hill where *Wodwo* had left Hughes: facing an issue part of which was out of range of the instruments at his disposal. Hughes was only able to focus those qualities in human behaviour which excite neither pity nor contempt by consigning them to a state of primal innocence, and so turning them into an object of pathos. He could say how it might feel to exercise an automatic purpose, but not how automatic purpose might destroy in those who exercise it and those who contemplate it the very capacity to feel. Hill was only able to focus similar qualities in social and political behaviour by deriving them from a lost kingdom where the exercise of law was wholly innocent, and where it might have been possible to act severely and yet justly. Thus the death of the noblemen in 'Funeral Music' signifies in so far as it echoes a world where such catastrophes might have had a reason. The deaths were brutal and quite probably meaningless, but their echo of a lost kingdom produces the pathos which is the meaning of the poem.

In 1971 Hill published *Mercian Hymns*, a sequence of thirty prose-poems about Offa, the Anglo-Saxon king who conquered a large part of England but left little other testimony to his power than an impressive coinage and a dyke built against the Welsh.

Out of such traces of law on metal and earth the Hill of *King Log* might well have devised another memorial to the lost kingdom, another lament whose heartless music would not have extinguished the pathos of subjectivity. But in fact the new sequence modified the procedures of his earlier work.

The switch to prose versets has more significance for Hill's work than it would have for a poet less adroit with elaborate poetic forms or less conscious of the rhetorical consequences of such forms. The relative occlusion of formal device in *Mercian Hymns* certainly encourages a greater variety of tone. Participial adjectives abound, but freed from the close-fitting constraints of stanza they find their place as one rhetoric among several. More importantly, the sequence constitutes a dramatic polylogue rather than a dramatic monologue. Offa himself defies grandeur so imperiously that he begins to sound like Crow in one of his less megalomaniac moods, as when the first hymn reels off the titles he can lay claim to, from 'overlord of the M5' to 'friend of Charlemagne': ' "I like that," said Offa, "sing it again".' Indeed, despite Andrew Waterman's belief that Hill would never stoop so low as 'the instant cartoon-myth of Ted Hughes's *Crow* and other recent crass bestiaries', Offa is something of a cartoon-character:

> A pet-name, a common name. Best-selling brand, curt graffito. A laugh; a cough. A syndicate. A specious gift. Scoffed-at horned phonograph.
>
> The starting-cry of a race. A name to conjure with.

Offa's subjectivity disperses among the uses that might be made of his name, among the different meanings the name might have for different people. It becomes a graphic effect: the spread of capital A's on the page.

As it qualifies the dominance of a certain rhetoric and a certain genre, so *Mercian Hymns* brings into focus something other than the pathos of history. For the traces Offa left were both fugitive and strangely impersonal: coins, a dyke, a journey, laws. They neither echo a lost kingdom, like the hacked and coveted crowns of the Plantagenet Kings, nor summon a personality, like Tiptoft's request that his head should be taken off with three strokes, 'in honour of the Trinity'. Instead they allow Hill to imagine how the exercise of power might determine individuality, and how the exercise of individuality might determine power, as his epigraph suggests:

> The conduct of government rests upon the same foundation and encounters the same difficulties as the conduct of private persons: that is, as to its object and justification, for as to its methods, or technical part, there is all the difference which separates the person from the group, the man acting on behalf of himself from the man acting on behalf of many.

The point is not to collapse public into private, as Hill's earlier poems had tended to do, but to recognise both the similarities and the differences. The quotation comes from C. H. Sisson's *Sevenoaks Essays,* which have much to say about the importance of a social and political definition of identity:

> The person who takes this orientation finds a kind of renewal. The 'individual' sinks from sight and is extinguished; in exchange, one has all the benefits of history, not as an emporium to choose from, but as they bear down upon one at a particular point of time, like a column of air. The famous 'conflict between the individual and society' – that Byronic conception – is resolved, because one term is lost . . . One chooses roles and tries to perfect them – not one role, but as many as one can discern. Instead of the 'problem of conduct' there is the matter of discernment. The attention is shifted from the subject to the object. Indeed one does not bother about the subject; perhaps it is not there.

I would guess that *Mercian Hymns* brought Hill a similar 'renewal', the freedom to choose and perfect roles rather than contemplate the pathos of subjectivity. The 'subject' is not there; Offa becomes like Crow a site across which impulses play without ever articulating a consciousness.

Offa seems convulsed less by laughter than by the force of law. Hill has spoken of the king's 'murderous brutality' as 'a means of trying to encompass and accommodate the early humiliations and fears of one's own childhood and also one's discovery of the tyrannical streak in oneself as a child'. Thus, Hymn XIX brings public and private tyranny into a relation which empties the pathos from both:

Behind the thorn-trees thin smoke, scutch-grass or wattle
smouldering. At this distance it is hard to tell.
Far cries impinge like the faint tinkling of iron.

We have a kitchen-garden riddled with toy-shards, with
splinters of habitation. The children shriek and
scavenge, play havoc. They incinerate boxes, rags
and old tyres. They haul a sodden log, hung with
soft shields of fungus, and launch it upon the flames.

The smoke might come from grass burning or from a house
burning. The cries might be of joy or anger or pain (a possibility
admitted only as an analogy: 'like the faint tinkling of iron'). It is
the predicament described by 'Ovid in the Third Reich': distant
events which we suspect to involve brutal persecution, but which
we can still explain to ourselves as perfectly natural, or even as
something we may have imagined. In the earlier poem, the issue
had been resolved by the device of dramatic monologue, which
assigned it to a particular subjectivity. We respond to the pathos
of the predicament, to the coherent if reprehensible self-
communing it has provoked. In Hymn XIX, on the other hand,
the experience has quite literally no subject: 'It is hard to tell at
this distance.' The demonstrative informs us that the experience
is specific, but the subject clause ('to tell at this distance') does not
identify an agent, and is itself replaced at the head of the sentence
by a dummy.

The first word of the second verset appears to fill the gap;
perhaps it was 'we' on whom the far cries impinged. The effect is
similar to a shot/reverse-shot sequence in a film: the first shot
giving a particular view of people or things, and the next one
identifying the character whose view it was. There is a sight of
smoke rising in the distance, and then the pronoun marking the
place of a possible observer. But any such retrospective
association of observer and observed has to leap the space
between versets, and it turns out that 'we' inhabit a rather
different world from the wattle and scutch-grass of the first scene.
'We' do not observe persecution, but rather the domestic tyranny
of children who scavenge and play havoc. No coherent
subjectivity links the two scenes, the public and the private
tyranny. And yet, on another level, there are connections. For the
pleasure the children find in launching the log upon the flames

echoes the cathartic pleasure societies have found, and still find, in the funeral rites of a ruler. The names given to their recreating derive from legal and military usage: 'scavage' was a toll levied by town corporations on goods sold within their precincts; 'havoc', which now carries the sense of general devastation, once meant purposeful pillage by any army. The hymn is entitled 'Offa's Laws', and it sets public and private law-enforcement in relation without ever allowing a single (and pathetic) consciousness to emerge from the encounter. It discovers a language for the anti-pathos, the desire to play havoc, which inheres in many kinds of behaviour.

Mercian Hymns brings out an aspect of historical process which Hill had not been able to describe before. I am not sure that it does so consistently, or that it means to do so consistently. There is still plenty of pathos around, and the final hymn is comparable in its effect to the conclusion of 'Funeral Music'. Maybe Offa will speak to us through the traces he has left, and so rise into subjectivity. Or has he vanished?

The major sequence in *Tenebrae* (1978), 'An Apology for the Revival of Christian Architecture in England', seems less concerned with the aspect of private and public behaviour uncovered by *Mercian Hymns*; indeed, it puts the pathos-machine back into full production. Nobody plays havoc any more. The switch of mode, from prose versets back to intricate pattern, again carries its full charge of connotation. Interviewed by Blake Morrison on the day *Tenebrae* received the Duff Cooper Memorial Prize, Hill remarked that Milton was right to insist on the simple, sensuous and passionate nature of poetry, but that recent manifestations of 'confessionalism' had debased these concepts. In such circumstances, an 'extreme concentration' on formal discipline had become 'the only true way of releasing the simple, sensuous and passionate'. Formal discipline is once more the only guarantee that poetry resembles unfallen speech, a speech which can awaken echoes of the lost kingdom of innocence and original justice.

So the England celebrated by the disciplined sonnets of 'An Apology' is, if not a paradise, then at least an object of overwhelming pathos. Not only is the poetry in the pity, but the pity is also in the poetry, as can be seen from the third of the sonnets entitled 'A Short History of British India':

Malcolm and Frere, Colebrooke and Elphinstone,
the life of empire like the life of the mind
'simple, sensuous, passionate', attuned
to the clear theme of justice and order, gone.

Gone the ascetic pastimes, the Persian
scholarship, the wild boar run to ground,
the watercolours of the sun and wind.
Names rise like outcrops on the rich terrain,

like carapaces of the Mughal tombs
lop-sided in the rice-fields, boarded-up
near railway-sidings and small aerodromes.

'India's a peacock-shrine next to a shop
selling mangola, sitars, lucky charms,
heavenly Buddhas smiling in their sleep.'

The public life of the servants of empire is assimilated directly to
the life of the mind, and to poetry in particular. It is not that they
were invariably correct or magnanimous, but that the *clarity* of the
theme of justice and order in their minds gave them a kind of
uprightness, a pathos comparable to that evoked by poetry. Hill
may or may not admire them, but his poem gives the reader little
chance to avoid registering the pathos of their lives. Its second
and third stanzas select those readers who are willing and able
to identify the hallmarks of colonial service: 'the Persian
Scholarship', 'the wild boar run to ground', 'the watercolours of
the sun and wind'. They recall the first movement of 'Spain
1937', with its appeal to 'the absolute value of Greek' and 'the
prayer to the sunset'. But Hill's poem, unlike Auden's, does not
go on to suggest how we might confront the legacy of the past we
have identified. The past is now derelict, but the paradox of
modern India does nothing to relieve it of pathos.

The commitment of these sonnets to formal splendour seems
absolute, right from the opening lines of the very first one,
'Quaint Mazes':

And, after all, it is to them we return.
Their triumph is to rise and be our hosts:
lords of unquiet or of quiet sojourn,
those muddy-hued and midge-tormented ghosts.

The line from Yeats's 'Byzantium' – 'That dolphin-torn, gong-tormented sea' – which rises to become the host of the fourth here has surely been resurrected for its gorgeousness rather than for any meaning it may contribute. The ghosts we return to are literary as well as architectural, an echo of the days when poetic speech could afford to be unabashedly grandiloquent. These ghosts will have little to tell us about the topics of *Mercian Hymns*, about law and havoc. So it is not surprising that the last poem in *Tenebrae,* the title poem, should attribute the spirit of anti-pathos to music rather than to poetry:

> Music survives, composing her own sphere,
> Angel of Tones, Medusa, Queen of the Air,
> and when we would accost her with real cries
> silver on silver thrills itself to ice.

*   *   *

If we were to look for a *poetry* which 'thrills itself to ice' when accosted, we might arrive eventually at another book published in 1971, J. H. Prynne's *Brass*. Here is a brief passage from it, the conclusion to an elegy for Paul Celan:

>   Only
> the alder thrown over the cranial push, the
> waged incompleteness, comes with the animals
> and their watchful calm. The long-tailed bird
> is total awareness, a forced lust, it is that
> absolutely. Give us this love of murder and
> sacred boredom, you walk in the shade of
> the technical house. Take it away and set up
> the table ready for white honey, choking the
> which cloth spread openly for the most worthless
> accident. The whiteness is a patchwork of
> revenge too, open the window and white fleecy
> clouds sail over the azure;
>
>   it is true. Over and
> over it is so, calm or vehement. You know
> the plum is a nick of pain, is so and is also
> certainly loved. Forbearance comes into the
> stormy sky and the water is not quiet.

Definite articles work overtime, but without putting us in the position to identify anything, as they had done in Auden's poems. The form of address is sometimes intimate, but without claiming the privilege of lyric verve, as the conclusion to 'Funeral Music' had. Like many poems in the book, this one (an elegy) turns a Medusa-head on anyone who accosts it with a demand for ready meaning.

It bears the title 'Es Lebe der König', a line from Georg Büchner's *Dantons Tod* which Celan commented on in a speech accepting the Büchner Prize in 1960. At the end of the play Lucille is left alone beside the scaffold after her lover Camille and his friends have been guillotined. A patrol of citizens passes:

> CITIZEN. Who is there?
> LUCILLE. (*remembering, then as if making a decision, suddenly*)
> Long live the king!
> CITIZEN. In the name of the Republic!
> *She is surrounded by the PATROL and led away.*

Celan remarks that although Lucille's 'Long live the King' ('es lebe der König') might seem like reactionary nostalgia for the *ancien régime,* it does in fact represent an act of freedom, a 'counter-word' (Gegenwort) which annuls the sham piety of political conformism; it pays homage not to political totems, but to the durable and humanising majesty of the absurd ('die Gegenwart des Menschlichen zeugenden Majestät des Absurden'). It is a majesty to which art also pays tribute.

In Büchner's prose fragment *Lenz*, the writer is out walking when he sees two girls sitting on a rock and remarks that he would like to become a 'Medusa-head' in order to preserve their appearance and the scene they compose. Celan suggests that Büchner was expressing through Lenz his own views about the nature of art, and that Lenz's desire represents 'a step beyond the human, a removal of oneself to an opposite, alien realm – a realm inhabited by ape-forms, automata and also . . . yes, indeed, art as well' ('ein Hinaustreten aus dem Menschlichen, ein Sichhinausbegeben in einen dem Menschlichen zugewandten und unheimlichen Bereich – denselben, in dem die Affengestalt, die Automaten und damit . . . ach, auch die Kunst zuhause zu sein scheinen'). Art is a Medusa-head not simply because it isolates a particular moment from the flux of experience, but because it demands a pact with the inhuman – in short, with anti-pathos. Lenz does not want to preserve the girls on the rock as an object of sentimental reflections; he wants to turn them to stone, and to turn his own feelings for them to stone, because art also requires self-forgetfulness ('Selbstvergessen') and distance from oneself ('Ich-Ferne').

Of course, Prynne's regard for Celan's regard for Büchner's regard for Lenz need not imply an immediate resort to ape-forms and automata. At the same time, that 'love of murder and sacred boredom' might represent a counter-word, a step beyond the human. When accosted by real cries, the poems in *Brass* do thrill themselves to ice, do turn a Medusa-head on the pathos of poet and reader alike. In this respect they revise the procedures of Prynne's earlier work.

His first book, *Force of Circumstance,* was published by Routledge and Kegan Paul in 1962, and took as its main concern the pathos of those moments in our lives which, although quite arbitrary, seem to date the emergence or the reassertion of subjectivity. These are perhaps the moments Eliot spoke of, which have a distinct but undefinable value for us because they represent 'the depths of feeling into which we cannot peer': the old woman on a mountain path, the ruffians playing cards in a railway junction where there was a water-mill. Prynne, however, does peer into the depths and (to judge by the title-poem) his memories have lost some of their whimsy:

> And so I must carry with me, through the course
> Of pale imaginings that leave no trace,
> This broken, idle mill-wheel, and the force
> Of circumstance that still protects the place.

The image of the mill-wheel can be lost but not changed, because it founds the subjectivity which now has to come to terms with it. No mere accessory, it has already identified that which would identify it. The force of circumstance which protects the place is itself protected by the demonstrative 'this', whose associations of closeness and intimacy lock it rigid in the mind. Poem after poem in the book extends a protective 'this' or 'here' over the poet's founding memories. These demonstratives do not really ask us to identify a margin, a Perilous Chapel, and so declare ourselves (the margins they indicate never tie into any system of mythic or religious or political belief). Rather, they assure us that the poet has been well and truly caught in the nets of feeling. He has no other being than the filaments of pathos which string him up.

Prynne entrusted his next important collection, *The White Stones* (1969), to a small press and to more open forms, thus breaking the literary and economic mould into which the previous book had been poured. These decisions gave it a different character, and we must expect to find the nets of feeling somewhat rearranged. Indeed, they gave it a character at variance with current English habit. Of course, poets like Charles Tomlinson and Christopher Middleton were already at variance with that habit, and Prynne may well have been encouraged by their example. But open forms and fugitive presses had made a bigger splash in America than they had in England, and *The White Stones* looked more intently to the example of Ed Dorn and Charles Olson (in whose Gloucester home one poem, 'FRI 13', was written). Its rhetoric has something in common with what Dorn once termed his 'adamant practice'.

Subjectivity now seems to be grounded less on moments locked rigid in the mind than on the 'responsibility to say how you feel about things' that Dorn remarked (and regretted) in *Hands Up!* Pathos inheres in responsibility and its vindication, in the poet's willingness to say something which bears to the full the stress of his own identity. So the poems in Prynne's book embark on lyrical argument, with an ambition to carry over the simple, sensuous and passionate idiom of poetry into the field of discourse. They do not undertake this project merely to find a home for troublesome opinions. For the fields they enter – politics, economics, geology – mark the limit to how far any subjectivity can be taken. A contemporary philosophical enquiry, Maurice Merleau-Ponty's *Phenomenology of Perception*, has some bearing here, through its definition of bodily space:

> If I stand in front of my desk and lean on it with both hands, only my hands are stressed and the whole of my body trails behind them like the tail of a comet. It is not that I am unaware of the whereabouts of my shoulders or back, but these are simply swallowed up in the position of my hands, and my whole posture can be read so to speak in the pressure they exert on the table.

Following this analogy, we might say that the whole 'posture' of a subjectivity can be read in the pressure it exerts on language, in the stress borne by specific utterances. That posture, Merleau-Ponty adds, is 'the darkness needed in the theatre to show up the performance, the background of somnolence or reserve of vague power against which the gesture and its aim stand out, the zone of not being *in front of which* precise beings, figures and points can come to light'. What can be read in Prynne's poems is the background of somnolence and reserve of vague power against which a specific utterance and its aim stand out: an entire social, political and economic condition.

But might there not be moments when the utterance articulates, rather than standing out against, its reserve of vague power? A poem like 'First Notes on Daylight' would suggest that Prynne thinks so, and that he is most deeply fascinated by the pathos of such moments. These first notes at first light attempt to capture the birth process of conviction, of the responsibility to say how you feel about things. Yet they seek its vindication in events far removed from a suburban loft at 5 a.m.:

> The open
> fields we cross, we carry ourselves by ritual
> observance, even sleeping in the library.
> The laggard, that is,
> whose patience
> is the protective
> shield, of the true
> limit to *size*.
> 'The ceremonial use of the things described',
> the *cinar* trees or the white-metal mirror, forms
> of patience, oh yes, and each time I even
> move, the strophic muscular pattern is *use*, in
> no other sense. The common world, how far we
> go, the practical limits of daylight.

Like those in Dorn's early work, the italicised terms bear the stress of a particular consciousness as it becomes responsible for what it is saying. Yet what it says is far from particular, having to do with the 'size' or condition or circumstances we all find ourselves in, and with the knowledge we might have of our 'practical limits'. Ritual observance would seem to be the answer to our problems. But it is not proposed glibly. Prynne knows how exotic the 'ceremonial use' he refers to must appear, how remote from our common world; rather, he knows how powerful the conviction must be – 'forms / of patience, oh yes, and each time I . . .' – which would pull ceremony and world together. (One can imagine Larkin endorsing the emphasis on ceremony, but not the white-metal mirror and the trees with a funny name.)

Prynne attributes true patience (true knowledge of the reserve of vague power which must support every moral act) only to a select band of extremely marginal figures, such as the laggard of 'First Notes' or the medieval pilgrims of 'Frost and Snow, Falling'. These figures seem to articulate through their behaviour the entire condition of the worlds they inhabit. Yet they are remote, hypothetical, perhaps impossible. Unlike Wordsworth's beggars and Hardy's itinerant, they cannot be identified and so identify us. Like the demonstratives in *Force of Circumstance*, they do not serve to select a readership, but rather to extend the play between subjectivity and its opposites: the pathos of the birth process of conviction is shadowed by something which threatens both to complete and to extinguish it, an implausible and enviable marginality. A fine poem, 'Aristeas', describes how the flight of a Greek shaman took him out over more primitive tribes whose social and spiritual organisation had given them a better sense of the 'true limit to size' than his own people. The flight completes his (Greek) subjectivity, and exceeds it:

> This movement was of
> course cruel beyond belief, as this
> was the risk Aristeas took
> with him. The conquests were for the motive of
> sway, involving massive slaughter as the
> obverse politics of claim. That is, slaves and
> animals, *life* and not value: 'the western Sar-
> matian tribes lived side by side not in a loose
> tribal configuration, but had been welded
> into organised imperium
> under the leadership of one
> royal tribe.' Royalty
> as *plural*. Hence the calendar as taking of
> life, which left gold as the side-issue, pure
> figure.

What Aristeas experiences is the fading of his own pathos. He comes up against the end of the Greek world, for the tribes he sees on his journey were pressing down all the time against the settlement he inhabited. It may also be that in writing about him Prynne came up against the limits of conviction, of the responsibility to say what you feel about things: in the passage I have just quoted, a historian's summary sits alongside the italicised words which bear the stress of thesis.

Force of Circumstance and *The White Stones* had paid their dues to the birth processes of mind. Sufficient dues, at any rate, for *Brass* to represent as striking a development in Prynne's career as *Crow* and *Mercian Hymns* had in the careers of Hughes and Hill. Indeed, all three poets might be said to have entered the realm of ape-forms and automata at more or less the same time. I would guess that Prynne was beginning to find the miscarriage of the birth processes of mind as interesting a phenomenon as the moments themselves in their fictitious purity. But his rhetorical procedures were still firmly committed to the pathos of those moments. The miscarriage of innocence and original justice probably did not seem like a topic which would yield to thesis, since the thesis itself would be invalidated by the first hint of falsification. Hence, I think, the Medusa-head flourished by *Brass*.

The title may allude to the second chapter of the *First Book of Urizen*, where Urizen, having been expelled from Eternity, promulgates the laws of the created universe:

> 7. 'Lo, I unfold my darkness and on
> This rock place with strong hand the book
> Of eternal brass, written in my solitude.
>
> 8. 'Laws of peace, of love, of unity,
> Of pity, compassion, forgiveness.
> Let each choose one habitation,
> His ancient infinite mansion,
> One command, one joy, one desire,
> One curse, one weight, one measure,
> One King, one God, one Law.'

In Blake's eyes, Urizen has sinned by trying to impose a single origin and a single law on all humankind, and the prophetic books describe the tyrannies he has performed with his book and his instruments of brass:

So he began to dig, forming of gold, silver & iron
And brass, vast instruments to measure out the immense &
    fix
The whole into another world, better suited to obey
His will, where none should dare oppose his will, himself
    being king
Of all, & all futurity be bound in his vast chain.

                   (*Four Zoas*, VI, 226–30)

But Urizen remitted not their labours upon his rock,
And Urizen read in his book of brass in sounding tones:

'Listen O daughters, to my voice! Listen to the words of
    wisdom!
So shall you govern over all. Let moral duty tune your
    tongue,
But be your hearts harder than the nether millstone . . .

                (*Four Zoas*, VIII, 108–12)

Brass is clearly the metal of law-giving and law-enforcement, so
we might expect that Prynne's Book of Brass will touch on some
of the themes of *Mercian Hymns*.

Blake had wanted to contest the tyranny of law, and his Bible of
Hell (in which the *First Book of Urizen* was to replace Genesis) did
so by ensuring that there could be no single authoritative version
of Creation and Fall. *Brass*, on the other hand, tends to anatomise
rather than repudiate its latter-day Urizens. It does include a
counter-Genesis, 'Of Sanguine Fire', but one which parodies the
Creation-myth proposed by Blake himself, or rather by his
sources: for this is the Blake of Kathleen Raine's *Blake and
Tradition* (1969), a poet steeped in mystical and alchemical lore.
Prynne seems to feel that Urizen has already repudiated himself,
and that what passes for tyranny these days is more like a coma
punctuated by the occasional spasm of all-purpose indignation.

According to one version of the downfall of the human race
offered by the prophetic books, Urizen (the power of conscious
thought) slept, and the Eternal Man became entranced by a
shadow of himself, an image of total pathos:

'When Urizen slept in the porch and the Ancient Man was
    smitten,

'The darkening Man walked on the steps of fire before his
    halls,
And Vala walked with him in dreams of soft deluding
    slumber.
He looked up and saw thee, prince of light, thy splendour
    faded,
But saw not Los nor Enitharmon, for Luvah hid them in
    shadow,

'Then Man ascended mourning into the splendours of his
    palace:
Above him rose a shadow from his wearied intellect
Of living gold, pure, perfect, holy; in white linen pure he
    hovered,
A sweet entrancing self-delusion, a watery vision of Man,
Soft exulting in existence, all the Man absorbing.'

Urizen is still asleep in his porch, to judge by the watery self-
deluding vision which percolates through the opening of one
poem in *Brass,* 'A New Tax on the Counter-Earth':

A dream in sepia and eau-de-nil ascends
from the ground as a great wish for calm. And
the wish is green in season, hazy like meadow-sweet,
downy & soft waving among the reeds, the
cabinet of Mr. Heath. Precious vacancy pales in
this studious form, the stupid slow down & become
wise with inertia, and instantly the prospect of
money is solemnised to the great landscape.
It actually glows like a stream of evening sun,
value become coinage fixed in the grass crown.
The moral drive isn't
    quick enough, the greasy rope-trick
has made payment an edge of rhetoric;
      the conviction of merely being
      right, that has
marched into the patter of balance.
               And here
the dream prevails, announced by Lord Cromer:
his warnings of crisis revert to hillside
and the market town: 'the great pyrotechnist

who did it all, red from head to foot' – inducing
disbelief stronger even than remedies. We become
who he is, the abandoned fishing, the asserted
instrument renewed as a cloud over the moor. What
he says is nothing, the hills and the trees, the
distant panorama washing the buried forest. Who
he is tells us that what he says need not be
true, in the dream to come it will not happen.

Lord Cromer (then Governor of the Bank of England) makes a
distinctly unappealing Urizen, not so much drowsy as
lobotomised.

Of course, there was nothing exceptional about the assertion
that economic criteria had supplanted moral criteria in public life,
or the assertion that politics had entered Disneyland. Donald
Davie was making much the same point in articles published by
the *Listener* just before he left for America in 1968:

English life has become an endless kaleidoscopic comedy in
which each of us both plays his part and applauds from the
stalls, in which financial crises and general elections recur at
predictable intervals like episodes of farce . . . The charade
that has been made of the national life is not anything that has
been wished upon us, but something that we crave. We like our
fancy dress, and will reward handsomely anyone who can
devise new scenes for us to wear it in . . . national politics is
itself a shadow-play, a histrionic illusion in which Heath can
play Wilson's role and Wilson Heath's.

Davie's response was to stop applauding from the stalls: to apply
the lash ever more fiercely to his own back and to the backs of our
political and cultural leaders, in the hope that one or two of them
might bring some genuine moral authority to his or her role. This
response has itself come to play an important part in the 'charade'
– the part of a chorus rather than a lone voice in the wilderness –
and I shall return to it in my next chapter. But it is not one
adopted by Prynne's poem, which seems more concerned to
analyse than to damn, and less concerned with the charade than
with our reasons for craving it:

It is cash so distraught

that the limbic mid-brain system has absorbed
its reflex massage. We move into sleep portioned
off in the restored liner, and the drowsy body
is closer to 'nature', the counter-earth. The nervous
system burns hissing down to its fluid base,
watched by the hermaphrodite from Coventry.

Prynne does not so much argue as assemble terms, modes of
explanation: from science, from Blake (whose hermaphrodites
symbolised sterile and irreconcilable opposition). He seems
unwilling to declare himself as he had in earlier poems, and reap
the pathos of conviction.

What I am suggesting is that Prynne now regards pathos as
part of the problem rather than part of the solution. This is how
the poem ends:

> The distance of being so reopens
> the millenial landscape, 'that we need not even
> think of it as possible.'
>   Then the possible seems
> a paltry art: 'the perceptual events of the dream
> produce a partial or temporary reduction in the
> state of need current in the organism.' Whether
> partial or temporary they release gratitude, the
> moment of joy self-induced as desire turned back
> into a globe itself infolding like a sun, or like
> a moon, or like a universe of starry majesty.
>   'The spot was the one which
> he loved best in the world'.
> And such affection curdles the effort to be just,
> the absolute perception spreads calm into the air
> and the air works like a sea. The horizon is lit
> with the rightness of wayward sentiment, cash
> as a principal of nature. And cheap at the price.

So entrancing is the watery vision of infinite pathos that nobody
bothers to ask whether the millennial landscape it has opened is
attainable, or even desirable. The effect of the management of
opinion in modern society is to perpetuate the vision, to suffuse us
with 'wayward sentiment'; we cannot remember a moment
when, like Redburn in Launcelott's-Hey, we acted decisively and
correctly, moved by the justice of a situation. For example,

watching reports of a strike on the television news, we may at first
feel angry; but after a while the anger becomes something we are
grateful for, a proof of our ability to feel rather than of the
wickedness of the strikers, a confirmation of identity. That 'at
first', the moment of immediate and immediately 'correct'
response, has lost even the ideal status it held under previous
moral systems. The sheer surplus of information, which can only
be regulated by an overproduction of pathos, has anticipated and
revised it out of existence. Prynne asserts, I think, that this
process should be considered in relation to the dominance of
economic criteria: cash nurtures the watery vision and adjusts the
'rightness' of the wayward sentiment lighting the horizon. And
from the Greek word for horizon, Blake (according to Kathleen
Raine) derived the name Urizen. Sentiment even lights up the
Book of Brass.

Anyone putting forward this hypothesis could not very well add
to the surplus by a further watery tribute to the pathos of origins.
On the contrary, Celan's admonition to cultivate self-
estrangement and to remove oneself into an alien realm inhabited
by ape-forms and automata must have seemed opportune.
Prynne brandishes a poetic Medusa-head in order to freeze
symptoms which would otherwise have melted away at his
approach. He does not elaborate a thesis, and so allow the pathos
of his own subjectivity to rise finally over the heartless music of
the verse. Any thesis is produced by the play between different
forms of explanation, each of which articulates its own grouping
of interests and values. A scientific analysis of dream-work leads
into a quotation from the first book of Blake's *Milton* (21–7):

> The nature of infinity is this: that everything has its
> Own vortex, & when once a traveller through Eternity
> Has passed that vortex, he perceives it roll backward behind
> His path, into a globe itself enfolding like a sun
> Or like a moon, or like a universe of starry majesty,
> While he keeps onwards in his wondrous journey on the
>   earth –
> Or like a human form, a friend with whom he lived
>   benevolent.

Blake's account of the way memory revises experience is not
preferred to the scientific one, or juxtaposed for ironic effect, but

called in evidence along with any other statement which may bear on the matter in hand. The poem's meaning is the work done by the reader's mind as it adjusts to the different texture and implication of each new turn of phrase.

A more recent book by Prynne, *Down Where Changed* (1979), shows some sign of a return to declarative utterance; its title even borrows a stockmarket idiom. But he has not followed the later Hughes and the later Hill back to the pathos of origins. If the emphasis of his writing has changed since *Brass*, it has changed in the direction of 'increasing scientific precision', as Douglas Oliver notes. A book like *High Pink on Chrome* (1975) is crucially concerned with the falsification of subjectivity, but the scientific language it employs is very much more elaborate, and indeed achieves a kind of autonomy. I myself think that the independence of this scientific language (the way it stands out in relief) may have weakened the political accountability of the writing. Scientific terms are no more recondite than those derived from Blake's prophetic books, but they proclaim more loudly the existence of the self-sufficient and enclosed community which supplied them. Scientists are a more identifiable and more powerful group in our society than connoisseurs of the prophetic books, and the identity and the power of their specialised vocabularies may impair the ability of many readers to move freely and with some equality of response from one form of statement to another within the poem. It is as though the Medusa-head has not simply frozen, but contracted and isolated, what it addresses. The language and the model of the scientific community come closer to coding the poems in *High Pink on Chrome* than they ever did the poems in *Brass*.

* * *

This chapter developed from my enthusiasm for three very distinct books, and I know that it is only too easy to construct a historical 'moment' out of the connections you see between things you happen to be fond of. However, it does seem to me that all three books take an interest in the spirit of anti-pathos and that they therefore represent, when seen against the course taken before and after them by the careers of the poets concerned, an opportunity for English writing which has since receded.

12 Conclusion

Books like this one often cap a morbid account of the defects of the 'contemporary situation' by presenting with magicianly pride the young poet whose work will put things right, or the older poet whose work (if properly understood) might yet help to put things right. This arrangement has not always been to the advantage of the poets concerned. Some have barely had time to mumble their thanks before disappearing without trace. For example, Leavis's *New Bearings in English Poetry* proclaimed Ronald Bottrall, whose plummet into relative obscurity was immediate and lasting. 'Mr Bottrall's work,' Leavis had written, 'clinches felicitously the argument of this book, and sanctions high hopes for the future.' The mistake so often made, and made with such majesty here, is to suppose that a poem is improved by the way it clinches the critic's argument. In any case, it seems unlikely that readers are much moved by the exercise: either they know more about the poet in question than the critic does, or they assume that the fondness of the one for the other is a sure sign of the imminent demise of both.

I want to take a different course myself, although not just in order to avoid polemic and controversy. (Diffidence always seems a lost cause; if you try to make a book unobjectionable, that is what people will object to.) The 'felicitous' end to my own argument will not involve specific poets so much as the conditions under which poetry is read today. I shall concentrate on England, partly because it is the country I know best, and partly because the situation in America seems more fluid. You do not have to like John Ashbery's poems to be glad that an uncompromising and idiosyncratic writer should have found a readership. In England, by contrast, the conditions under which poetry is read threaten to become so specialised and so rigid that certain kinds of writing will not reach even the relatively small number of people who might take an interest in them.

231

I have described in Chapters 9 to 11 the rhetorical orientation
of various contemporary poems, the play between a declarative
voice and its opposites; and I have argued that these poems either
abandon the selective and identifying strategies found in poems
from the first half of the century, or arrange them by means of a
different imperative. The only explanation I have been able to
advance is that the growth of institutional audiences of one kind
or another has shifted the responsibility for making readers *away
from* the rhetorical and thematic layout of the poems themselves.
Thus my remarks about the language of recent poetry have
tended towards practical criticism; they have been remarks about
the coherence of a poem, about significant form, rather than
about the way it invokes its secret complement. And they could
not perhaps have done otherwise, since practical criticism is now
one of the most important of the conventions we use to make sense
of poems: a convention devised with the disappearance of the
Common Reader in mind, elaborated in schools and academies,
and absorbed by the poets who pass through those schools and
academies. To put it crudely, if you are aware that a sizeable part
of your potential audience will scan your poem in search of
significant form and in search of the subjectivity which authorised
the significance of that form, then you may not bother with the
selective and identifying strategies of a Yeats or an Eliot or an
Auden; you may simply ensure that the poem can be practically
criticised and that a certain subjectivity can be seen to articulate
it.

The shift in the balance of power between poem and reader has
important consequences. 'The next event,' Jane Tompkins
reports,

> in the drama of the reader's emergence into critical prominence
> is that instead of being seen as instrumental to the
> understanding of the text, the reader's activity is declared to be
> *identical with* the text and therefore becomes itself the source of
> all literary value. If literature *is* what happens when we read,
> its value depends on the value of the reading process.

Once the reader's activity has been recognised in theory as 'the
source of all literary value', then literary value becomes the
product of the specific ways in which that activity is controlled by
the institutions which now make readers. Of course, there has

been much debate about whether the reader of a text produces or consumes its meaning. What concerns me here is the power acquired by institutions which openly admit that their business is to produce meaning, and thus literary value. If it is a matter of power, then it is a matter of dispute, and we surely need to examine the rules under which the game is played. We must ask how and why it is that some kinds of writing have found a readership, while others have not. The answer will of course have a lot to do with the energy and fortitude of the individuals concerned. But it may also have something to do with circumstances under which they operate. I suspect that it now takes an institution rather than a way with words to create 'high hopes for the future'.

* * *

Despite the power of the institutions, Common Readers – readers identified by assimilation into a 'homogeneous culture' rather than by their response to a segregating rhetoric, or by membership of an academy – have not altogether disappeared. However heterogeneous the culture in question, however segregated it may always have been and may still be, it does make readers. Unfortunately, it has proved more and more difficult to attract the attention of those readers, and the very few poets who do manage to attract it (notably John Betjeman and Philip Larkin) have sometimes been put to strange antics; at least, they have been put to the cultivation of 'personality'.

When Seamus Heaney, in his essay on the language of contemporary English poetry, comes to discuss Larkin, his argument alters for the first time from a preoccupation with tonal and mythic resource to a preoccupation with personality:

> He too returns to origins and brings something back, although he does not return to 'roots'. He puts inverted commas round his 'roots', in fact. His childhood, he says, was a forgotten boredom. He sees England from train windows, fleeting past and away. He is urban modern man, the insular Englishman, responding to the tones of his own clan, ill at ease when out of his environment.

Unlike Hughes and Hill, Larkin personifies something. 'He *is* urban modern man, *the* insular Englishman . . .' At that an image familiar to every reader of his poems floats into view: an alert and fastidious observer whose anorexic wit has for so long needled the national decline, a will-have-been among has-beens. This image is the convention according to which each new poem will be read. 'From *The Less Deceived* on,' writes Anthony Thwaite, 'the personality is an achieved and consistent one, each poem restating or adding another facet to what has gone before.'

But the personality has also gained a certain currency outside the poems. It is customary for newspapers to pay some attention to poets who have just published a book or won a prize, but Larkin has on occasion been interviewed because he is Larkin (that is, 'urban modern man'). Each occasion restates or adds another facet to what has gone before. Thus an interview with Miriam Gross in the *Observer* of 16 December 1979 warms over all the old tales about uneventful childhood, lack of interest in any literature except novels or biography, xenophobia, and so on. Did Larkin ever dance, as well as listen, to jazz? 'Dance,' he replies incredulously, 'you mean dance?' Would he like to visit, say, China? Hmm, yes, 'if I could come back the same day.' Politics? 'Oh, I adore Mrs. Thatcher . . . Recognising that if you haven't got the money for something you can't have it – this is a concept that's vanished for many years.' Why does he live in Hull? 'I love all the Americans getting on to the train at King's Cross and thinking they're going to come and bother me, and then looking at the connections and deciding they'll go to Newcastle and bother Basil Bunting instead.' A photograph shows him on his haunches in a nest of bicycles, and the piece is entitled 'A Voice for Our Time'. It is that voice, defined here in relation to social and political issues, which we look for behind the poems.

Of course, Larkin is not to be seen climbing through the potted plants which adorn the quarter-deck of a TV chat-show. To suggest that he has cultivated a personality is simply to say that he is one of the few English poets whose readers are made in the way we imagine an eighteenth-century poet's readers to have been made: socially, rather than rhetorically or institutionally. He has certainly claimed as much: 'What I don't like about subsidies and official support is that they destroy the essential nexus between the writer and the reader. If the writer is being paid to read, the element of compulsive contact vanishes.' In Larkin's eyes that element of compulsive (or socially produced) contact is the only right reason for reading. He has therefore disavowed, although he may well benefit from, the institutional readerships upon which other poets depend. A report in the *Sunday Times* of 11 January 1981 suggests that some students choose Hull University because Larkin is Librarian there; they will, we learn, be sorely disappointed, because the Librarian refuses to discuss poetry with undergraduates. For the same reason, he has also spurned the trappings of literary status. 'Nowadays,' he told Miriam Gross, 'you *can* live by being a poet. A lot of people do it: it means a blend of giving readings and lecturing and spending a year at a university as poet in residence or something. But I couldn't bear that: it would embarrass me very much. I don't want to go around pretending to be me.' Larkin's strategy is honest and successful, but it also looks like hard work. To get people to read his poems for the right reasons, he has to do an awful lot of pretending not to be pretending to be a poet. If all those Americans had found their way to Hull, the game would really be up.

However, very few English poets can hope to be enlisted as a voice for our time. Larkin's poems have evidently made compulsive contact with a large number of readers, but few of those readers seem compelled to read poems by anyone else. It is as though the Common Reader cannot cope with more than (say) three poets at once. The major publishing houses have either provoked, or more likely adjusted to, this tendency (a tendency whose implications are studied in an excellent essay by Blake Morrison, 'Poetry and the Poetry Business'). Some firms publish no poetry at all, some publish nothing but anthologies, while others rely almost exclusively on a single established poet. Only three – Faber, OUP and Secker and Warburg – have what might be described as a poetry list. 'For the rest,' Morrison concludes, 'poetry is left almost entirely to the small presses like Carcanet, Anvil, Bloodaxe, and Peterloo, all of which depend on Arts Council support for their survival; or indeed to smaller presses than these, private operations run by enthusiastic individuals in back-rooms and garden sheds.' Nowadays it takes more than a handful of definite articles to identify a readership. You need a Certificate of Registration for your own press, a garden shed to nail it to ('This certificate is required by the Act to be exhibited in a conspicuous position at the principal place of business'), and the temerity to impose your variously-shaped products on booksellers whose shelves were built to hold Penguins and Picadors. Then you can get started.

There are perhaps other, easier ways. But since small presses now produce more books of poems every year than the major publishing houses, they cannot be left out of any account of the audience for contemporary writing. Rather, we cannot leave out those presses which have persuaded people to read the books they produce. For that reason, I shall concentrate here on Carcanet, an intelligently conceived and relatively well-funded operation which sponsors a particular group of poets and critics and is directed at a particular audience. Whatever one thinks of those poets and critics, it is hard to avoid the conclusion that Carcanet has done what has to be done better than anyone else: namely, made and distributed the books it wishes people to read, while at the same time creating an audience which will read those books for the 'right reasons'. 'Carcanet,' Morrison observes, 'set up twelve years ago as a small press, now publishes eighteen to twenty poetry titles a year; it still relies on the Arts Council for about twenty per cent of its income, but is now sufficiently stable to be planning further significant additions – including a fiction list – to its rapidly expanding programme.' The reasons for its success bear thinking about.

One reason is that Carcanet does not simply publish books. It also tries, more strenuously than any other small or smallish press, to define and promote the conventions according to which those books should be read. The process can be glimpsed in the introduction to a recent Carcanet book, *British Poetry since 1970. A Critical Survey*, where someone called the 'serious reader' puts in a first ever appearance on the literary scene. The editors, Peter Jones and Michael Schmidt, begin with a remark about the seventies: 'The overdue recognition of Geoffrey Hill's uncompromising work, the rediscovery of Edgell Rickword, indicate a change in the quality of seriousness of some readers and writers.' Whatever this 'quality of seriousness' might represent in the abstract, it would seem in the here and now to be not altogether unconnected with the activities of Carcanet Press, which publishes Sisson and Rickword and allows both space in its associated journal, *PN Review*. The press and the journal have together created a 'seriousness', a set of conventions, which enables certain readers to appreciate certain writers. Their 'serious reader' is thus as much of a construct as the various Super-readers and Implied Readers who throng the corridors of the academy.

This construct has recognisable features which do not belong to any reader of any book of poems, and which can be seen in what Jones and Schmidt have to say about the success enjoyed by poets from Northern Ireland: 'The inflation of the "Ulster school" has occurred for quite understandable extrapoetic reasons; but for the serious reader, there is no reason to re-draw the map of English *poetry* around the six counties.' One doubts whether 'extrapoetic reasons' could ever be separated satisfactorily from poetic reasons; and whether, if they could, the result would not be widespread torpor. Still, the serious reader must be assumed to engage continually in such activities. Introducing a Carcanet anthology, *Ten English Poets*, Michael Schmidt took it upon himself to proscribe 'unspeakable epic poets, tearful lyricists, rhetoricians of a political kidney, adolescent angst peddlers, geriatric lovers, spineless satirists, sinless confessional writers, pasticheurs of modernism'. All these are tainted by indulgence in extrapoetic reasons. For the serious reader, on the other hand, poetry is an encounter with form, where convention disposes what man proposes. An editorial in the first number of *Poetry Nation* (which later became *PN Review*) announced that the journal would support 'a renewed popularity and practice of clearly formal writing, a common bridling at vacuous public and private rhetoric'. In a supporting essay on 'The Politics of Form', Schmidt attacked poets who seek 'to cajole or bemuse the readers'.

When *Poetry Nation* became *PN Review* in 1976, he returned to the theme from a slightly different angle:

> Among modern English writers we have sensed, and gone some way in our early issues towards defining, a failure of seriousness, a flippancy before formal and social choices, and an unwillingness to examine the human implications of certain ideas expressed as it were casually in particular works of imaginative writing, or in underlying attitudes.

Social choices now took their place beside formal choices, a change of emphasis announced by the addition of the term 'Review' to the journal's title. Seriousness had now to be defined in broader terms. Commenting in an editorial on the refusal of booksellers to stock *PN Review*, Donald Davie wrote: 'It's the level of seriousness that is the inexcusable thing, not at all the topics that we choose to be serious about.' To Davie this meant the absence of an 'educated electorate' which might purchase such a journal, an audience distinguished from the accidental and temporary among citizens by its response to serious debate about political and literary issues. *PN Review*, he concluded, 'like any other responsible journal at the present time, must have as a main objective the bringing into being of an electorate that shall once again be educated.' As C. H. Sisson, also a joint editor, put it in the next issue: 'Our problem is therefore with an audience which is not there or – less ambitiously – with one which is just beginning to appear, here and there, in a scattered way . . .' Setting out quite consciously to make a readership, the editors of *PN Review* had decided that the level of seriousness demanded by a certain kind of poetry was the same as that demanded by a certain kind of politics.

This decision took shape against the horrors of the sixties, when demonstrators who were also unspeakable epic poets ran riot. 'The critic's task,' Schmidt said,

> is to help direct contemporary literature and the modern reader back into the main-stream, reclaiming for both a little of their lost authority. This it may be able to do if there are creative writers worth serious attention, who have refused, with the contraction of the responsive audience and the retreat of the critics, to chasten the scope of their art.

Only those who have authority can set and maintain an appropriate level of seriousness, and authority was something which the demonstrators and/or unspeakable epic poets had all but destroyed. Donald Davie, then Pro-Vice-Chancellor of Essex University, argued in his 1968 articles for the *Listener* that student unrest and the moral cowardice it met with among academics were symptomatic of a widespread fear of authority. He claimed that good writing depends on 'the drive towards authority, the authoritative note and tone,' and that Britain in the sixties had abandoned this note and tone:

> The pastor in his manse didn't wield much power, but he was magnificently an image of authority. And it's just those images

that Britain today won't tolerate . . . What's new with us is that authority is as unpopular with those who deal it out as with those who take it. It's people like me who, because they can't stand being hated, refuse the authority that makes them hateful: 50-year olds determined to be young for ever.

As long as such people remained silent there would be no seriousness, no way of sorting out the accidental and temporary among citizens or among readers of poetry.

At this point, Davie retired to California. But his preoccupation with the authority-shy persisted, developing into (among other things) a critique of Larkin's *Oxford Book of Twentieth-Century English Verse*, which he reviewed for the *Listener* in 1973. In Davie's eyes, Larkin had not provided the rigorous and decisive view of modern English verse which we would expect from 'an anthology backed by the authority of a famous publishing house, and by his own authority as the best-loved poet of his generation'. Larkin's choice of poems had been swayed by histrionic considerations; it showed him to be 'a man who thinks that poetry is a private indulgence or a professional entertainer's patter or, at most, a symptom for social historians to brood over'. This pastor has not exactly abandoned his manse, but he has thrown a wild party and invited every rock star and debutante he could think of: teenagers pet heavily in the upstairs rooms, while bearded social workers stand around scrunching plastic cups. The pastor does not exactly enjoy it, but he thinks they might love him for his Led Zeppelin records.

Davie was equally forthright about his own failures. In 1973 he criticised 'Creon's Mouse', a poem he had written twenty years earlier, for advocating loss of nerve:

> What I didn't envisage then, which there is no excuse for not envisaging now, is that there would be people who would think it too daring of Creon to be a king at all, however self-limited and vowed to consultation and compromise. It is possible, I now have to realise, to think that it is audacious presumption for a man to get into any position of authority over his fellows, to take on any kind of institutionalized responsibility for directing them.

When his *Collected Poems* was published in 1972, it became clear

that he had answered that failure of nerve by recourse to a
particular kind of institutionalised responsibility, scholarship.
The recourse has puzzled at least one of his admirers, Neil
Powell:

> But the extent and the obscurity of allusion, and the
> deliberation with which he refuses to be helpful in some recent
> poems, are new and disturbing. Two long poems at the end of
> the *Collected Poems*, 'Trevenen' and 'Vancouver', are provided
> with J. H. Prynne-like notes which would be of little use to
> anyone outside one of the copyright libraries.

But the deliberation with which Davie refused to be helpful was, I
think, a political deliberation, a reassertion of the authority
implicit in a certain level of scholarly seriousness. The notes to
'Trevenen' help establish a precise historical moment, which can
be said to represent 'an age much like our own', an age when few
things were as fashionable as 'indignant righteousness'. In talking
about this age, Davie is able to talk about ours as well.
Brandishing his footnotes, the pastor has stormed back into the
manse and kicked out all the groupies and sociologists and
unspeakable epic poets. Prynne's Medusa-head had frozen the
spectacle of indignant righteousness, anatomising it while holding
it in place; Davie sought to abolish it altogether, by a less devious
but less incisive moralism.

Of the two rhetorics, Davie's has proved the more successful in
gathering a readership. This is partly because the appeal to
authority has found a particular language in present-day political
journalism, a language which has proved popular and influential.
Writing in the *Sunday Telegraph* of 13 September 1981, Peregrine
Worsthorne argued that the true reactionary must always be
warning people against idealism and high-mindedness, and that
such warnings are 'bound often to take the form of a
contemptuous sneer, an angry jibe, a deflating rudeness, and a
certain verbal brutality, at best witty but at worst merely abusive,
simply because these are the most effective corrosives with which
to dissolve liberal waffle'. By way of example he cited the
Victorian Prime Minister Lord Salisbury, who defined universal
education as 'pumping learning into louts'. Such 'corrosives' are
very popular in England today (they have a lot to do with the
success of *Private Eye*). We admire them less for their wit, although

they are sometimes very witty, than for their sadism: the brutality with which they lay bare pretensions and reassert the authority of self-evident truths.

Literary men have also found a use for these corrosives, as can be seen from a review by Kingsley Amis, which does to Donald Davie's *New Oxford Book of Christian Verse* what Davie did to Larkin's *Oxford Book of Twentieth-Century Verse* (the pastors like to keep each other up to the mark). Reaching for the corrosives, Amis observes that Davie has included a translation of the 'Dream of the Rood' which 'has words like "durst" and "corse" in it and has small letters at the beginnings of the lines. A useful rough rule says that no good poems do that'. Thus the true reactionary punctures the pretensions of all the unspeakable epic poets who have abandoned capital letters, and of all those readers who have been foolish enough to admire them for doing so. Although it would be wrong to identify *PN Review* in general, and Davie and Schmidt in particular, with such posturing, there can be little doubt that the journal has benefited from its loose association with the rhetoric of political and literary reaction. For if one had to name the English critic who most forcefully combined Toryism with a witty and brutal commentary on literature, it would be C. H. Sisson. Introducing the latter's collected essays, Schmidt points out that there 'is often a polemical edge to what Sisson says: he does not wish to persuade us of anything, but to disabuse us – he is impatient that some men so readily misunderstand'. And the essays do indeed steam with indignation whenever they encounter such whimsical notions as 'democracy' or 'Stephen Spender'. Their fashionable disabusing rhetoric has clearly had some influence on the tone of the journal Sisson helps to edit.

I must confess that the young writers Carcanet publishes seem to me less interesting than the older ones it has re-published. But whatever its virtues and shortcomings, it can be said to represent a Leavisite project for the making of readers, sharpened by the horrors of the sixties and strengthened by a more astute handling of institutional audiences and the excellence of Donald Davie's writing. Like *Scrutiny*, the project is characterised by a tension between liberalism and reaction which usually resolves itself in favour of reaction. It is exemplary because of its success, a success I would attribute in part to its collusion with a certain political posture.

There are of course other small presses and other journals. The Ferry Press, for example, has published books (by Andrew Crozier, John James, Douglas Oliver, J. H. Prynne, Peter Riley) of a high standard with rare consistency. Libraries which take an interest in contemporary English poetry should buy everything it prints, as well as every issue of the *Grosseteste Review*. But these other presses and journals have not been as successful as Carcanet at reaching and identifying those who might want to read the poets they sponsor. Sometimes one of their books does break surface. In 1975 the *Spectator* gave Ashbery and Crozier and James and Prynne what must be about the only favourable reviews they have ever received in the daily or weekly press. 'By refusing to become a readily accessible and intelligible writer,' Peter Ackroyd said of Prynne, 'he has ensured that poetry can no longer be treated as a deodorised museum of fine thoughts and fine feelings; he is creating, instead, a complete and a coherent language.' But the *Spectator*-initiative did not last long (revolt in the rectories? blank stares in the Athenaeum?), and in the absence of a sustained effort of exposition it is hard to see how Prynne can be said to have 'ensured' anything. For the success of Carcanet has shown that the making of readers in England today is an arduous business, and one requiring a range of consistent strategies.

* * *

But however sweet the appeal to authority, it can hardly match the real authority vested in the men and women who teach literature in our schools. According to David Holbrook, these people are 'helping train the sensibility of three-quarters of the nation: and they are helping create its capacities for living and its potentialities as an audience for new forms of literary expression'. That was said in 1961, and twenty years later it looks an ambitious claim. But literature is still very much on the curriculum, and we must attempt some analysis of the way it continues to be taught.

Influential commentators like Holbrook and Frank Whitehead have always emphasised the difficulty of clearing a space for poetry among rival attractions. So unaccustomed are we to poetry, Holbrook observes, that we 'have to train ourselves self-consciously to respond'; according to Whitehead, poetry has been relegated to 'the utmost periphery of normal human activity', and we forget that there were times when hearing it spoken or sung 'formed part of the background in which all children grew up'. Since the disappearance of the Common Reader, the reader primed by living in a homogeneous culture, we have had to *make* an audience for poetry, and the classroom now seems like a good place to start. Whitehead argues that the modern teacher should therefore 'supply as far as he can the deficiencies of the environment'.

This understandably defensive view of the role of poetry in modern life has determined to a large extent the way it is taught in schools. Because the process is felt to be a struggle against great odds, it has come more and more to resemble a minimum programme, a programme which teaches people to recognise not so much 'new forms of literary expression' as the place poetry might hold in their imaginative lives, what it has to offer against counter-attractions. We must learn to know the poetic, not as a discourse whose value lies in its autonomy, but as a mode of perception dormant within our daily lives. Poetry is no longer seen as a series of conventions (prosodic, generic, rhetorical) which have been used to produce new versions of subjectivity, but as a capacity to imagine freshly and unconventionally. 'Every new child,' according to Ted Hughes, 'is nature's chance to correct culture's error.'

A sign of the shift of emphasis I am talking about can be seen in the thematising approach adopted by anthologies designed for use in schools. 'Throughout the poetry course,' Whitehead suggests, 'we should be looking first and foremost for poems which can make contact, in an intimate way, with the child's most vital experience and interests.' This means that the poems must be coded in such a way as to break through any expectations about the kind of discourse they are and 'make contact' with the child's capacity to imagine his or her world. They are therefore classified not according to, say, prosodic convention, but according to the customary disposition of the vital interests they are supposed to make contact with. Maurice Wollman's 1968 anthology, *7 Themes in Modern Verse,* contains the following categories: Work and Leisure; Travel and Adventure; Personal Relationships; Coming to Terms with People and Life; With People and Away from People; Communication; 'The Age of Anxiety'. In 1969, eye-deep in the Age of Anxiety, Rhodri Jones edited for Heinemann Educational a series of anthologies entitled *Themes*: Men and

Beasts; Imagination; Conflict; Generations; Sport and Leisure; Men at Work; Town and Country. Not so much the Age of Anxiety, more like the Age of Themes. Of course, anthologies have to be categorised somehow, and classification according to theme has traditionally been one way of doing it. But it may be that what was once a matter of convenience has become an indispensable coding, a way of labelling poems so that they make contact with the vital interests of the pupil.

I have been dealing with a minimum programme for the training of readers. No doubt other kinds of reading, including a study of prosodic conventions and so on, can follow from it. But the minimum programme, with its attention to *the poetic* rather than to *poems*, may take such a firm hold on the habits of young readers that only a powerful counter-argument will dislodge it. Since the majority of readers learn how to read in the classroom, and publishers favour poets who are likely to be read there, this specialisation of reading-habits must eventually have some consequence for literary practice.

Features of the minimum programme for the training of young readers in school are reproduced in the overall context for the writing and reception of poetry. Consider the possible effect of the emphasis placed on creative writing in the schools today. Hughes's influential *Poetry in the Making*, first published in 1967, was intended to encourage ten- to fourteen-year-olds to 'more purposeful efforts in their writing'. He argued that 'by showing to a pupil's imagination many opportunities and few restraints and instilling into him confidence and a natural motive for writing, the odds are that something – may be not much, but something – of our common genius will begin to put a word in'. As Whitehead remarks, creative writing fosters 'the acceptance of poetry as something which is neither esoteric nor precious, but a normal and natural facet of human life'. The shift from poems to the poetic is achieved by encouraging pupils to write themselves, and by showing them many opportunities and few restraints (that is, few conventions).

As the discipline of teaching English has become more codified, so the emphasis on opportunity rather than restraint (capacity rather than convention) has become firmly established. It governs not only the teaching of pupils, but the teaching of teachers. When in the late sixties the universities took on a greater responsibility for teacher-training, there was some concern that the courses they provided should not be too 'academic'. 'A teacher,' Holbrook wrote, 'who has written at some time or other honest creative work about his inmost self, and who has often been truly moved by word-art, will be able to respond to children's own creative writing.' Such honest creative work, Whitehead argued, 'should form part of the in-service training of all teachers of English, whatever their age'.

These may well be sensible provisions, and the emphasis given to creative writing by the syllabus may well be amply justified. The problem arises when such specialised activities begin to dominate not only the classroom but the literary world as a whole. This could be happening now. For example, poetry competitions are here to stay, and their immense popularity – anything up to 35 000 entries in some cases – must surely be attributed in part to an educational system which insists that an achieved poem by someone else is simply the stimulus to the poetic capacity in oneself, an incentive to produce more of the same.

The way poetry is taught in schools may have other, more precise consequences for the literary world as a whole, although these are hard to establish. It may perhaps help to determine what kinds of writing are recognised as 'poetic'. If we are to understand how, we must look more closely at particular techniques of reading taught in the schools.

Whitehead has suggested that the teacher needs to devise

> ways of helping the pupils to give to the words and their meanings the right kind of attentiveness . . . The process is one of drawing attention (usually by questioning) to some of the key points in the meaning of the poem – those focal points or nodes around which the total poetic meaning is organised and concentrated. In searching, during the preparation of the lesson, for these nodes of meaning it will be found that the 'tip' commended by F. R. Leavis to the critic, 'scrutinise the imagery', holds good for the teacher as well.

The emphasis is on the focal point of a poem, the single detail around which it has been organised; and that focal point will almost invariably be an image. So the first step in our recognition of the poetic will be to isolate within the discourse of the poem a significant detail. This is what we imagine the poet to have done when he scanned the 'discourse' of experience in the first place and isolated the germ of his poem. This is what we ourselves will be attempting to do in our own creative writing. Description, Hughes says, is a matter of picking out and remembering significant details: 'then it is just a matter of presenting those vividly in words.'

But what is it that makes the detail we pick out of the poem significant? What will render the detail we have picked out of experience vivid? Comparison. 'It is one of those curious facts,' Hughes claims, 'that when two things are compared in a metaphor or a simile, we see both of them much more distinctly than if they were mentioned separately as having nothing to do with each other.' Comparisons are what we notice in a poem, and what we want to produce in our own writing:

> You are forced to look more closely, and to think, and make distinctions, and be surprised at what you find – and all this adds to the strength and vividness of your final impression. And it all happens in a flash. Just give yourself a few odd similes or metaphors and see how they set your imagination going:
>
> > How is a dragonfly like a helicopter?
> > How is a tramp-steamer in a rough sea like an old man?
> > How is a ball like an echo?
>
> So, in this business of bringing people to life in words, comparisons can be helpful.

Having scanned experience for significant detail, the poet will reproduce the detail by means of a comparison, which is what the reader will recognise as the poetic part of his activity. Poems are, in the first instance, metaphors or similes. Other instances will follow, other recognitions (of prosody or genre or whatever). But the chances are, particularly if the process of reading is short-circuited by creative writing, that the first instance will remain primary: the indelible mark of the poetic. When we think of poetry, we will think first – and maybe last – of vivid comparisons: 'it all happens in a flash'.

This is certainly the assumption behind *Touchstones,* a series of five anthologies edited by Michael and Peter Benton and widely used in the middle school. *Touchstones* I opens with a discussion of 'word-pictures', using Japanese haiku as a model:

Imagination is difficult to define but we go some way towards it if we say that it is being able to look at things in a fresh or original way. Comparisons help the poet to do this, for he puts together two things which we do not normally connect and gives us a new and vivid picture of them. Dylan Thomas, for example, describes milk-churns standing at the corner of the village street 'like short, silver policemen'. D. H. Lawrence sees bats flying in the evening air as 'bits of old umbrellas'.

So the Bentons define poetic thinking as an ability to 'look at things in a fresh or original way', an ability to look at bats as though they were pieces of umbrella. They go on to consider other aspects of poetry, but comparison remains for them the primary element, and one they return to again and again. Thus their next topic is the ballad, but even here they remark that 'the ballad composer has stressed a few significant details and kept the picture he wants you to imagine bold and simple'. Generic considerations are less important than seeing familiar things in a fresh or original way; what the reader does in effect is to isolate the haiku (the vivid comparison) within the ballad.

That, at any rate, is the basis upon which the creative writing of the pupils must proceed. Here are a couple of exercises from the third volume of *Touchstones*:

> You may be able to think of comparisons for some of the following and write two or three lines of free verse where you use them: petrol or oil on the surface of a puddle, the surface of your desk, electricity pylons, the London underground. These are only suggestions; find your own subjects if you can.

> Look carefully at your desk lid. Possibly it is new and shiny but it is quite likely that on it there are marks, initials, doodles, 'train lines', blots and stains dating back over many years. What is the texture of the wood like? Why and when were the different marks made? If a minute insect were to make its way across this desk 'landscape' what features would it notice? What obstacles would it encounter? one or two of these questions may suggest ideas for a poem.

In this way familiar objects can be revived by the exercise of comparison, and the poetic faculty vindicated. Comparison, one of the many different ways in which poems signify, has become a sign for poetry itself: for the entire scope and value of the art.

No doubt the *Touchstones* approach works in the classroom. No doubt many teachers supplement it with an emphasis on other aspects of poetic form. But it does predispose one rather heavily towards a certain kind of writing, and if the assumptions which support it were to take root outside the classroom as well as inside, we might have a problem. This could happen directly, through the making of readers in the schools and in teacher training programmes, or indirectly, through the pressure exerted on publishers. (The schools remain the only large market for books of poetry, a market which has determined such ventures as the joint paperback selection of work by Thom Gunn and Ted Hughes, two poets who are usually taught together; Faber have sold well over 100 000 copies.) I want to argue that the assumptions I have described are already taking root outside the classroom, and so determining which poets get to be read.

The establishment of Craig Raine as a popular and respected poet has been, as Alan Hollinghurst points out, 'a conspicuous feature of British literary life during the last three years . . . And the result of this rapid creation of . . . taste is of course a dangerous over-definition of his skills which any young writer might find restricting and which can easily threaten an atrophy through excessive self-consciousness.' Hollinghurst suggests that the taste has been created – in part, at least – by a burst of praise from important people (Peter Porter, John Carey, John Bayley). I think we need to look beyond such factors, to the skills which have been over-defined and the assumptions which have defined them.

On 30 December 1979 the *Observer* said goodbye to the seventies. Christopher Booker recalled the 'gloom and confusion' of the decade in a gloomy and confused manner; someone else decided that sex, apparently an 'invention of the sixties', was now 'in retreat'. But the paper also looked forward to the eighties, and to the young men and women who might be expected to make their mark in the coming decade. Among the young hopefuls were two poets:

CRAIG RAINE, 35, poet and critic who leapt to fame last year with the publication of his first slim volume *The Onion, Memory*, which earned him the title of founding father of a new school of poetry – the Metaphor Men. A second volume, *A Martian Sends a Postcard Home*, has just appeared.

CHRISTOPHER REID, 30, a young poet whose first book, *Arcadia,* published last summer, introduced a new note of brilliant stylishness and subtle feeling.

The soubriquet 'Metaphor Man' indicates that the popularity of this new school is based on a rhetorical choice, rather than on a choice of subject-matter. Prestige attaches to the exercise of a particular skill. Faber and Faber, who missed out on Raine and Reid, have acknowledged as much by signing up another metaphor-fiend, David Sweetman, and by appointing Raine poetry editor.

The skill defined and over-defined by the work of Raine and Reid is the skill which has become in our society a sign for the entire scope and value of poetry. Readers trained to identify poetry with the art of noting visual correspondences will inevitably favour poets who are better at comparing things than they are at handling genre or rhythm or argument. Several critics have commented on the relative inconspicuousness of genre and rhythm and argument in Raine's writing. His poems are coded by our expectations about what their metaphors will yield, to the point at which we more or less ignore anything else they might have to offer. Thus, like the Bentons' pupils, he has been thinking of things to compare with electricity pylons: in one poem, pylons go for their guns; in another, they pull out their pockets. The basis of these metaphors is almost always visual, and their purpose to demonstrate the enduring validity in everyday life of the poetic faculty. In Raine's world, a packet of cigarettes looks like a miniature organ and a rose has a shark-infested stem. In Reid's world, glasses lie in a lotus position and violinists do a futile side-stroke; his sequence 'The Haiku Adapted for Home Use' even brings the Bentons' favourite form to bear on the domesticity which is one of the favourite subjects of the Metaphor Men. When Ian Hamilton, reviewing *A Free Translation,* observed that 'Raine continues to fish out the flashy similes, as if from a bottomless school satchel,' his own simile was perhaps less flashy and more apposite that he knew.

Of course, comparison is not a sin. It only becomes dangerous when a significant number of readers identify it with the entire scope and value of poetry, and use it to distinguish good from bad. The success of the Metaphor Men suggests that this has already happened. I cannot explain why it has happened. But if the identification of poetry with comparison does derive from the way the subject is taught in the schools, then a particular institution can indeed be said to have become responsible for the making of a large number of readers.

On the other hand, Carcanet has shown that it is possible to make a readership for poets who do not necessarily at first appeal to that institutional audience. In doing so, the press has had to collude to some extent with a certain political stance. Not for the first time, dismay at the awfulness of the contemporary world has made a place in our culture for the defence of a particular kind of writing.

I believe it is the responsibility of criticism to sustain a plurality of readerships, if necessary against the monopoly power of any institution or rhetoric. That means tolerance, and something more than tolerance, namely the ability to recognise the different conventions of reading invoked by different poetries and the ability to understand how such conventions find their reason in society.

References

Where several references to the same text appear in close succession, they will be grouped under the entry for the first reference. All books cited were published in London, unless otherwise indicated.

CHAPTER 1. THE SECRET COMPLEMENT

p.1 'just boundaries'   Laurence Sterne, *Tristram Shandy*, II, XI.
     'Every work'   Quoted by Jonathan Culler, *Structuralist Poetics* (1975) p.158.
     'The action'   Paul Valéry, *Collected Works* Vol. 7 (1958) p.158.
p.2 'to convert'   Jonathan Culler, *Structuralist Poetics* p.114.
     'reader response'   See the useful anthology edited by Jane Tompkins, *Reader-Response Criticism* (Baltimore 1980); and Culler's *The Pursuit of Signs* (1981).
     'to be born'   F. R. Leavis, *How to Teach Reading: A Primer for Ezra Pound* (Cambridge 1933) pp.1, 3.
p.3 'the cohesion'   Malcolm Bradbury, *The Social Context of Modern English Literature* (1971) pp.75–6, xxxiv.
p.4 'do not read'   E. de Selincourt (ed.), *Letters of William Wordsworth and Dorothy Wordsworth: The Middle Years, Part 1*, revised by Mary Moorman (Oxford 1969) p.150.
     'My glory'   Letter to J. H. Reynolds, 9 April 1818; in *Letters*, H. E. Rollins (ed.), Vol. 1 (Cambridge Mass. 1958) p.267.
     'But how'   Barbara Rook (ed.), *The Friend* Vol. 1 (1969) p.51.
     'since the strangely' Marilyn Butler, *Romantics, Rebels, and Reactionaries* (Oxford 1981) p.91.
     'To consider'   Paul Valéry, *Collected Works* Vol. 7 pp.153–4.
p.6 'are neither'   Victor Turner, *The Ritual Process* (Pelican edition 1974) pp.81–2.

251

p.7 'open and'   Victor Turner, 'Pilgrimages as Social
                             Processes', in *Dramas, Fields and Metaphors*
                             (Ithaca 1974) p.202.

    'essential and'   Victor Turner, *The Ritual Process* pp.82–3.
    'A pilgrim'   Victor Turner, *Image and Pilgrimage in
                             Christian Culture* (Oxford 1978) p.15.
p.8 'momentarily free'   Friedrich Schiller, *On the Aesthetic Education
                             of Man*, trans. E. M. Wilkinson and L. A.
                             Willoughby (Oxford 1967) pp.139, 151.
                             After completing this chapter, I read
                             Geoffrey Hartman's *Criticism in the
                             Wilderness* (New Haven 1980); he also
                             (p.262) juxtaposes Turner and Schiller,
                             although without elaborating.

p.9 'I am convinced'   E. L. Griggs (ed.), *Collected Letters* Vol. 1
                             (Oxford 1956) p.74.

    'pure and equal'   Thomas Cooper, *Some Information respecting
                             America* (1974) pp.37–8.

    'These, Tom'   Quoted by William Haller, *The Early Life
                             of Robert Southey* (New York 1917) p.136.
p.12 'when we come'   W. G. Hutchinson (ed.), *The Nemesis of
                             Fate* pp.112–13.

    'live for humanity'   'Family Life', in *On Society* (1918) p.42.
    'The longer'   Maurice de Guérin, R. R. H. Super,
                             (ed.), *Complete Prose Works* Vol. 3 (Ann
                             Arbor 1964) p.31.

p.13 'Simile'   E. S. Dallas, *Poetics: An Essay in Poetry*
                             (1852) pp.203–5.

    'can only be met'   John Ruskin, *Modern Painters*, in E. T.
                             Cook and A. Wedderburn (eds.), *Works*
                             Vol. 3 (1903) p.136.

p.14 'the system'   Charles Hartman, *Free Verse. An Essay on
                             Prosody* (Princeton 1980) p.14.

    providing cohesion   The classic account is by M. A. K.
                             Halliday and R. Hasan, *Cohesion in
                             English* (1977). My attention was drawn
                             to this book by Colin MacCabe (ed.).

p.15 'few and scattered'   William Wordsworth, *Prose Works*, W. J.
                             B. Owen and J. W. Smyser (eds.) Vol. 3
                             (1974) p.83.

p.16 'co-operating power'   Ibid. p.81.
p.17 'It was quite'   Ford Maddox Ford,   *Memories and
                             Impressions* (Penguin edition 1979) p.351.

CHAPTER 2. THE DURATION OF MORTMAIN

p.22 as Robert Langbaum   Robert Langbaum, *The Poetry of
                             Experience* (Penguin edition 1974) p.86.
p.23 'Having the young man's' Robert McAlman, *Being Geniuses Together*,
                             revised by Kay Boyle (1970) p.5

p.23 as Ronald Bush | Ronald Bush, *The Genesis of Ezra Pound's Cantos* (Princeton 1976) p.6.

'silent and aloof' | J. M. Keynes, *The Economic Consequences of the Peace* (1919), quoted by Bush, ibid. p.273.

'the duration' | Ezra Pound in W. Cookson (ed.), *Selected Prose 1909–1965* (1973) p.226.

'It is such' | William Wordsworth, 'Essays upon Epitaphs', *Prose Works*, Vol. 2 (1974) pp.633–4, 59, 93, 51, 54.

p.24 'the awful doom' | Henry James, Preface to Vol. 17 of the New York edition of the *Novels and Tales* p.viii.

'a medium' | Paul Fussell, *The Great War and Modern Memory* (Oxford 1975) p.3.

'conventional' | Sigmund Freud, 'Thoughts for the Times on War and Death', *Standard Edition of the Complete Psychological Works,* trans. James Strachey, Vol. 14 (1957) p.291.

p.25 'find the strange' | Edmund Blunden, *Undertones of War* (1928, 1956) pp.58–9.

'I daresay' | James Joyce, *Ulysses* (Bodley Head edition) pp.137, 143.

p.26 'We may assume' | Sir James Frazer, *Adonis, Attis, Osiris* (1906) p.281.

p.27 'neurotic ceremonial' | Sigmund Freud, 'Obsessive Acts and Religious Practices', *Standard Edition*, Vol. 9 (1959) pp. 117–18, 123.

p.28 'the puberty rites' | Sigmund Freud, *Introductory Lectures Standard Edition*, Vol. 16 (1963) p.335.

p.29 'I yearn' | Quoted by Lyndall Gordon, *Eliot's Early Years* (Oxford 1977) p.17.

'a new' | Sigmund Freud, 'On Narcissism', *Standard Edition*, Vol. 14 (1957) pp.77, 95.

p.31 'special psychical' | Ibid. p.95.

'an Eye' | T. S. Eliot, 'The Preacher as Artist', *Athenaeum* (28 November 1919) p.1253.

p.33 'in a class' | Lyndall Gordon, *Eliot's Early Years* p.30.

'In mourning' | Sigmund Freud, 'Mourning and Melancholia', *Standard Edition*, Vol. 14 (1957) p.246.

'the man in the world' | Henry James, 'The Beast in the Jungle', New York edition of the *Novels and Tales,* Vol. 17 (1909) pp.125, 119, 124–5.

p.34 'recall' | Lyndall Gordon, *Eliot's Early Years* p.101.

'lurid comfort' | Hugh Kenner, *The Invisible Poet: T. S. Eliot* (1960) pp.121–2.

254

References

CHAPTER 3. IN THE CAGE

p.36 'Psychology' — T. S. Eliot, *'Ulysses*, Order and Myth' (1923), in Frank Kermode (ed.), *Selected Prose* (1975) p.178.

'that which' — Ezra Pound, 'A few don'ts', in T. S. Eliot (ed.), *Literary Essays* (1954) p.4.

'dissociation' — Bernard Hart, *The Psychology of Insanity* (Cambridge 1912) pp.41–5.

'dissociation of sensibility' — T. S. Eliot, 'The Metaphysical Poets', in Kermode (ed.), *Selected Prose* p.64.

p.37 'the subjective' — Roger Vittoz, *Treatment of Neurasthenia* second edition, trans. H. B. Brooke (1913) pp.1, 7, 19, 21.

'mythical method' — T. S. Eliot, *'Ulysses,* Order and Myth', pp.177–8.

'to re-establish' — Claude Lévi-Strauss, *L'homme nu* (Paris 1971) pp.603–4.

p.38 'capable of' — T. S. Eliot, *International Journal of Ethics* 17 (1916) p.116.

'The Grail romances' — Jessie Weston, *From Ritual to Romance* (Cambridge 1920) pp.176, 172, 117.

p.39 'whole process' — Julien Benda, *Belphégor,* trans. S. J. I. Lawson (New York 1929) pp.84, 122.

p.40 'sound of rending' — Max Nordau, *Degeneration* (1895) pp. 5–6, 11.

p.41 'the critical' — T. S. Eliot, 'The Perfect Critic', in Kermode (ed.), *Selected Prose* pp.11–12.

'boundless empire' — Arthur Symons, *Studies in Elizabethan Drama* (1920) pp.11–12.

p.42 'The subject' — *Practitioner* (July 1923) pp.2, 4, 24.

'psychologically' — *Report of the Fifth International Neo-Malthusian and Birth Control Conference* (1922) p.167.

'what should be' — *Practitioner* (July 1923) pp. 34, 29, 74, 4.

p.43 'lowest stratum' — *Nature* 113 (1924) pp. 669, 774.

p.44 'sustained' — Donald Davie, *The Poet in the Imaginary Museum* (Manchester 1977) p.101.

p.46 'extreme scepticism' — Robertson Smith, *Lectures on the Religion of the Semites,* revised edition (1894) p.23.

'But the prevailing' — George Adam Smith, *Historical Geography of the Holy Lane* (1894) pp. 307, 310.

'peculiarly sterile' — 'Semites', *Encyclopaedia of Religion and Ethics*, James Hastings (ed.) Vol. 11 (1910–27) p.382.

p.47 Eliot reviewed — T. S. Eliot, review of L. M. Bristol, *Social Adaptation; New Statesman* (29 July 1916) p.405.

'The dry, pure air' — Ellen Churchill Semple, *Influences of Geographic Environment* (1911) pp.512, 510.

p.48	'real for us'	F. H. Bradley, *Appearance and Reality* (1893) pp. 224–5.
	'All significant'	T. S. Eliot, *Knowledge and Experience in the Philosophy of F. H. Bradley* (1964) pp. 165, 24.
p.50	'staging'	Sigmund Freud, *Beyond the Pleasure Principle, Standard Edition* Vol. 18 (1955) pp. 15, 16.
p.57	Hugh Kenner remarks	Hugh Kenner, *The Invisible Poet: T. S. Eliot* (1960) p.145.
	'A gentleman'	*Cornhill Magazine* 5 (1862) p.337.
p.52	'I'll take no'	George Eliot, *Felix Holt the Radical* (Penguin edition) p.144.
	'to assert'	E. M. Forster, *Howards End* (Penguin edition) p.44.
	'Jack London'	Wyndham Lewis, 'Cantleman's Spring Mate', in *A Soldier of Humour and Selected Writings* (New York 1966) p.109.
p.53	'From the close'	Lyndall Gordon, *Eliot's Early Years*, p.111.

CHAPTER 4. WORDS FULL OF FAR-OFF SUGGESTION

p.58	'alike strange'	W. B. Yeats, 'What is "Popular Poetry?"', *Essays and Introductions* (1961) pp.6–11.
p.59	'I had not wanted'	W. B. Yeats, 'Discoveries', in ibid. p.265.
	'Then,' Eliot concluded	T. S. Eliot, *The Use of Poetry and the Use of Criticism* (1933, 1964) p.140.
p.60	'at *prise*'	Ezra Pound, review in *Poetry* (May 1914) *Literary Essays* (1960) p.380.
p.62	'I know more'	Ezra Pound, review in *Poetry* (December 1914) in ibid. p.384.
p.63	'only for the few'	Ezra Pound, *'Noh' or Accomplishment* (1916) p.5.
	'an aristocratic form'	W. B. Yeats, 'Certain Noble Plays of Japan', *Essays and Introductions*, pp.221, 232.
p.64	'create for myself'	W. B. Yeats, 'A People's Theatre', reprinted in *Plays and Controversies* (1923) p.212.
	'one character'	T. S. Eliot, *The Use of Poetry* p.153.
p.67	'What brought him'	W. B. Yeats, *Letters*, Allan Wade (ed.) (1954) p.646.
	'The Nekuia'	Ezra Pound in D. D. Paige (ed.), *Selected Letters* (1950) p.274.

CHAPTER 5. THE SPIRIT OF ANTIPATHOS

p.70	Brecht sat	Bertholt Brecht, *Diaries 1920–1922*, trans. John Willett (1979) pp.105, 74, 3.
	'something'	Henry Ford, *My Life and Work* (1922) p.3.
p.71	'In America'	Antonio Gramsci, *Selections from the Prison Notebooks*, trans. Q. Hoare and G. Nowell-Smith (1971) pp.286, 281.
	'morsel'	R. M. Rilke, *Selected Letters*, trans. R. F. C. Hull (1947) p.394.
	'Once the process'	Antonio Gramsci, *Prison Notebooks* p.309.
p.72	'Repetitive Work'	Dexter Kimball, *Industrial Economics* (New York 1929) p.79.
	'The alienation effect'	Bertholt Brecht, *Brecht on Theatre*, trans. John Willett (1964) p.94.
	'Even I'	George Grosz, *A Little Yes and a Big No* trans. K. Winston (Middletown 1972) p.185.
	'singing cowboy'	Wyndham Lewis, *Blasting and Bombardiering* (1937, 1967) pp.257–8.
p.74	'Going over there'	Ernest Hemingway, Letter of 9 March 1922, Carlos Baker (ed.), *Selected Letters 1917–1961* p.62.
	'Why do American artists'	William Carlos Williams, 'The Somnambulists', *Imaginations*, W. Schott (ed.), (1970) p. 341.
p.75	'an inexplicable'	Bertholt Brecht in *Collected Plays*, John Willett and Ralph Manheim (eds.), Vol. l, Part 4 (1980) p.2. Translated by Gerhard Nellhaus.
p.76	'I am a large'	Wyndham Lewis, 'A Soldier of Humour', *The Wild Body* (1927) pp. 3–4.
	'Within five yards'	Wyndham Lewis, 'Inferior Religions', *The Wild Body* pp.238, 240.
p.78	'the satyr-poem'	Harold Bloom, *Wallace Stevens. The Poems of our Climate* (Ithaca 1976) p.70.
	'weary pilgrimage'	Joseph Conrad, *The Heart of Darkness* (Penguin edition) pp.21, 75, 78, 79.
p.79	'like a task'	R. M. Rilke, *Selected Letters* p.355.
p.80	'Violence'	Wyndham Lewis, *The Wild Body* pp. 158–9.
	'wild' comedy	W. B. Yeats, *Letters* , pp.625, 590, 668, 632, 693, 716.
p.81	'a sustained nightmare'	Frank Kermode, *Wallace Stevens* (Edinburgh 1960) p.45.

CHAPTER 6. FORM-SENSE AND DICTATOR-SENSE

p.82 'Only from about'   T. S. Eliot, *Criterion*, 18 (1939) p.271.

'Form sense'   Ezra Pound, *Guide to Kulchur* (1938, 1966) p.134.

p.83 'If you will not'   T. S. Eliot, *Idea of a Christian Society* (1939) p.63.

'Never in Italy'   Ezra Pound, 'A Social Creditor Serves Notice', *Fascist Quarterly*, 2 (1936) p.496.

William Chace   William Chace, *The Political Identities of Ezra Pound and T. S. Eliot* (Stanford 1973).

'I remain'   Ezra Pound, *ABC of Economics* (Glasgow 1933) p.53.

'Ole Henry Ford'   Ezra Pound, *Selected Letters* p.221.

'artists'   Henry Ford, *My Life and Work* p.104.

p.84 'Nordic capitalist'   Hamilton Yorke, *The Dawes Report and Control of World Gold* (New York 1925) p.2.

'Over a decade'   Ezra Pound, *ABC of Economics* p.37.

'In the end'   John Diggins, *Mussolini and Fascism. The View From America* (Princeton 1971) p.21.

'Executive actions'   Merle Thorpe, *Nations Business* (December 1927), quoted by Diggins p.60.

p.85 'I don't believe'   Ezra Pound, *Jefferson and/or Mussolini* (1935) p.33.

'common sense'   Kenneth Roberts, *Black Magic* (Indianapolis 1924) pp.5, 105.

'the will for you'   Quoted by Adrian Lyttelton, *The Seizure of Power. Fascism in Italy 1919–1929* (1973) p.367.

p.86 'the existence'   Ezra Pound, *ABC of Economics* p.27.

'This possibility'   Ezra Pound, *Criterion* 15 (1935) p.40.

'The real views'   Quoted by Lyttleton, *The Seizure of Power* p.369.

p.87 'Pound, however'   Quoted by Noel Stock, *The Life of Ezra Pound* (New York, 1970) p.101.

'Sometimes, when'   Romano Bilenchi, 'Rapallo 1941', trans. David Anderson, *Paideuma*, 8 (1979) p.439.

'if America'   Quoted by Stock, *The Life of Ezra Pound* p.313.

p.88 'never wrote'   Quoted by Stock, *The Life of Ezra Pound* p.278.

'guided'   Ezra Pound, *Jefferson and/or Mussolini* p.15.

'From sheer force'   Ezra Pound, *Guide to Kulchur* p.259.

'the range'   Adrian Lyttelton, *Seizure of Power* p.400.

p.91 'burden of meaning' Roland Barthes, 'Diderot, Brecht, Eisenstein', in *Image-Music-Text,* trans. Stephen Heath (1977) p.72.

'strict, frame-like' Walter Benjamin, *Understanding Brecht,* trans. Anna Bostock (1973) p.3.

Jefferson wrote Letter of 17 August 1787. Cantos 31 and 37 can be read alongside their sources in Stephen Spender's useful anthology, *The American Long Poem: an Annotated Selection* (1977). For a different view of the American History Cantos from my own, see his perceptive essay, 'Ezra Pound and the Words off the Page; Historical Allusions in Some American Long Poems', *Yearbook of English Studies* 8 (1978).

p.94 Alan Durant Alan Durant, *Ezra Pound: Identity in Crisis* (Brighton 1981).

'comes to a half' Sigmund Freud, 'Fetishism', *Standard Edition* Vol. 21 (1961) pp.155, 153.

p.95 He copied Matthew Arnold, in H. F. Lowry et al., (eds.) *Notebooks* (Oxford 1952) p.524.

p.96 'victorious life' W. B. Yeats, *Uncollected Prose* Vol. 2 (1975) p.319.

'heroic sanction' Ursula Bridge (ed.), *W. B. Yeats and T. Sturge Moore: Their Correspondence* (1953) p.319.

'test art' W. B. Yeats, *A Vision*, revised edition (1962) p.52.

p.97 as Helen Gardner Helen Gardner, *The Composition of Four Quartets* (1978) pp.209–11.

p.98 'is built like' John Gunther, *Inside Europe* (New York 1938) p.194.

p.99 'A language' Bertholt Brecht, 'On Gestic Music', in *Brecht on Theatre* p.104.

p.100 'the issuing' J. L. Austin, *How to do Things with Words* (Oxford 1962) pp.6, 8.

'These experiences' Bertholt Brecht, *Brecht on Theatre*, pp.118, 120.

p.102 'Mussolini speaking' Ezra Pound, *Criterion* 14 (1935) pp. 302–4.

CHAPTER 7. GOING OVER

p.105 'Immediately' David Caute, *The Fellow-Travellers* (1973) p.6. Paul Hollander's informative chronicle of fellow-travelling, *Political Pilgrims* (Oxford 1981), unfortunately appeared after I had finished work on this chapter.

p.105 'have access'	*Our Tours* (Berlin 1929) p.5.
'The streets'	*Moscow, Past, Present, Future* (1934) p.22.
'Oh, you will find'	Walter Citrine, *I Search for Truth in Russia* (1936) p.1.
p.106 'in spite of'	R. Boothby, *Britain and the Soviets. The Congress of Peace and Friendship with the U.S.S.R.* (1936) pp.2, 9, 50, 101.
'While that speech'	Vyvyan Adam, *For Peace and Friendship. Proceedings of the Second National Congress.* (1937) p.85.
p.107 'that the mind'	Cecil Day Lewis (ed.), 'Introduction', *The Mind in Chains* (1937) p.17.
'In 1934'	Alistair Browne, 'Psychology and Marxism', ibid. p.178.
'The instruments'	W. H. Auden, *The Dance of Death* (1933) p.37.
'In the classless'	Edward Upward, 'A Marxist Interpretation of Literature', *Mind in Chains* pp. 53–4.
p.108 'Recurrent as'	John Lehmann, *The Whispering Gallery* (1955) p.220.
a 'distemper'	Andrew Boyle, *The Climate of Treason* (1979) p.448.
'the arguments'	Julian Bell, 'The Proletariat and Poetry: An open Letter to C. Day-Lewis', in *Julian Bell. Essays, Poems and Letters.* Quentin Bell (ed.), (1938) pp.323, 318.
'it averts'	'War and Peace: A letter to E. M. Forster', ibid. p.387.
'Julian's tips'	E. M. Forster, 'Notes for a Reply', ibid. p.392.
p.109 'Just as'	Julian Bell, 'The Proletariat and Poetry', ibid. p.323.
'a classic'	Julian Bell, 'Notes for a Memoir', ibid. p.20.
'kept painting'	Anthony Blunt, 'Self-consciousness in Modern Art', *The Venture*, 1 (1928) p.49.
'non-rational'	Anthony Blunt, *Spectator* (23 September 1938) p.1480.
'the essential'	Anthony Blunt, *Spectator* (26 June 1936) p.1182.
p.110 'reservation'	'War and Peace', *Julian Bell*, p.387.
p.111 'The symbolic position'	Stephen Spender, *The Destructive Element* p.268.
'the privelege'	Edward Mendelson, *The Early Auden* (1981).
'Through the hesitant'	Oswald Mosley, *Fascism: 100 Questions Asked and Answered* (1936). Foreword.
p.112 cannot have been unaware	As Barbara Everett suggests: *Auden* (Edinburgh 1964) p.32.

p.112 'a romantic' Edward Mendelson, *Early Auden*, p.251.
'is a daily' Captain Gordon-Canning, *The Inward Strength of a National Socialist* (1938) pp.34–5.
p.114 'These are excellent' Stephen Spender, *The Destructive Element* p.270.
'The poet' E. Mendelson (ed.), *The English Auden* (1977) p.327.
p.115 'the decline' W. H. Auden, *The Dance of Death* p.7.
'is that they' Stephen Spender, *The Destructive Element* p.270.
'I longed to be' Stephen Spender, *World Within World* (1951) p.135.
Thus he contrasted John Cornford, 'Left?' *Cambridge Left* (Spring 1934); quoted by Peter Stansky and William Abrahams, *Journey to the Frontier* (1966) p.224.
'Mr. Bell's verse' *Spectator* (28 August 1936) p.354.
'the futile chatter' Christopher Isherwood, *Mr. Norris Changes Trains* (1935, 1977) p.56.
p.117 'It is goodbye' George Orwell, *Collected Essays, Journalism and Letters,* Vol. 2 (Penguin edition) p.109.
'eau de Cologne' Rex Warner, *Poems* (1937) p.39.
p.118 'If the poet' Cecil Day Lewis, 'A Reply', in *Julian Bell* p.333.
'the Angel' E. M. Forster, 'The Last Parade', *Two Cheers for Democracy* (Penguin edition) p.22.
'The bombs' George Orwell, *Coming up for Air* (Penguin edition) pp.223–4.
p.119 'I imagined' Stephen Spender, *World Within World* p.118.
p.120 'the struggle or moral choice' Samuel Hayes, *The Auden Generation,* (1976) p.252.
p.121 'crossing the frontier' Bernard Bergonzi, *Reading the Thirties* (1978) p.73.
as Mendelson has Edward Mendelson, *Early Auden* pp.317–23
p.124 'the whole of' T. S. Eliot, *The Use of Poetry* p.148.
p.125 'in a way from which' T. S. Eliot, *The Idea of a Christian Society* (1939) pp.63–4.
p.126 'esthetic sanction' T. S. Eliot, 'Poetry and Propaganda', *Bookman* 70 (1930) p.598.
'a hypothetical' T. S. Eliot, *Idea of a Christian Society* pp.38, 22.
p.127 'proclaims' Helen Gardner, *Composition of Four Quartets* p.58.
p.128 'And T. S. Eliot' Laura Riding, *Poems,* a new edition (Manchester 1980) pp.410, 407–8.

p.128 'the most absorbing' — Wallace Stevens in Holly Stevens (ed.), *Letters* (New York 1966) p.309.

CHAPTER 8. THE SERIOUS ACTION

p.132 'We're national' — Graham Greene, *England Made Me* (Penguin edition) pp.135, 138, 12, 120, 61.

p.134 The proportion — The following figures show the incidence of definite articles in major collections from 1933 to 1960, considered as a percentage of the word-total: *Poems* (1933), 6%; *Look Stranger* (1936), 8.9%; *Another Time* (1940), 7.8%; *Nones* (1951), 6.5%; *The Shield of Achilles* (1955), 4.4%; *Homage to Clio* (1960), 3.7%. Figures from Vilas Savary 'Articles in the Poetry of W. H. Auden,' *Language and Style*, 7 (1974) pp.77–89.

p.135 he even found — See George S. Lensing, 'Wallace Stevens in England', in *Wallace Stevens. A Celebration* Frank Doggett and Robert Buttel (eds.) (Princeton 1980) pp.130–48.

p.136 'Academic is' — Donald Davie, *The Poet in the Imaginary Museum* pp.72–4.

'the English poet' — John Wain, 'The Strategy of Victorian Poetry', *Twentieth Century* (May 1953); quoted in Blake Morrison's excellent study, *The Movement* (Oxford 1980) p.111.

'small, compact' — Cecil Day-Lewis, *A Hope for Poetry* (1934) p.37.

p.137 'The revival' — Cecil Day Lewis, *A Hope for Poetry* (second edition, 1936) p.79.

'clerisy' — Ben Knights, *The Idea of the Clerisy in the Nineteenth Century* (Cambridge 1978).

'fittest persons' — John Stuart Mill, in F. A. von Kayek (ed.), *The Spirit of the Age* (Chicago 1942) pp.35–6.

'Looking backward' — W. B. Yeats, 'Autobiography' (1916–17), in Denis Donaghue (ed.), *Memoirs* (1972) p.60.

p.138 'The modern' — Yeats, *Autobiographies* (1955) p.559. Written 1924.

'spent much' — W. B. Yeats, 'Windlestraws', *Samhain* (October 1901), quoted by Elizabeth Cullingford, *Yeats, Ireland and Fascism* (1981) p.44.

'They assert' — James Joyce in Richard Ellman (ed.) *Selected Letters* (1975) p.117.

p.139 'a complete outsider'   H. G. Wells, *Experiment in Autobiography*, Vol. 2 (1934) pp.651, 648, 659.

'authoritative'   W. B. Yeats, 'From Democracy to Authority', *Irish Times* (16 February 1924) in *Uncollected Prose*, Vol. 2, p.435.

'In the close'   Quoted by H. W. Koch, *The Hitler Youth*, (1975) p.40.

p.140 'This cult'   F. Matzke, *Jugend bekennt: so sind wir!* (1930); quoted in translation by Koch, *The Hitler Youth* p.42.

'I recognise'   B.U.F. Membership Form (1932) recto.

'those creeds'   Oswald Mosley, *Fascism in Britain* (1933) p.3.

'an unconscious'   Christopher Dawson, *Beyond Politics* (1939) pp.14, 24, 57.

p.141 'an ever more'   Wyndham Lewis, *The Art of Being Ruled* (1926) p.420.

'man himself'   J. D. Bernal, *The World, the Flesh and the Devil* (1929, 1970) pp.32, 39, 68.

p.142 'propaganda'   Ezra Pound, 'Allen Upward Serious', *Selected Prose* p.381.

'an attempt'   Michael Ledeen, *Universal Fascism* (New York 1972) p.7.

'the 243'   Ezra Pound, *Selected Letters* p.221.

'An intelligentzia'   Ezra Pound, 'Intellectual Money', *British Union Quarterly*, 1 (1937) p.33.

one pamphlet   J. F. C. Fuller, *March to Sanity* (n.d.) p.13; A. Raven Thompson, *The Coming Corporate State* (n.d.) p.42.

'To ORGANISE'   Ezra Pound, 'National Culture', *Selected Prose* p.135.

p.143 'I am not'   Ezra Pound, *Literary Essays*, p.32.

'you cannot'   Ezra Pound, Preface to *Active Anthology*, in *Selected Prose* p.367.

'a technique'   F. R. Leavis, *How to Teach Reading*, pp.40, 4.

p.144 'how a properly-qualified'   William Empson, *Seven Types of Ambiguity* (Penguin edition) p.248.

'the properly'   Northrop Frye, *Anatomy of Criticism* (Princeton 1957) pp.102 12, 16.

p.145 'Books are already'   Geoffrey Hartman, *Criticism in the Wilderness* (New Haven 1979) pp.165, 170, 99, 68.

Anthony Wilden   Anthony Wilden, *System and Structure* (1972) pp.187, 396, 400, 405, 413, 458-9; Stephen Heath, Colin MacCabe and Christopher Prendergast (eds.), *Signs of the Times* (Cambridge 1971) pp.3, 8-9, 23-5, 43-5.

p.146 'countercultural'   Geoffrey Hartman, *The Fate of Reading* (Chicago 1975) p.272.

'Academics have'   Christopher Logue, Interview in the *Guardian* (9 May 1981) p.10.

'Like a Sermon'   Seamus Heaney, *Viewpoints. Poets in Conversation with John Haffenden* (1981) p.73.

p.147 'A wholly new'   Charles Hartman, *Free Verse* p.21.

CHAPTER 9. *LES BLANCS DÉBARQUENT*

p.150 'a degree'   David Lehman, 'Introduction' in David Lehman (ed.), *Beyond Amazement. New Essays on John Ashbery* (Ithaca 1980) p.15.

'My friend'   John Ashbery, 'The invisible Avant-Garde', John Ashbery and Thomas Hess (eds), *Avant-Garde Art* (New York 1968) pp.181–2.

p.151 'It's a collection'   John Carey, 'Grunts and Groans', *Sunday Times* (9 December 1979) p.51.

p.152 'simultaneously'   David Lehman, 'Introduction', pp.23, 18.

'a precursor'   David Shapiro, *John Ashbery. An Introduction to the Poetry* (New York 1979) p.1.

'When my first'   Gerrit Henry 'In Progress', *Spectator* (31 July 1979) p.1.

p.154 'the necessity'   Donald Davie, 'American Lines', *Spectator* (22 November 1975) p.669.

p.155 'These two disclaimers'   Robert Pinsky, *The Situation of Poetry* (Princeton 1976) pp.15–16.

'reveals but does not'   John Bayley, *The Uses of Division* (1976) pp.157, 160–1.

Marjorie Perloff's study   *Frank O'Hara. Poet among Painters* (New York 1977).

'only recently'   Frank O'Hara, 'An interview', in Donald Allen (ed.), *Standing Still and Walking in New York* (New York 1975) pp.16, 8, 24.

p.157 'the many'   John Ashbery, 'Introduction' to O'Hara's *Collected Poems* (1971) p.x.

p.158 'O'Hara has a line'   Helen Vendler, *Part of Nature, Part of Us* (Cambridge 1980) p.185.

p.163 'As Marjorie Perloff'   Marjorie Perloff, *Frank O'Hara* p.145.

p.164 'a wonderful'   Frank O'Hara, Letter to John Ashbery, (1 February 1961) quoted by Perloff p.216.

p.165 'My readers'   Ed Dorn, Donald Allen (ed.), *Interviews* (Bolinas 1980) pp.66, 32.

p.165 'From the beginning'	Ed Dorn, 'Preface' to *Collected Poems 1956–1974*, p.v.
p.166 'have most interestingly'	Douglas Oliver, 'J. H. Prynne's "Of Movement towards a Natural Place"', *Grosseteste Review*, 12 (1979) p.96.
'When people'	Ed Dorn, *Interviews* pp.99, 101.
p.167 'Leaving'	Herman Melville, *Redburn*, Chapter 37 (Penguin edition) p.254.
'as a placement'	Ed Dorn, *What I see in the Maximus Poems* (Migrant Press 1960) p.12.
p.168 'trying for'	Ed Dorn, *Interviews* pp.76–7.
'space of time'	Charles Olson, *A Bibliography on America for Ed Dorn* (San Francisco 1964) p.6.
'The thing to be'	John Leighly (ed.), *Land and Life. A Selection from the Writings of Carl Ortwin Sauer* (Berkeley 1963) pp.337, 342, 326, 333.
p.170 'very dogmatic'	Ed Dorn, *Interviews* p.98.
p.171 'The social basis'	Ibid. p.38.
p.172 an account of	Harry Sinclair Drago, *Wild, Woolly and Wicked*; cited in *Interviews* pp.87–8.
Johnson's hilarious	*Adventurer* 84, reprinted in *Selected Writings* R. T. Davies (ed.) (1965) pp.143–6.
ironic or Sarcastic	Ed Dorn, *Interviews* p.98.
p.173 'the moan'	C. Seelye (ed.), *Charles Olson and Ezra Pound* (New York 1975) Reference mislaid.
p.174 'However our present'	Quoted by Merrill D. Peterson, *Thomas Jefferson and the New Nation* (New York 1970) p.746.
'It is not a line'	Walter Prescott Webb, *The Great Frontier* (1953) pp.2, 64, 5–6.
p.175 'American development'	Frederick Jackson Turner, 'Significance of the Frontier', in *Frontier and Section. Selected Essays*. R. A. Billington (ed.) (Englewood Cliffs 1961) p.38.
'With the closing'	Quoted by William Appleman Williams, *The Contours of American History* (1961) p.468.
p.176 'last stage'	Walter Prescott Webb, *The Great Plains* (New York 1931) pp.205–6.

CHAPTER 10. DECLARATIVE VOICES

p.182 'I don't mind'	Philip Larkin, 'A Voice for Our Time', *Observer* (16 December 1969) p.35.
'quite spectacular'	Anthony Sampson, *Anatomy of Britain Today*, second edition (1965) pp.668, 669, 91, 617. Wilson's remark about the

language of the technical age is quoted on p.94.

p.184 'take up the moralistic'　　Peter Richards, *Parliament and Conscience* (1970) p.19.

p.184 'I believe'　　Quoted by David McKie, 'The Quality of Life', in McKie and Chris Cook (eds.), *The Decade of Disillusion: British Politics in the Sixties* (1972) p.201.

p.187 'the most trusted'　　Christopher Ricks, 'The Mount, the Meal and the Book', *London Review of Books* (8 November 1979) p.4.

'From that moment'　　Seamus Heaney, 'Feeling into Words', in *Preoccupations. Selected Prose 1968–1978*, (1980) pp.56–7.

'declarative voice'　　Seamus Heaney, *Viewpoints* p.70.

p.188 'It would be'　　Blake Morrison, 'Speech and Reticence' pp.110, 107.

a 'kind of somnambulist'　　Seamus Heaney, '1972', *Preoccupations* p.34.

p.189 'requires a knowledge'　　Karl Miller, 'Opinion', *The Review*, 27–8 (1971–2) pp. 48–51.

'I hate'　　Seamus Heaney, *Viewpoints* p.61.

p.190 'incubating mind'　　Seamus Heaney, 'The Makings of a Music', *Preoccupations* p.61.

p.191 'his rehearsal'　　John Foster, 'The Poetry of Seamus Heaney', *Critical Quarterly* 16 (1974) p.36.

CHAPTER 11. PLAYING HAVOC

p.196 'All of them'　　Seamus Heaney, 'England of the Mind', *Preoccupations* p.151.

p.197 'enormous'　　Geoffrey Thurley, *The Ironic Harvest* (1974) pp.186, 175.

'leap off'　　Keith Sagar, *The Poetry of Ted Hughes,* second edition (Cambridge 1978) p.14.

'language'　　John Carey, 'Grunts and Groans' p.51.

'a solid phalanx'　　Robert Stuart 'Ted Hughes' in Peter Jones and Michael Schmidt (eds.), *British Poetry since 1970* (1980) p.77.

p.198 'The greater part'　　John Keats, *Letters* Vol. 2 p.79.

p.199 'We suspend'　　Robert Langbaum, *The Poetry of Experience* p.77.

on 'a wild'　　Ekbert Faas, *Ted Hughes: the Unaccommodated Universe* (Santa Barbara 1980) p.102.

p.202 David Lodge has　　David Lodge, 'Crow and the Cartoons', *Working with Structuralism* (1981) p.170.

p.206 'optimism'　　Ted Hughes, 'A Reply to My Critics',

p.207 'We are dreaming'   Books and Issues, 3–4 (1981) pp. 4–5.
                            Ted Hughes, interview with Ekbert Faas,
                            reprinted in Faas, *Ted Hughes* p.198.
      'We were'   Michael Herr, *Dispatches* (1978) p.210.
p.209 'contention'   Eric Homberger, *The Art of the Real* (1977)
                            p.210.
p.209 'the lost kingdom'   Geoffrey Hill, *Viewpoints* p.88.
p.210 'Hill's power-pack'   Andrew Waterman, 'The Poetry of
                            Geoffrey Hill, in Peter Jones and Michael
                            Schmidt (eds.), *British Poetry since 1970*
                            p.91.
p.211 'says what'   Christopher Ricks, 'Cliché as "Res-
                            ponsible Speech": Geoffrey Hill', *London
                            Magazine*, n.s. 4. (1964) p.100.
p.212 'grave abstractness' Andrew Waterman, 'The Poetry of
                            Geoffrey Hill' p.94.
p.213 'the instant'   Ibid. p.87.
p.214 'The person'   C. H. Sisson, 'Sevenoaks Essays', 1967,
                            in *The Avoidance of Literature* (Manchester
                            1978) p.211.
      'murderous brutality' Geoffrey Hill, *Viewpoints* p.94.
p.216 'confessionalism'   Geoffrey Hill, *New Statesman* (8 February
                            1980) p.212.
p.219 'CITIZEN'   Georg Büchner, *Danton's Death*, trans.
                            James Maxwell (1968) p.83.
      Gegenwort   Paul Celan, *Der Meridian* (Frankfurt-am-
                            Main 1961) pp.8, 11.
p.221 'adamant practice'   Ed Dorn, *Interviews* pp. 15, 19. There is a
                            good introductory essay by Nigel Wheale,
                            'Expense: J. H. Prynne, *The White
                            Stones*', *Grosseteste Review* 12 (1979)
                            pp.103–18.
      'If I stand'   Maurice Merleau-Ponty, *The
                            Phenomenology of Perception:* trans. Colin
                            Smith (1962) pp.100–1.
p.227 'English Life'   Donald Davie, 'Views', *Listener* (11 April
                            1968) p.461.
p.230 'increasing'   Douglas Oliver, 'J. H. Prynne's "Of
                            Movement towards a Natural Place"'
                            p.95.

CHAPTER 12. CONCLUSION

p.231 'Mr. Bottrall's'   F. R. Leavis, *New Bearings in English
                            Poetry.* New edition (1971) p.211.
p.232 'the next event'   Jane Tompkins, 'An Introduction',
                            Reader-Response Criticism p.xvi.
p.233 'He too returns'   Seamus Heaney, 'England of the Mind'
                            p.167.

p.234 'From *The Less Deceived* — Anthony Thwaite, *Twentieth Century English Poetry* p.105.

'Dance' — Philip Larkin, 'A Voice for our Time', *Observer* (16 December 1979) p.35.

p.235 'For the rest' — Blake Morrison, 'Poetry and the Poetry Business', *Granta*, 4 (1981) pp.100, 102.

p.235 'This certificate' — Certificate of Registration, as required by the Registration of Business Names Act, 1916.

p.236 'The overdue' — Peter Jones and Michael Schmidt, *British Poetry Since 1970* pp. ix, xi.

p.237 'unspeakable' — Michael Schmidt, Introduction to *Ten English Poets* (Manchester 1976) p.9.

'renewed' — *Poetry Nation* 1 (1973) pp.3, 50.

'Among modern' — Michael Schmidt, *PN Review, 1* (1973) p.1.

p.238 'It's the level' — Donald Davie, *PN Review* 2 (1977) p.1.

'Our problem' — C. H. Sisson, *PN Review* 3 (1977) p.1.

'The critics task' — Michael Schmidt, *PN Review* 1 (1976) p.3.

'the drive' — Donald Davie, 'Views' *Listener* (21 March 1968) p.365.

p.239 'an anthology' — Donald Davie, *Listener* (29 March 1973) pp. 420–1.

'What I didn't' — Donald Davie *Thomas Hardy and English Poetry* (1973) p.86.

p.240 'But the extent' — Neil Powell, *Carpenters of Light* (Manchester 1979) p.77.

p.241 'has words like' — Kingsley Amis 'Jerusalem and the Heavenly Aeroplane', *Sunday Times* (4 October 1981) p.44.

'is often' — Michael Schmidt, *The Avoidance of Literature* p.6.

p.242 'By refusing' — Peter Ackroyd, 'Verse and Worse?' *Spectator* (20 December 1975) p.793.

'helping train' — David Holbrook, *English for Maturity. English in the Secondary School* (Cambridge 1961) pp.7, 64.

'the utmost periphery' — Frank Whitehead, *The Disappearing Dais* (1966) p.94.

p.243 'Every new child' — Ted Hughes, 'Myth and Education' G. Fox et al. (eds.) in *Writers, Critics and Children* (1976) p.91.

'Throughout' — Frank Whitehead, *The Disappearing Dais,* p.99.

p.244 'more purposeful' — Ted Hughes, *Poetry in the Making* (1967) pp. 11–12.

'the acceptance' — Frank Whitehead, *The Disappearing Dais* p.96.

p.245 'A teacher' — David Holbrook, *The Exploring Word* (Cambridge 1967) p.128.

p.245 'should form part' Frank Whitehead, *Creative Experiment. Writing and the Teacher* (1970), Foreword.

'ways of helping' Frank Whitehead, *The Disappearing Dais* pp.103–4.

p.246 'then it is' Ted Hughes, *Poetry in the Making* pp.47, 44.

p.247 'Imagination is difficult' Michael and Peter Benton (eds.), *Touchstones* 1 (1968) pp.8, 15,

'You may be able' *Touchstones* 3 (1969) pp. 28, 147.

p.248 'a conspicuous feature' Alan Hollinghurst, 'Best things', *London Review of Books* 3 (1981) p.14.

'CRAIG RAINE' 'Eighty for the Eighties' *Observer* (30 December 1979) p.27.

p.249 'Raine continues' Ian Hamilton, 'View from a Backyard in Cumbria', *Sunday Times* (21 June 1981) p.43.

Index